THE **BIG** BOOK OF
LOW-CARB
RECIPES

NICOLA GRAIMES

THE **BIG** BOOK OF LOW-CARB RECIPES

365

**FAST AND FABULOUS DISHES FOR
SENSIBLE LOW-CARB EATING**

dbp

DUNCAN BAIRD PUBLISHERS

LONDON

To Silvio for his help, patience, and support.

The Big Book of Low-carb Recipes
Nicola Graimes

First published in the United Kingdom and Ireland
in 2005 by Duncan Baird Publishers Ltd
Sixth Floor
Castle House
75–76 Wells Street
London W1T 3QH

Conceived, created, and designed
by Duncan Baird Publishers Ltd

Copyright © Duncan Baird Publishers 2005
Text copyright © Nicola Graimes 2005
Photography copyright © Duncan Baird Publishers 2005

The right of Nicola Graimes to be identified as the
Author of this text has been asserted in accordance
with the Copyright, Designs, and Patents Act of 1988.

Managing Editor: Julia Charles
Editor: Louise Bostock
Managing Designer: Manisha Patel
Designer: Sailesh Patel
Studio Photography: William Lingwood
Photography Assistant: Estelle Cuthbert
Stylists: David Morgan (food) and Helen Trent

Library of Congress Cataloging-in-Publication
Data is available

Distributed in the United States by
Publishers Group West

ISBN-10: 1-84483-137-X
ISBN-13: 9-781844-831371

10 9 8 7 6 5 4 3 2 1

Typeset in Interstate
Color reproduction by Scanhouse, Malaysia
Printed in China by Imago

Publisher's Note: While every care has been taken
in compiling the recipes in this book, Duncan Baird
Publishers, or any other persons who have been
involved in working on this publication, cannot
accept responsibility for any errors or omissions,
inadvertent or not, that may be found in the
recipes or text, nor for any problems that may
arise as a result of preparing one of these recipes.

CONTENTS

INTRODUCTION

Carbohydrates are an essential part of our diet and a primary source of energy. However, there are different types of carbohydrate and each has a differing effect on blood glucose and insulin levels, which in turn affect how we feel. Controlling the effects of carbohydrates in the body is important if you want to lose weight, and maintain a healthy weight in the long term, without being left feeling hungry, frustrated, and miserable. The nutritious recipes in this book offer ideas for using so-called "good carbs" and carbs with a low glycemic index to avoid these effects, while cutting out refined and processed foods that help pile on the weight. Healthy eating should always be combined with plenty of exercise and drinking enough water, both vital for good health.

CARBOHYDRATES
–THE "GOOD" AND "BAD" GUYS

Although carbohydrates are an essential part of our diet, there are certain carbs that play no role and are basically nutritionally redundant. These are the refined types, such as sugar and white flour, which during processing are stripped of their fiber content and of many of their nutrients. These "bad" carbohydrates are not only lacking in nutrients and fiber, but they also influence blood glucose and insulin levels, resulting in peaks and troughs in energy levels, cravings for more carbohydrates, and hunger pangs. Foods made up of refined flour and sugar also tend to contain significant amounts of fat, responsible for adding excess weight. The following are the most familiar of the "bad" carbohydrates:

• WHITE PASTA AND RICE

• WHITE BREAD

• REFINED SUGAR

• COOKIES AND CAKES

• CHOCOLATE AND CANDIES

• POTATO CHIPS AND SALTED NUTS

• SUGARY BREAKFAST CEREALS AND CEREAL BARS

• FIZZY DRINKS, CORDIALS, AND JUICE DRINKS

• PRE-PACKAGED CONVENIENCE MEALS

• READY-MADE SAUCES AND GRAVY MIXES

• PIZZAS AND PIES

By contrast, the "good" carbs (such as, whole wheat pasta, pulses, wholegrain seedy bread, and brown rice) provide valuable vitamins and minerals as well as fiber. By eating these in controlled amounts (one slice of bread, not two or more; 2oz pasta or rice, not a huge plateful) and in combination with other food groups, you'll avoid highs and lows in blood glucose levels that result in peaks and troughs in energy, and hunger pangs. Nutritionists recommend a carbohydrate intake of around 40 per cent of your daily calorie intake, but this varies from person to person depending on activity levels and metabolism.

When deciding which carbs to include in your diet, avoid overloading on wheat. Eating too much wheat is easy–a wheat-based cereal for breakfast, sandwich for lunch, and pasta for dinner, and perhaps the snacks in between. Many people are intolerant to wheat, leading to uncomfortable bloating and weight gain. Try including other types of grain in your diet, such as oats, barley, rye, and rice.

INSULIN RESISTANCE

The hormone insulin plays a major role in converting carbohydrates into energy in the body, but if you are not very active, or overweight, and eat too many sugary, refined foods, you may become insulin resistant. This means that insulin levels remain too high and in turn contribute to excess fat in the blood. If you have high insulin resistance, you may have to be more cautious about how many carbs you can eat on a daily basis. By losing weight, eating less sugar, and taking plenty of exercise, you will be in a better position to curb excessive insulin production and improve levels of fats and glucose in the bloodstream. Signs of unstable blood glucose levels include cravings for carbohydrate foods, mood swings, tiredness, and feeling sluggish.

GLYCEMIC INDEX

Eliminating "bad" carbs and replacing them with "good" carbs may not be enough to significantly influence weight loss, especially if insulin resistance is an issue. All carbohydrates have a ranking of 0 to 100, which indicates how quickly a food is broken down by the body and its subsequent effect on blood glucose levels. This value is known as the glycemic index (GI). The lower a food's GI value, the longer it takes to be digested and the smaller the rise in blood glucose levels and insulin response after a meal. In other words, low GI foods produce a steady release of energy and satisfy the appetite for longer. On the other hand, those foods with a high GI value have a more dramatic effect on blood glucose levels and trigger a quick release of insulin into the bloodstream in order to steady blood glucose. This leads to yo-yoing energy levels and hunger pangs. It is believed that a diet based on low (rather than high) GI foods can help to regulate weight by controlling appetite.

There are some surprises in the glycemic index. Whole wheat bread, for example, has a relatively high GI of 69, although multigrain bread has a medium GI of 55. This doesn't mean that you should ignore healthy foods with a high GI, but when you eat them, combine them with a low GI food (a level of less than 55) to reduce the effect on blood glucose levels. Other simple ways to switch to a low GI diet are to eat breakfast cereals based on oats, barley, and bran; buy grainy breads made with whole seeds; reduce the amount of potatoes you eat; eat plenty of salad vegetables as well as other types of vegetables and fruit. Furthermore, combining these carbohydrate-based foods with a protein food will help to control blood glucose levels.

GLYCEMIC INDEX SAMPLE VALUES

LOW GI—less than 55		MEDIUM GI—55–70	HIGH GI—more than 70
GLUCOSE	100	WHITE PASTA	41
BAKED POTATO	98	APPLE	39
CORNFLAKES	82	NATURAL YOGURT	38
RICE CAKES	82	BASMATI RICE	58
WHITE BREAD	72	NOODLES	46
WHOLE WHEAT BREAD	69	ORANGE	44
RAISINS	61	PEACH	42
OATMEAL	61	PORRIDGE	42
PITTA BREAD	57	PLUMS	38
SOURDOUGH RYE BREAD	57	WHOLEGRAIN PASTA	37
MULTIGRAIN BREAD	55	STRAWBERRIES	32
BUCKWHEAT	54	LENTILS	30
BANANA	53	TOMATOES	28
PEAS	51	CHERRIES	26
BULGHUR	48	FRUCTOSE	20
GARBANZOS	42	SOY BEANS	15
RYE BREAD	42	PEANUTS	14

LOW AND MEDIUM GI VEGETABLES

Arugula, asparagus, bean sprouts, bell peppers, broccoli, Brussels sprouts, cabbage, cauliflower, eggplant, green beans, greens, kale, leeks, mustard greens, okra, onions, peas, pumpkin, salad greens, spinach, Swiss chard, tomatoes, watercress, and zucchini.

LOW AND MEDIUM GI FRUIT

Apples, apricots, bananas, blackberries, cherries, grapefruit, lemons, limes, melon, oranges, papaya, peaches, plums, raspberries, rhubarb, strawberries, tangerines.

FIBER

There is another factor in the weight-loss equation, and that is fiber. To maximize the effect of appetite-regulating GI foods, you also need foods high in fiber which suppress hunger pangs, and have no effect on blood glucose levels. It is believed that increasing fiber intake from the currently recommended level of ¾oz (although most of us only eat around 12g) to 1oz a day can help to reduce calorie intake by 15–20 per cent and that means weight loss. This translates into three or more portions of vegetables and two of fruit, as well as two servings of complex unrefined carbohydrates, say whole wheat pasta or rice or multigrain whole wheat bread, spread throughout the day.

FAT

No, not a dirty word, fat plays a crucial role in our bodies, essential for our brain, eyes, and skin; to keep tissues in good repair; for the production of hormones; and to transport some vitamins around the body. Yet just as there are good and bad carbs, so there are good and bad fats. Say goodbye to foods that contain hydrogenated or trans fats (these are found in processed foods such as ready-meals, cookies, and some margarines) and minimize intake of foods that contain saturated fat, cheese for example. Instead, welcome plant-based fats, such as olive oil, omega-3 fatty acids, found in oily fish and flaxseed oil, and omega-6 fatty acids, found in nuts, seeds, and plant oils.

Research shows that the body metabolizes plant-based fats and omega-3 fats more rapidly than animal fats, and the latter may also help to burn calories derived from carbohydrates more quickly. Additionally, omega-3 fats have been found to improve mood, concentration, and memory.

GOOD SOURCES OF OMEGA-3

- TUNA
- MACKEREL
- SARDINES
- PILCHARDS
- HERRING
- SALMON
- TROUT
- SMALL AMOUNTS IN WHITE FISH
- EGGS
- WALNUTS
- PUMPKIN SEEDS
- SOY BEANS

PROTEIN

Protein plays a crucial role in maintaining and repairing our bodies. It is also said to satisfy the appetite for longer than carbohydrate-based foods. Proteins are made up of 25 amino acids. Eight of these are known as "essential" amino acids because they are not made in the body and so have to be provided by diet. Foods that contain all eight are known as "complete" proteins and they include fish, meat, poultry, and dairy products. Fruit, vegetables, beans, and pulses are "incomplete" proteins and need to be combined in order to get the desired range of amino acids. Soy—along with its by-products tofu, soy milk, soy yogurt, and soy cheese—is one of the few plant foods to be a complete protein. Additionally, it is low in fat and can help to reduce both insulin and harmful cholesterol levels in the body.

To keep your metabolism working at optimal levels and to keep hunger at bay, combine a portion of protein with carbohydrate at every meal. Quality is key: opt for lean red meat, and poultry, fish, shellfish, eggs (no more than four a week), beans, and tofu.

WHAT YOU NEED EVERY DAY

Eating regular, nutritionally balanced meals makes it easier to avoid the lure of snacks. It just takes the odd cookie here and slice of cake there to pile on the weight. It's tempting when slimming to skip meals, but this often has the reverse effect of that desired, leading to unmanageable hunger, a preoccupation with food, and poor energy levels. Regular meals based on the main food groups (good carbs, as well as protein, unsaturated fats, and plenty of vegetables) help to control appetite and how we store fat in the body.

A decent breakfast that contains a protein element (eggs, fish, meat, yogurt, or a small amount of cheese) along with unrefined carbs will give flagging energy levels a boost as well as satisfy the appetite for the morning ahead. Protein-based foods also have a motivational effect on the brain, influencing concentration and mood. An afternoon dip in energy levels is not uncommon and this can be more pronounced after a carbohydrate-based lunch (sandwich, pizza, baked potato). Instead, curb the amount of carbs you eat and up the protein element, but keep it lean and good-quality, such as chicken or fish.

Many diets suggest cutting carbs out of the evening meal, but they do have an influence on serotonin levels in the brain and consequently on how well you sleep, so it is advisable to include some form of unrefined carbohydrate food in tandem with protein in your last meal of the day.

ABOUT THE RECIPES

Each individual's tolerance to carbohydrates is different. This is why at the end of each recipe you will find a carb count and not a carbohydrate indicator such as "high" or "low." This enables you to choose and balance the dishes according to the guidelines above, depending on whether you are looking to lose weight or maintain a healthy weight level. The figures are, however, approximations, giving a guideline to each recipe's net carbohydrate content (fiber is excluded from the figure as it does not increase blood glucose levels).

The recipes have been created to fit our fast-paced lives; they're simple and in the main quick to prepare, making the most of fresh, quality ingredients. They take their inspiration from the many cuisines of the world, including Thai, Spanish, North African, Indian, Japanese, and Italian. You'll find nutritious ideas for breakfast, light meals, salads, side dishes, main meals, and desserts. The recipes in the main meals chapter are accompanied by a suggestion for a suitable carbohydrate-based accompaniment, which will help you to create a nutritionally balanced meal. However, this doesn't mean you can overload your plate with pasta, rice, or potatoes. Make sure the protein element always plays a prominent part on the plate and reverse the ratio of vegetables to starchy carbs.

Most of us are born with a naturally sweet tooth, which can make it really difficult to cut out sugary foods. Bearing this in mind, I've included a selection of desserts, mainly fruit-based, which satisfy the desire for something sweet yet provide vitamins, minerals, and fiber and don't blow the carb count. Fructose is used instead of normal table sugar or artificial sweeteners. This natural fruit sugar has a low GI and doesn't have a dramatic effect on blood glucose or insulin levels. It's also sweeter than sugar so you need less. Again, don't overdo the desserts, but a little of what you fancy definitely makes you feel good.

chapter 1

BREAKFASTS & BRUNCHES

Breakfast is traditionally high in carbohydrates but it doesn't have to be, as the varied selection of recipes in this chapter demonstrates. Whether you're looking for ideas for a quick weekday breakfast or a more leisurely weekend brunch, there's a recipe for you. It's tempting to skip breakfast when weight loss is an issue, but research has shown that cutting what is often considered to be the most important meal of the day, can lead to an undesirable pattern of snacking on unhealthy foods mid-morning. We need to eat a good breakfast to replace some of the glycogen stores diminished overnight, to refuel the body with essential nutrients, and to provide energy for the morning ahead. Protein foods, such as lean meat, poultry, fish, tofu, eggs, nuts, and seeds rapidly satiate the appetite for long periods, keeping hunger pangs at bay. However, don't forget your good carbs, particularly those with a low glycemic index value, as these will help to keep blood sugar levels steady, providing much-needed sustained energy as well as fiber. The following breakfast recipes have all been selected bearing these dietary considerations in mind and the emphasis is on taste, variety, and health, rather than deprivation.

001 ROASTED MUSHROOMS WITH CRÈME FRAÎCHE & BACON

2 large portobello
mushrooms
1 tbsp extra-virgin
olive oil

2 free-range eggs
2 tbsp reduced-fat crème
fraîche

2 slices bacon, broiled
until crisp
salt and freshly ground
black pepper

1 Preheat the oven to 200°C/400°F/Gas 6. Place the mushrooms in a piece
of foil large enough to make a package. Spoon over the oil and season. Fold up
the foil to encase the mushrooms. Place the package on a baking sheet and
roast for 20 minutes until tender.
2 Meanwhile, half-fill a skillet with water and bring to a boil, then reduce
the heat to low. Break the eggs into the pan and cook them at a gentle
simmer for about 3 minutes, then remove using a slotted spoon and drain.
3 Place a mushroom on each serving plate and top with a poached egg.
Place a spoonful of crème fraîche on top of each one and sprinkle
with the bacon snipped into small pieces. Season with salt and pepper.

SERVES 2
3G CARBOHYDRATE PER SERVING

002 MOZZARELLA & ROASTED TOMATO TOWER

2 large plum tomatoes,
halved and seeds
scooped out

1 tbsp extra-virgin olive
oil, plus extra
for greasing
6 slices mozzarella

3 tsp pre-made
pesto
salt and freshly
ground black pepper

1 Preheat the oven to 190°C/375°F/Gas 5. Lightly oil a roasting pan.
Place the tomatoes, skin-side down, in the pan and roast for
15-20 minutes until they are tender but still retain their shape.
2 Divide the mozzarella slices between two plates and top with
the tomatoes. Mix together the remaining olive oil and pesto,
and spoon the dressing over; season well.

SERVES 2
2.5G CARBOHYDRATE PER SERVING

003　SMOKED SALMON OMELET

small knob of butter
2 free-range eggs,
  beaten
freshly ground
  black pepper

few strips smoked salmon
extra-virgin olive oil, for
  brushing
2 vine-ripened tomatoes,
  thickly sliced

½ tsp balsamic vinegar,
  optional

1　Melt the butter in a medium-sized skillet and swirl it around to coat the bottom.
2　Pour in the egg and as it sets, gently push the edges toward the center, allowing the raw egg to run to the edges of the pan. Place the salmon down the center then cook until the egg is lightly set but still runny on top.
3　Season the omelet with pepper, then fold in half to enclose the salmon and heat briefly.
4　Meanwhile, heat a broiler to medium. Line a broiler pan with foil and brush with a little olive oil. Arrange the tomato slices on top and broil for about 3 minutes, turning, until tender.
5　Place the omelet and broiled tomatoes on a plate. Spoon the balsamic vinegar over the tomatoes, if using.

SERVES 1
2.5G CARBOHYDRATE

004　SMOKED TROUT ROLLS

3 strips smoked trout,
  about 2oz
  total weight
3 tsp reduced-fat
  cream cheese

3 matchsticks
  peeled cucumber
1 tbsp snipped
  fresh chives

1 tbsp lemon juice,
  plus extra to serve
freshly ground
  black pepper
3 long chives, to garnish

1　Lay out the strips of trout on a chopping board. Place a spoonful of cream cheese at one end of each strip, then place a stick of cucumber crosswise on top. Sprinkle with the chives.
2　Squeeze over the lemon juice, season with pepper, and roll up each strip of trout to make a roll.
3　Tie a chive around each roll, and serve with extra lemon juice, if liked.

SERVES 1
1G CARBOHYDRATE

005 **HAM ROULADE**

4 slices lean
  good-quality ham
8 tsp half-fat
  cream cheese

2 scallions
2 tbsp finely chopped
  red bell pepper

freshly ground
  black pepper

1   Place the ham slices on a chopping board. Spread 2 teaspoons of cream cheese down one half of each slice of ham.
2   Sprinkle each one with scallions and red bell pepper. Season with pepper and roll up the ham slices.

SERVES 2
1.5G CARBOHYDRATE PER SERVING

006 **COOL DOGS**

4 gluten-free turkey
  sausages

1 small whole wheat
  tortilla
1 tsp mild mustard

2 vine-ripened tomatoes,
  sliced

1   Preheat the broiler to medium and line the broiler pan with foil. Broil the sausages until cooked through and golden.
2   Warm the tortilla and slice into 4 strips. Spread each strip with a little mustard.
3   Place a sausage horizontally on the top of each slice of tortilla and roll up to make a sausage roll. Serve with the tomato.

SERVES 2
9G CARBOHYDRATE PER SERVING

007 **SMOKED FISH & SPINACH**

½lb undyed smoked fish,
  such as cod or haddock

9-oz bag fresh spinach,
  tough stalks removed
  and rinsed
2 tsp lemon juice

freshly ground
  black pepper
2 tbsp reduced-fat
  crème fraîche

1   Place the smoked fish in a sauté pan. Carefully cover with boiling water and poach the fish until cooked. Peel off the skin, and cut the fillet into 2 portions.
2   Steam the spinach for 3 minutes until wilted. Drain and divide the spinach between two plates, then pour over the lemon juice.
3   Place the fish on top of the spinach. Season with pepper, and serve with a spoonful of crème fraîche.

SERVES 2
4G CARBOHYDRATE PER SERVING

008 SUNDAY BREAKFAST PLATTER

4 slices prosciutto
1 hard-cooked free-range
  egg, quartered
1 cup Gruyère,
  thinly sliced
6 spears of asparagus,
  trimmed and steamed
2 slices rye bread

RICOTTA DIP:
5 tbsp ricotta cheese
2 tbsp snipped fresh
  chives
1 tbsp fresh basil
1 tbsp lemon juice
salt and freshly ground
  black pepper
paprika, to garnish

1   Arrange the prosciutto, egg, Gruyère, asparagus, and rye bread on a
    serving platter.
2   Put the ricotta, chives, basil, and lemon in a blender. Mix until creamy.
    Season to taste, and spoon into a small serving bowl. Sprinkle with paprika
    to serve.

SERVES 2
15G CARBOHYDRATE PER SERVING

BREAKFASTS & BRUNCHES

009 **TORTILLA EGG ROLLS**

2 small whole wheat
   tortillas or
   pitta bread
8 vine-ripened cherry
   tomatoes, broiled, or
   oven-baked, to serve

FILLING:
1 tbsp unsalted butter
1 tsp olive oil
¼ red bell pepper,
   seeded and diced
1 scallion, finely chopped

2 sun-dried
   tomatoes in oil,
   finely chopped
4 free-range eggs,
   lightly beaten
2 tbsp milk
salt and freshly
   ground black pepper

1   Heat the butter and oil in a heavy-based saucepan, add the bell pepper, scallion,
    and sun-dried tomatoes and cook for 5 minutes until softened.
2   Mix together the eggs and milk, season well, then pour into the pan. Using
    a wooden spoon, stir the egg constantly but gently, to ensure it doesn't stick.
    Cook for about 2–3 minutes until the scrambled egg is semi-solid but creamy.
3   Meanwhile, warm the tortillas in an oven or dry skillet, then spoon the egg on
    top, and roll up. Serve with the broiled tomatoes.

SERVES 2
18G CARBOHYDRATE PER SERVING

010   SOUFFLÉ CHEESE OMELET

2 free-range eggs,
   separated
salt and freshly
   ground black pepper
small knob of butter

¼ cup grated mature
   Cheddar
1 tbsp snipped fresh
   chives, to garnish

1   Whip the egg whites in a large, grease-free bowl until they form stiff peaks.
Beat the egg yolks, season, then carefully fold them into the egg whites using
a metal spoon.

2   Gently melt the butter in a medium-sized heavy-based skillet and swirl it around
to cover the base. Spoon in the whipped, frothy egg mixture and gently flatten
it (without losing too much air) using a spatula until it covers the base of the
pan. Cook over a medium heat for 1 minute.

3   Sprinkle the cheese along the center of the omelet and cook for
another 1 minute until the bottom of the omelet is set and golden.

4   Carefully fold the omelet in half to encase the cheese. Slide it onto a plate,
and garnish with chives before serving.

SERVES 1
1G CARBOHYDRATE

011   BREAKFAST FRITTATA

4 good-quality gluten-free
   sausages (or vegetarian
   alternative)

sunflower oil, for frying
8 cherry tomatoes
4 free-range eggs, beaten

salt and freshly ground
   black pepper

1   Preheat the broiler to medium-high. Arrange the sausages on a foil-lined broiler
pan and cook until golden. Let cool slightly, then slice into bite-sized pieces.

2   Meanwhile, heat a little oil in a medium-sized skillet with a heatproof
handle, add the tomatoes and cook for 2 minutes. Arrange the sausages
in the pan so the tomatoes and sausages are evenly distributed.

3   Add a little more oil to the pan if it seems dry. Season the beaten eggs
and pour the mixture over the ingredients in the pan. Cook for 3 minutes
without stirring the omelet. Place the pan under the preheated broiler for
an additional 3 minutes until the top is just cooked. Serve cut into wedges.

SERVES 3
4G CARBOHYDRATE PER SERVING

012   EGGS FLORENTINE

9-oz bag small leaf spinach, rinsed well	a little grated nutmeg	salt and freshly ground black pepper
3 tbsp reduced-fat crème fraîche	2 large free-range eggs	
	⅓ cup grated mature Cheddar	

1   Steam the spinach for 2 minutes until wilted. Let drain, then squeeze out any excess water using your hands. Finely chop the spinach, then mix with the crème fraîche and a little grated nutmeg. Season, and spoon the spinach mixture into a small baking dish.

2   Preheat the broiler to medium. Make two hollows in the spinach mixture, large enough to accommodate the eggs. Break the eggs into the holes, top the eggs with cheese and broil for 2-3 minutes until the eggs are just set.

SERVES 2
3G CARBOHYDRATE PER SERVING

013   EGGS EN COCOTTE

sunflower oil, for greasing	salt and freshly ground black pepper
2 large free-range eggs	1 tbsp snipped fresh chives, optional
2 tbsp reduced-fat crème fraîche	

1   Preheat the oven to 180°C/350°F/Gas 4. Lightly oil 2 ramekins, about 3 inches diameter, 1½ inches deep, then break an egg into each dish. Place a spoonful of crème fraîche on top of each egg and season.

2   Place the ramekins in a roasting pan. Pour boiling water into the pan until it comes halfway up the sides of the ramekins. Bake for 15 minutes. Sprinkle with chives before serving.

SERVES 2
1G CARBOHYDRATE PER SERVING

014   BAKED EGGS & HAM

sunflower oil, for greasing	2 large free-range eggs	salt and freshly ground black pepper
1 slice lean good-quality ham, cut in half	2 tbsp reduced-fat crème fraîche	¼ cup grated mature Cheddar

1   Preheat the oven to 180°C/350°F/Gas 4. Lightly oil 2 ramekins, about 3 inches diameter, 1½ inches deep. Place a slice of ham into the bottom of each ramekin, then break an egg into each dish.

2   Put a spoonful of crème fraîche on top of each egg and season. Sprinkle with the cheese.

3   Place the ramekins in a roasting pan. Pour boiling water into the pan until it comes halfway up the sides of the ramekins. Bake for 15 minutes.

SERVES 2
1G CARBOHYDRATE PER SERVING

015 BOILED EGG WITH ASPARAGUS

1-2 free-range eggs
5 spears asparagus

salt and freshly ground
black pepper

1 Boil the egg(s) for about 4 minutes or to your liking.
2 Meanwhile, steam the asparagus for about 3 minutes until just tender.
3 Season and dip the asparagus into the runny egg.

SERVES 1
1G CARBOHYDRATE

016 GRIDDLED TOMATOES WITH PARMESAN

olive oil, for brushing
1 vine-ripened tomato,
thickly sliced
1 tsp balsamic vinegar
1 slice whole wheat
soda bread

Parmesan shavings,
for sprinkling
salt and freshly
ground black pepper

1 Brush a griddle pan with oil and heat. Add the tomato and cook for about 2 minutes, turning once. Add the balsamic vinegar and heat briefly.
2 Meanwhile, lightly toast the bread and place the tomatoes on top. Pour over any juices left in the pan. Season, and sprinkle with Parmesan.

SERVES 1
1G CARBOHYDRATE

017 MOZZARELLA MUSHROOMS WITH CRISPY BACON BITS

oil, for brushing
2 large, flat cap
mushrooms
1 bacon slice

salt and freshly
ground black pepper
2 slices mozzarella
cheese

1 Preheat the broiler to medium. Lightly brush a large piece of foil with oil. Place the mushrooms in the center of the foil and brush with a little oil. Season, and broil for 10-15 minutes, turning once.
2 Meanwhile, broil the bacon until crisp, then cut it into small pieces.
3 Arrange the bacon pieces on top of the mushrooms, then place a slice of mozzarella on top of each one.
4 Broil for a further 3 minutes until the cheese has melted.

SERVES 2
3G CARBOHYDRATE PER SERVING

018 COTTAGE CHEESE PANCAKES

2½ tbsp soy flour
1 tbsp butter, softened
⅓ cup cottage cheese
2 free-range eggs

2 tbsp semi-skimmed
  milk
sunflower oil, for frying

⅓ cup grated mature
  Cheddar

1   Mix together the flour, butter, cottage cheese, eggs, and milk in a blender to make a batter. Let rest for 15 minutes.
2   To make each pancake, heat a little oil in a heavy-based skillet. Pour a quarter of the batter into the pan and swirl until it coats the base. Cook the pancake for 2 minutes, then sprinkle a quarter of the cheese over one side. Fold the pancake in half and cook for another minute.

MAKES 4 PANCAKES
2G CARBOHYDRATE PER PANCAKE

019 MORE FISH THAN RICE KEDGEREE

¼ cup brown rice, rinsed
1 bay leaf
¾lb undyed smoked
  haddock or cod
1 tbsp sunflower oil
1 onion, chopped

2 tsp garam masala
1 tsp turmeric
3 cardamom pods, split
1 tsp bouillon powder
2 free-range eggs,
  soft-cooked

salt and freshly ground
  black pepper

1   Put the rice in a saucepan and pour over cold water so that it covers the rice by ½ inch, then add the bay leaf. Bring the water to a boil, then cover the pan with a tight fitting lid, and reduce the heat to a very low simmer. Cook the rice, without removing the lid, for 30-35 minutes until the water has been absorbed. Taste the rice and if it is tender, cover the pan, remove it from the heat and let stand for 5 minutes. If the rice is still a little hard, add a touch more hot water, replace the lid, and return to the heat.
2   Put the fish in a large sauté pan and cover with water. Bring the water to a simmer and cook the fish, occasionally spooning the water over the fish, for about 5 minutes until just cooked and opaque. Remove the fish from the pan with a slotted spoon, and remove the skin and any bones. Break the fish into large chunks and set aside. Reserve 1 cup of the cooking water.
3   Meanwhile, heat the oil in a skillet and cook the onion for about 8 minutes until tender and beginning to brown. Stir in the spices and cook for 1 minute.
4   Pour the reserved water into the skillet and stir in the bouillon powder. Stir well, then add the rice and the fish, carefully mixing it in with a wooden spatula; heat through.
5   Season to taste and divide the rice between two bowls. Halve the eggs and place on top before serving.

SERVES 2
23G CARBOHYDRATE PER SERVING

020 SOUFFLÉ BERRY OMELET

**2 free-range eggs,
separated
½ tsp fructose**

**¾ cup frozen mixed
berries, defrosted
small knob of butter**

1   Whip the egg whites in a large, grease-free bowl until they form stiff peaks.
    Beat the egg yolks, then carefully fold into the egg whites with the fructose,
    using a metal spoon.
2   Gently melt the butter in a medium-sized heavy-based skillet and swirl it around
    to cover the base. Spoon in the whipped, frothy egg mixture and gently flatten
    it (without losing too much air) using a spatula until it covers the base of the
    pan. Cook over a medium heat for 1 minute.
3   Spoon the berries down the center of the omelet and cook for another
    2 minutes until the bottom of the omelet is set and golden. Fold the omelet
    in half to encase the berries, and slide onto a plate to serve.

SERVES 1
16G CARBOHYDRATE

BREAKFASTS & BRUNCHES

021 CHOCOLATE SOY DRINK

1 tbsp drinking
  chocolate powder

scant 1¼ cups soy milk
½ tsp pure vanilla extract

1   Mix together the chocolate powder with a little of the soy milk in a cup.
2   Warm the remaining soy milk and vanilla extract, then mix little by
    little into the chocolate paste. Stir well until combined. Serve warm.
    If you want to serve chilled, let cool then chill in the refrigerator for
    30 minutes to 1 hour. Stir well and add a few ice cubes before serving.

SERVES 1
2G CARBOHYDRATE

022 NUTTY BANANA SHAKE

½ cup whole
  blanched almonds
1¼ cups soy milk
1 small banana, halved

1 tsp pure vanilla
  extract
ground cinnamon,
  to sprinkle

1   Grind the almonds in a food processor until very finely chopped.
2   Add the milk, banana, and vanilla extract and mix until smooth and creamy.
3   Pour into glasses. Serve immediately, or chill for 30 minutes (but no longer
    as the banana will discolor). Sprinkle with cinnamon just before serving.

SERVES 2
13.5G CARBOHYDRATE PER SERVING

023 RASPBERRY OAT CRUNCH

1 tbsp sunflower seeds
1 cup thick natural bio
  yogurt

2 tbsp toasted
  wheat germ
scant 1 cup raspberries,
  fresh or frozen

1   Place the sunflower seeds in a dry skillet and cook over a
    medium heat for 1-2 minutes until lightly toasted and golden
    in color (take care—they can easily burn). Let cool.
2   Spoon the yogurt into a large bowl. Stir in the wheat germ
    and sunflower seeds, leaving a few to sprinkle over the top.
3   If using frozen raspberries, let them defrost. Gently
    fold the raspberries into the yogurt and stir to give a
    marbled effect. Spoon into 2 glasses, and top with the
    reserved seeds before serving.

SERVES 2
18G CARBOHYDRATE PER SERVING

024 BERRY SCRUNCH

1 tbsp sunflower seeds
1 tbsp whole
  porridge oats
¾ cup strawberries,
  hulled and sliced, or
  raspberries

2 Brazil nuts, chopped
¼ cup broken
  cashew nuts
6 heaped tbsp
  natural bio yogurt
⅓ cup soy milk

1　Place the sunflower seeds in a dry skillet and cook
  over a medium heat for 1-2 minutes until lightly toasted and
  golden in color (take care—they can easily burn). Let cool.
2　Place the oats, fruit, sunflower seeds, and nuts in a serving
  bowl. Add the yogurt and milk, and mix until combined.

SERVES 1
14.5G CARBOHYDRATE

025 LOW-CARB MUESLI

1 tbsp sunflower seeds,
1 tbsp pumpkin seeds
3 tbsp flaked almonds
½ cup broken
  cashew nuts

⅓ cup whole
  porridge oats
1 dessert apple, grated
soy milk, to serve

1　Place the seeds and nuts in a dry skillet and cook
  over a medium heat for 1-2 minutes until lightly toasted and
  golden in color (take care—they can easily burn). Let cool.
2　Mix together the seeds, nuts, and oats and divide between 2 bowls.
  Spoon the grated apple over the top and serve with a little soy milk.

SERVES 2
17.5G CARBOHYDRATE PER SERVING

026 STRAWBERRY & RICOTTA OATCAKES

8 tsp ricotta cheese
½ tsp pure vanilla extract
4 fine-milled oatcakes

4 strawberries,
  hulled and sliced

1　Beat together the ricotta and vanilla in a bowl.
2　Place 2 teaspoons of ricotta on top of each oatcake.
3　Divide the strawberries between the oatcakes and arrange
  on top of the ricotta.

SERVES 2
13G CARBOHYDRATE PER SERVING

chapter 2

SOUPS

Fresh, vibrant, healthy, and generally low in carbohydrates and fat, soup is the perfect fuel for those watching their weight, without wanting to miss out on vital nutrients. As the following recipes demonstrate, soups are incredibly versatile. There are thick, hearty soups, which can be meals in themselves, as well as lighter broths. These make excellent appetizers or even snacks, taking the edge off hunger pangs. There are also chilled soups for the hotter summer months. Two recipes for homemade stock are included in this chapter: one vegetable and one chicken. These can be used as the base for all the soup recipes. Homemade stocks contain minimal amounts of carbohydrate, while shop-bought alternatives vary in their content and can even be alarmingly high because some contain carbohydrate-based fillers and additives. If buying ready-made stocks do check the label first. The vegetable bouillon powders are about the best alternative to homemade. Most of the soups in this chapter freeze well, so it makes sense to make double and freeze the surplus, but avoid freezing those that contain fish or shellfish.

027 CHICKEN STOCK

1 chicken carcass (you could use the one left from the Best Ever Roast Chicken recipe, see page 123)

1 onion, roughly chopped
1 carrot, roughly chopped
1 stick celery, roughly chopped
1 bay leaf

6 black peppercorns
handful of fresh parsley
6¾ cups water

1 Place all the ingredients in a deep, narrow saucepan, making sure they are covered by the water, and bring to a boil.
2 Reduce the heat and simmer, uncovered, for 1½ hours, skimming off any fat that rises to the surface. Replenish with more cold water if the ingredients become uncovered.
3 Strain the stock and discard the solids. Let cool, pour the stock into a container, and store in the refrigerator for up to 3 days or freeze until required.

MAKES ABOUT 3¾–4½ CUPS
3G CARBOHYDRATE

028 VEGETABLE STOCK

2 onions, cut into ½-inch dice
2 carrots, cut into ½-inch dice

2 sticks celery, cut into ½-inch dice
1 leek, cut into ½-inch dice

1 bay leaf
2 sprigs fresh thyme
handful of fresh parsley
6¾ cups water

1 Place all the ingredients in a deep, narrow saucepan, making sure all the ingredients are covered.
2 Bring the water to a boil, then reduce the heat and simmer for 40 minutes, skimming off any scum that rises to the surface.
3 Strain the stock and discard the solids. Let cool, pour the stock into a container, and store in the refrigerator for up to 3 days or freeze until required.

MAKES ABOUT 3¾–4½ CUPS
3G CARBOHYDRATE

029 THAI CHICKEN BROTH

3¾ cups chicken stock (see recipe above)
1 stick lemon grass, peeled, halved lengthwise, and crushed with the back of a knife
4 slices fresh root ginger, plus 2 slices, peeled and cut into

matchsticks
4 kaffir lime leaves
2 tsp Thai fish sauce
2 chicken breast halves, about 5oz each
2 cloves garlic, thinly sliced
⅔ cup fresh spinach leaves

2 tbsp rice vinegar
1 tbsp lime juice
1 bird's eye chili, seeded and finely chopped
salt
1 tbsp chopped fresh cilantro

1 Put the stock, lemon grass, 4 ginger slices, the lime leaves, and fish sauce into a saucepan. Add the chicken breasts and bring to a boil. Reduce the heat and simmer, half-covered, for 20 minutes. Remove the chicken, set aside, and strain the stock, discarding the solids.
2 Return the stock to the pan and add the ginger matchsticks, garlic, spinach, rice vinegar, lime juice, and chili, then simmer for 2-3 minutes.
3 Slice the chicken into strips and divide between 2 bowls. Pour over the stock. Season with salt, if necessary, and garnish with fresh cilantro.

SERVES 2
7G CARBOHYDRATE PER SERVING

030 CHICKEN SOUP

1 tbsp olive oil
1 onion, finely chopped
1 stick celery,
  finely chopped
1 small carrot,
  finely chopped

1 bay leaf
¾ cup skinless
  chicken breast halves,
  cubed
3¾ cups chicken stock
  (see page 30)

1 tbsp reduced-fat
  crème fraîche
salt and freshly
  ground black pepper

1 Heat the oil in a saucepan and fry the onion, celery, carrot, and bay leaf for 8 minutes, half-covered, until softened.
2 Add the chicken and cook for 3–4 minutes until sealed and golden on all sides.
3 Pour in the stock and bring to a boil, then reduce the heat and simmer for 20–25 minutes until the chicken is cooked. Stir in the crème fraîche; season.

SERVES 2
7G CARBOHYDRATE PER SERVING

031 MOROCCAN SPINACH & GARBANZO SOUP

1 tbsp olive oil
1 red onion, roughly
  chopped
1 clove garlic, chopped
1 tsp ground coriander

1 tsp ground cumin
handful of fresh cilantro
9-oz bag fresh spinach,
  tough stalks removed
3¾ cups vegetable stock
  (see page 30)

¾ cup canned garbanzos,
  rinsed
salt and freshly
  ground black pepper
2 tbsp sour cream,
  to serve

1 Heat the oil in a saucepan and fry the onion, half-covered, for 8 minutes until softened. Add the garlic and spices and cook for a further 1 minute.
2 Add the cilantro and spinach to the pan and stir to coat them in the oil and spices, then pour in the stock. Bring to a boil, then reduce the heat and simmer for 10 minutes.
3 Add the garbanzos and simmer for a further 10 minutes. Transfer to a blender and process until a semi-chunky soup. Season, and serve topped with a spoonful of sour cream.

SERVES 2
11G CARBOHYDRATE PER SERVING

032 SPINACH & PEA SOUP

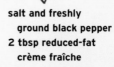

1 tbsp olive oil
1 onion, finely chopped
1 carrot, finely chopped
3¾ cups vegetable stock
  (see page 30)

2¾ cups fresh spinach,
  tough stalks removed
1 cup frozen
  petit pois
1 tbsp chopped fresh mint

salt and freshly
  ground black pepper
2 tbsp reduced-fat
  crème fraîche

1 Heat the oil in a saucepan and fry the onion for 7 minutes, stirring frequently, until softened. Add the carrot and cook for a further 3 minutes.
2 Pour in the stock and bring to a boil. Reduce the heat and simmer for 10 minutes.
3 Add the spinach, petit pois, and mint and cook for 3 minutes until the vegetables are tender. Transfer to a blender and mix until smooth. Season, and serve with a spoonful of crème fraîche.

SERVES 2
13G CARBOHYDRATE PER SERVING

033 **PISTOU**

1 tbsp olive oil
1 leek, sliced
1 small carrot,
    finely chopped
1 stick celery,
    finely chopped
3 green beans,
    thinly sliced

2½ cups vegetable
    stock (see page 30)
⅔ cup passata
1 bay leaf
⅔ cup conchigliette
    (small shells) pasta
sprig fresh rosemary

salt and freshly ground
    black pepper
1 tbsp pesto, to serve
few shavings of
    Parmesan, to serve

1   Heat the oil in a large saucepan and add the leek. Cook over a medium heat for
    5 minutes, stirring occasionally, until tender. Add the carrot, celery, and green
    beans and cook for a further 5 minutes.
2   Pour in the stock and passata and add the bay leaf, stir well. Bring to a boil,
    then reduce the heat and simmer, half-covered, for 15 minutes. Remove the bay
    leaves, and using a hand-blender or food processor, semi-purée the vegetables.
3   Return the bay leaf to the soup, add the pasta and rosemary and bring to a boil.
    Reduce the heat slightly and cook for 10 minutes until the pasta is tender. You
    may need to add some extra stock or water if the soup seems too thick.
    Remove the bay leaf and rosemary, and season to taste.
4   Divide between 2 bowls. Serve with the Parmesan shavings and a spoonful
    of pesto.

SERVES 2
27G CARBOHYDRATE PER SERVING

034 ROASTED VEGETABLE SOUP

2 tbsp olive oil
1 cup peeled butternut
  squash, cubed
1 carrot, cut into chunks
1 onion, quartered

1 small fennel bulb,
  thickly sliced
1 bay leaf
2 sprigs fresh oregano
1 sprig fresh rosemary

3¾ cups vegetable stock
  (see page 30)
salt and freshly
  ground black pepper
freshly grated Parmesan,
  to serve

1 Preheat the oven to 200°C/400°F/Gas 6. Put the olive oil into a large roasting pan. Add the vegetables and turn to coat them in the oil. Spread them out in a single layer. Tuck the herbs among the vegetables.
2 Roast the vegetables for 30-40 minutes until tender, turning them occasionally to ensure they brown evenly.
3 Remove from the oven, discard the herbs, and transfer the vegetables to a saucepan. Cover with the stock and bring to a boil. Reduce the heat and simmer for 15 minutes. Transfer the soup to a blender and mix until smooth. Season, and sprinkle with grated Parmesan.

SERVES 2
15G CARBOHYDRATE PER SERVING

035 VEGETABLE & BEAN SOUP

1 tbsp olive oil
1 onion, diced
1 stick celery, diced
1 carrot, finely sliced
1 bay leaf
⅓ cup dry
  white wine

3¾ cups vegetable stock
  (see page 30)
¾ cup (drained weight)
  canned borlotti beans,
  rinsed

2 cups fresh
  spinach, tough
  stalks removed
salt and freshly ground
  black pepper
¼ cup grated Parmesan,
  to serve

1 Heat the oil in a saucepan and fry the onion for 7 minutes until softened. Add the celery, carrot, and bay leaf, then cook for 3 minutes, stirring frequently.
2 Pour in the wine and stock, and bring to a boil. Reduce the heat and add the beans. Simmer the soup for 15 minutes until reduced and the vegetables are tender. Add the spinach 2 minutes before the end of the cooking time.
3 Season well, and serve sprinkled with Parmesan.

SERVES 2
16G CARBOHYDRATE PER SERVING

036 FAVA BEAN & BACON SOUP

2 cups shelled fava beans
1 stick celery, finely sliced
3 Romaine lettuce leaves,
  torn into pieces
2 tbsp fresh parsley

3¾ cups vegetable stock
  (see page 30)
3 slices lean bacon, cut
  into ½-inch pieces

2 tbsp fat-reduced
  crème fraîche
salt and freshly
  ground black pepper

1 Steam the beans for about 3 minutes until just tender, then cool under cold running water and peel off the tough outer shell.
2 Put the celery, lettuce, parsley, stock, and bacon into a saucepan and bring to a boil. Reduce the heat and simmer for 10 minutes.
3 Add the beans and transfer the soup to a blender. Mix until fairly smooth. Return the soup to the pan, and stir in the crème fraîche. Season, and heat through gently.

SERVES 2
11G CARBOHYDRATE PER SERVING

037 MIXED MUSHROOM SOUP

¼oz dried porcini
  mushrooms
3¾ cups vegetable stock
  (see page 30)

1 tbsp extra-virgin
  olive oil
1 onion, roughly chopped
2 large, flat mushrooms
1 stick celery, finely sliced

1 clove garlic, chopped
3 tbsp fat-reduced crème
  fraîche
salt and freshly ground
  black pepper

1   Soak the porcini in 1 cup of the hot vegetable stock for 20 minutes
    until softened. Strain the mushrooms and reserve the soaking liquor.
2   Heat the oil in a saucepan and fry the onion for 7 minutes until softened.
    Add the fresh and dried mushrooms, the celery and garlic, and cook,
    stirring frequently, for 4 minutes until softened.
3   Pour in the stock and the reserved mushroom liquor and bring to a boil,
    then lower the heat and simmer for 15 minutes until reduced. Transfer
    to a blender and mix until smooth. Return the soup to the pan and
    stir in the crème fraîche. Season and heat gently before serving.

SERVES 2
10G CARBOHYDRATE PER SERVING

038 RED ONION SOUP

2 tbsp olive oil
1lb red onions, chopped
½ cup dry
  white wine

3¾ cups vegetable stock
  (see page 30)
1 sprig fresh rosemary
1 tsp fresh thyme

1 tsp Dijon mustard
¼ cup grated Gruyère
  cheese
salt and freshly
  ground black pepper

1   Heat the oil in a saucepan and add the onions. Fry the onions,
    half-covered, for 10 minutes over a medium-low heat until softened.
    Add the wine and bring to a boil. Cook until most of the wine
    has evaporated and the smell of alcohol has disappeared.
2   Pour in the stock, rosemary, and thyme and bring to a boil, then
    lower the heat and simmer for 20 minutes until reduced and
    thickened. Stir in the Dijon mustard, and season.
3   Remove the rosemary, and pour half of the soup into a blender.
    Mix until smooth, then return the puréed onion mixture to the
    pan, and stir well. Ladle into bowls and sprinkle with the cheese.

SERVES 2
10G CARBOHYDRATE PER SERVING

039 CAULI-CHEESE SOUP

1 tbsp olive oil
2 leeks, finely chopped
2½ cups cauliflower
  florets
1 tsp dried oregano

3¾ cups vegetable stock
  (see page 30)
1 tbsp reduced-fat
  crème fraîche

½ cup grated mature
  Cheddar
salt and freshly
  ground black pepper

1   Heat the olive oil in a saucepan and fry the leeks for 4 minutes until softened.
    Add the cauliflower and oregano, then cook, stirring, for 2 minutes.
2   Pour in the stock and cook for 20 minutes until the cauliflower is tender.
    Transfer to a blender and mix until smooth.
3   Return the soup to the pan and add the crème fraîche and Cheddar. Heat
    through, stirring, until the cheese has melted. Season well before serving.

SERVES 2
6G CARBOHYDRATE PER SERVING

040 RIBOLITTA

1 tbsp olive oil
1 onion, diced
1 stick celery, diced
1 carrot, finely sliced
1 cup cabbage, shredded

2 slices bacon,
 cut into pieces
1 bay leaf
⅓ cup red wine
3¾ cups vegetable stock
 (see page 30)

¾ cup canned haricot or
 cannellini beans, rinsed
salt and freshly
 ground black pepper
¼ cup Parmesan, grated

1 Heat the oil in a saucepan and fry the onion for 7 minutes
 until softened. Add the celery, carrot, cabbage, bacon,
 and bay leaf, then cook for 3 minutes, stirring frequently.
2 Pour in the wine and stock and bring to a boil.
 Reduce the heat and add the beans. Simmer the soup
 for 15 minutes until reduced and the vegetables are tender.
3 Season well and serve sprinkled with Parmesan.

SERVES 2
18G CARBOHYDRATE PER SERVING

041 MISO SOUP WITH TOFU

2 packages instant
 miso soup powder
½ cup fine green
 beans, thinly sliced
1 small carrot,
 finely shredded
1½ cups fresh spinach
 leaves, shredded

2 toasted nori strips,
 broken into small pieces
½-inch piece fresh root
 ginger, peeled and
 sliced into thin strips
3oz Japanese tofu, thinly
 sliced

1 tbsp soy sauce
1 scallion, finely
 shredded
2 tsp sesame seeds,
 toasted
½ tsp crushed
 dried chili flakes

1 Make the miso soup following the package instructions.
2 Steam the beans and carrot for 3 minutes or until tender, adding the spinach 2
 minutes before the end of the cooking time, then place the vegetables in two bowls.
3 Add the nori, ginger, and tofu, then pour the hot miso soup over the top.
 Stir in the soy sauce. Sprinkle with the scallion, sesame seeds, and
 chili before serving.

SERVES 2
9G CARBOHYDRATE (EX MISO)

042 HOT & SOUR SOUP

2 cups vegetable stock
 (see page 30)
1 stick lemon grass,
 peeled and crushed
 using the back of
 a knife

1 bird's eye chili, seeded
 and finely chopped
2 kaffir lime leaves
1 clove garlic, finely sliced
2 scallions, finely sliced
1 small carrot, cut into
 fine strips

3oz Japanese tofu, sliced
2 tbsp chopped fresh
 cilantro
salt
juice of ½ lime

1 Put the stock in a saucepan with the lemon grass, half of the chili,
 the kaffir lime leaves, garlic, and half the scallions. Bring to a boil, then
 reduce the heat and simmer for 10 minutes. Strain the stock and discard
 the solids.
2 Return the stock to the pan with the reserved chili and scallions, the carrot and
 tofu. Season with salt, and heat for 2 minutes. Stir in the lime juice and serve
 sprinkled with cilantro.

SERVES 2
5.5G CARBOHYDRATE PER SERVING

043 ROASTED TOMATO & ROSEMARY SOUP

6 vine-ripened plum
  tomatoes
2 tbsp olive oil
1 leek, sliced

1 clove garlic, chopped
2 sprigs fresh rosemary
1 bay leaf
½ cup passata

2½ cups vegetable stock
  (see page 30)
salt and freshly ground
  black pepper

1 Preheat the oven to 180°C/350°F/Gas 4. Put the tomatoes in a roasting
   pan with half of the oil and roast for 20 minutes until tender. Leave until
   cool enough to handle, then peel away the skin, and deseed. Chop the flesh.
2 Heat the remaining oil in a heavy-based saucepan and fry the leek for
   4 minutes until softened. Add the garlic, rosemary, and bay leaf and cook
   for a further 1 minute.
3 Pour in the passata and stock, then bring to a boil. Reduce the heat
   and simmer for 15 minutes until thickened. Add the chopped tomatoes,
   and cook for a further 5 minutes.
4 Remove the rosemary and bay leaf, and transfer the soup to a blender.
   Mix until smooth and creamy; season well.

SERVES 2
7G CARBOHYDRATE PER SERVING

044 CREAMY TOMATO & LENTIL SOUP

¼ cup split
  red lentils, rinsed
1 tbsp olive oil
1 onion, chopped
1 carrot, finely chopped

1 stick celery,
  finely chopped
½ cup passata
2½ cups vegetable stock
  (see page 30)

1 bay leaf
3 tbsp reduced-fat
  crème fraîche
salt and freshly
  ground black pepper

1 Place the lentils in a saucepan, cover with water and bring to a boil.
   Reduce the heat and simmer, half-covered, for 15 minutes until just tender.
   Remove any scum that rises to the surface using a spoon. Drain the lentils
   well and set aside.
2 Meanwhile, heat the oil in a saucepan. Add the onion and cook, half-covered,
   for 8 minutes until softened. Add the carrot and celery, cover, and cook,
   stirring occasionally, for a further 3 minutes.
3 Add the passata, stock, lentils, and bay leaf. Bring to a boil, then reduce
   the heat and simmer, half-covered, for 20 minutes until the lentils and
   vegetables are tender and the soup has thickened.
4 Transfer the soup to a blender and mix until smooth. Return the soup
   to the pan, season, stir in the crème fraîche, and heat gently.

SERVES 2
12.5G CARBOHYDRATE PER SERVING

045 SPICY FISH & GARBANZO SOUP

2 tbsp sunflower oil
2 onions, finely sliced
3 cardamom pods, seeds removed
1 tsp cumin seeds
1 tsp ground coriander
½-inch piece fresh root ginger, peeled and grated
1 red chili, seeded and finely sliced

2 large cloves garlic, crushed
1 bay leaf
1⅓ cups peeled butternut squash, cubed
2½ cups vegetable stock (see page 30)
salt and freshly ground black pepper

squeeze of fresh lemon juice
½ cup canned garbanzos, rinsed
2 thick cod fillets, skinned, about ½lb each
2 tbsp natural bio yogurt
1 tbsp chopped fresh cilantro, to serve

1   Heat half the oil in a large saucepan and fry one of the onions for 7 minutes until softened. Add the spices, garlic, and bay leaf and cook for another minute.
2   Add the squash and stock to the pan. Bring to a boil, then reduce the heat and simmer, half-covered, for 10-12 minutes until the squash is tender. Remove the bay leaf and mix until puréed. Season to taste, add a squeeze of lemon juice and the garbanzos and cook for a further 5 minutes, half-covered.
3   Meanwhile, preheat the broiler to its highest setting. Line a broiler pan with foil, then lightly oil. Season the fish, then broil for about 4-5 minutes each side.
4   Heat the remaining oil in a skillet and fry the second onion until crisp.
5   Ladle the soup into 2 shallow bowls, and top with the fish fillets. Place a spoonful of yogurt on top of the fish, then sprinkle with the crisp onion and cilantro.

SERVES 2
22G CARBOHYDRATE PER SERVING

046 GAZPACHO WITH AVOCADO SALSA

1 slice day-old whole
   wheat bread
1lb vine-ripened tomatoes,
   peeled, seeded, and
   chopped
1 small cucumber, peeled,
   seeded, and chopped
1 small red bell pepper,
   seeded and chopped
1 green chili, seeded
   and sliced

1 clove garlic, crushed
1 tbsp extra-virgin
   olive oil
juice of 1 lime
few drops Tabasco sauce
salt and freshly
   ground black pepper
4 ice cubes, to serve
fresh basil, to garnish

AVOCADO SALSA:
1 ripe avocado, pitted,
   peeled, and diced
1 tsp lemon juice
1-inch piece
   cucumber, diced
½ red chili,
   finely chopped

1   Soak the bread in a little water for 5 minutes. Place the bread with the
    tomatoes, cucumber, red bell pepper, chili, garlic, oil, lime juice, and Tabasco in
    a food processor or blender. Add 1 cup of water and mix until combined but still
    chunky. Season to taste and chill for 2-3 hours.
2   Just before serving make the avocado salsa. Toss the avocado in the lemon
    juice to prevent it browning. Combine with the cucumber and chili.
3   Ladle the soup into bowls, add the ice cubes, and top with a spoonful of salsa.
    Garnish with the basil just before serving.

SERVES 2
22G CARBOHYDRATE PER SERVING

047 ROASTED RED BELL PEPPER SOUP WITH SCALLOPS

2 red bell peppers, seeded
 and quartered
2 tbsp olive oil
1 onion, roughly chopped
1 clove garlic, chopped

1 bay leaf
3¾ cups vegetable stock
 (see page 30)
handful of fresh basil

salt and freshly
 ground black pepper
4 scallops

1   Preheat the oven to 200°C/400°F/Gas 6. Brush the bell peppers with a little oil
    and place them in a roasting pan. Roast the bell peppers for 25-30 minutes,
    turning once. Remove from the oven and leave until cool enough to handle.
    Peel off the skin, and roughly chop the bell peppers.
2   Heat 1 tablespoon of the oil and fry the onion for 8 minutes, stirring frequently,
    until softened. Add the garlic and bay leaf and cook for 1 minute.
3   Add the bell peppers, stock, and basil and cook for 10 minutes.
    Remove the bay leaf, and mix in a blender until semi-puréed; season well.
4   Heat the remaining oil in a skillet and fry the scallops for 1 minute
    each side. Serve the soup in shallow bowls topped with the scallops.

SERVES 2
9G CARBOHYDRATE PER SERVING

048 CHILLED AVOCADO SOUP

2 avocados, pitted and
 flesh scooped out
1 small cucumber, peeled,
 seeded, and chopped
1 clove garlic, chopped
1 leek, sliced

2 handfuls of
 fresh cilantro,
 plus extra to garnish
juice and finely
 grated zest of 1 lime

2 cups vegetable or
 chicken stock
 (see page 30)
1 green chili, seeded
 and chopped
salt

1   Place all the ingredients in a food processor or blender and mix until smooth
    and creamy.
2   Chill the soup for 1-2 hours, and serve garnished with extra cilantro.
    For an interesting variation, try adding a similar amount of basil in place of
    the cilantro and substitute the lime juice and zest with the juice and zest of
    ½ a lemon.

SERVES 2
11G CARBOHYDRATE PER SERVING

049 PORK BALLS IN FRAGRANT BROTH

2 cups chicken stock (see page 30)
2 kaffir lime leaves
1 stalk lemon grass, peeled and crushed using the back of a knife
1 tsp fish sauce
½-inch piece fresh root ginger, peeled and sliced into 3
1 tbsp sunflower oil

1¾ cups fresh spinach, tough stalks removed, rinsed
1 tbsp chopped fresh cilantro

PORK BALLS:
16oz lean pork fillet
1 bird's eye chili, thinly sliced

1-inch piece fresh root ginger, peeled and chopped
handful of fresh cilantro
1 stalk lemon grass, peeled and finely chopped
2 scallions, chopped
salt and freshly ground black pepper

1 Put the ingredients for the pork balls in a food processor and mix until they form a coarse paste. Season, and chill for 30 minutes.
2 Put the stock, lime leaves, lemon grass, fish sauce, and ginger in a saucepan. Bring to a boil, then reduce the heat and simmer for 10 minutes. Strain the stock, discard the solids, and return it to the pan.
3 Form the pork mixture into 8 equal-sized balls. Heat the oil in a skillet. Add the pork balls and cook for 4 minutes, turning occasionally, until golden.
4 Place the balls in the broth and cook for a further 8 minutes, adding the spinach 2 minutes before the end of the cooking time. Serve garnished with cilantro.

SERVES 2
2G CARBOHYDRATE PER SERVING

050 PORK & VEGETABLE RAMEN

olive oil, for brushing
5oz lean pork fillet
⅔ cup buckwheat noodles
2½ cups chicken stock (see page 30)
½-inch piece fresh root ginger, peeled and sliced into matchsticks

1 tbsp miso paste
2 tbsp dry sherry
2 tbsp soy sauce
1 carrot, thinly sliced
1 scallion, finely chopped
2 heads pak choi, sliced lengthwise
⅔ cup bean sprouts

½ tsp dried crushed chili flakes
2 tbsp chopped fresh cilantro

1 Heat a griddle pan until hot and brush with a little oil. Griddle the pork fillet for 4 minutes each side. Set aside.
2 Meanwhile, cook the noodles following the package instructions, and refresh under cold running water.
3 Heat the stock in a saucepan and stir in the ginger, miso paste, dry sherry, and soy sauce. Bring to a boil and cook for 5 minutes. Reduce the heat, add the carrot, scallions, and pak choi and simmer for 3 minutes, adding the bean sprouts in the last minute.
4 Thinly slice the pork, and divide the meat and noodles between two bowls.
5 Pour over the vegetables and stock and sprinkle with the chili and cilantro.

SERVES 2
26.5G CARBOHYDRATE PER SERVING

051 SPICED CANNELLINI BEAN SOUP WITH SHRIMP KEBABS

1 tbsp sunflower oil
1 onion, finely chopped
½ red bell pepper,
  seeded and chopped
1 clove garlic, chopped
1½ cups (drained weight)
  canned cannellini beans,
  rinsed
1 tsp dried oregano

½ tsp cayenne pepper
3¾ cups vegetable stock
  (see page 30)
3 tbsp passata
juice of ½ lime
1 tbsp reduced-fat
  crème fraîche

SHRIMP KEBABS:
2 tbsp lime juice
½ tsp cayenne pepper
1 clove garlic, crushed
1 tsp sunflower oil
6 large raw shrimp,
  peeled and tails on
salt

1 To make the shrimp kebabs, mix together the lime juice, cayenne, garlic, and oil in a bowl. Season with salt and add the shrimp. Turn to coat them in the marinade, and chill for 30 minutes.
2 Heat the oil in a saucepan and cook the onion, half-covered, for 7 minutes, until soft. Add the bell pepper and garlic and cook for 3 minutes, stirring frequently.
3 Add the oregano, beans, cayenne, stock, and passata and bring to a boil. Reduce the heat and simmer for 15 minutes. Stir in the lime juice, transfer to a blender and mix until smooth. Return to the pan, season, and stir in the crème fraîche.
4 Preheat the broiler to medium. Remove the shrimp from the marinade and thread them onto 2 skewers. Broil the shrimp for 2-3 minutes each side. Ladle the soup into bowls and top with the kebabs.

SERVES 2
22.5G CARBOHYDRATE PER SERVING

052 VIETNAMESE BEEF BROTH

3¾ cups vegetable stock
  (see page 30), or beef
  stock
1 tbsp fish sauce
2 star anise
2 bird's eye chilies,
  seeded and halved

1-inch piece
  fresh root ginger,
  peeled and sliced
1 stalk lemon grass,
  peeled and crushed
2 cloves garlic, sliced
2 kaffir lime leaves
9oz lean fillet beef,
  thinly sliced

1 large head pak choi
1⅓ cups bean sprouts
juice of 1 lime
1 tsp soy sauce
2 scallions,
  finely sliced
½ cup chopped
  fresh cilantro

1 Put the stock, fish sauce, star anise, chilies, ginger, lemon grass, garlic, and lime leaves in a saucepan. Bring to a boil, then reduce the heat and simmer for 15 minutes. Strain, discard the solids, and return the flavored stock to the pan.
2 Add the beef and cook for 4 minutes, then add the pak choi and bean sprouts and cook for a further 2 minutes. Stir in the lime juice, soy sauce, scallions, and cilantro.

SERVES 2
7G CARBOHYDRATE PER SERVING

053 CHILI SHRIMP IN COCONUT BROTH

1 tbsp sunflower oil
1 shallot, finely chopped
1 stalk lemon grass, peeled, and crushed using the back of a knife
½ yellow bell pepper, seeded and cut into long strips

½ cup fine green beans, thinly sliced
2 cloves garlic, crushed
3¾ cups vegetable stock (see page 30)
1-1½ tbsp tom yum soup paste
1-inch piece fresh root ginger, peeled and finely chopped

1 cup reduced-fat coconut milk
2 kaffir lime leaves or juice of ½ lime
1 cup medium-sized raw shrimp, peeled
2 tbsp chopped fresh cilantro

1   Heat the oil in a large saucepan then add the shallot and lemon grass and cook for 2 minutes. Add the yellow bell pepper, green beans, and garlic then cook over a medium heat for another 2 minutes, stirring frequently.
2   Stir in the stock and bring to a boil. Reduce the heat, add the tom yum paste, ginger, coconut milk, and lime leaves, or lime juice, and simmer for 12-15 minutes until thickened slightly.
3   Stir in the shrimp and cook for 2-3 minutes until cooked through. Sprinkle with cilantro before serving.

SERVES 2
11.5G CARBOHYDRATE PER SERVING

054 THAI FISH SOUP

3¾ cups vegetable stock (see page 30) or fish stock
2 tsp tom yum soup paste
1-inch piece fresh root ginger, peeled and finely chopped

1 stalk lemon grass, peeled, and crushed using the back of a knife
2 kaffir lime leaves
2 scallions, finely sliced
2 tsp lime juice
1 tsp fish sauce

¼ cup reduced-fat coconut milk
½lb firm white fish, cut into pieces
⅔ cup cooked medium shrimp
1 tbsp chopped fresh cilantro

1   Put the stock, soup paste, ginger, lemon grass, and lime leaves in a saucepan and bring to a boil. Reduce the heat and simmer for 15 minutes, then strain and discard the solids.
2   Return the flavored stock to the pan and add the scallions, lime juice, fish sauce, coconut milk, and fish and simmer for 3 minutes. Add the shrimp and simmer for a further 2 minutes. Serve sprinkled with the cilantro.

SERVES 2
5G CARBOHYDRATE PER SERVING

055 MARINATED SALMON IN TAHINI BROTH

2 salmon fillets,
   about ¼lb each
2 cups vegetable stock
   (see page 30)
1 tbsp soy sauce
1 clove garlic, crushed
¼ tsp crushed
   dried chili flakes

1-inch piece fresh
   root ginger, peeled
   and thinly sliced
1 heaped tbsp tahini paste
2oz cooked
   buckwheat (soba)
   noodles
1 scallion,
   thinly sliced

½ carrot, cut into
   thin strips

MARINADE:
1 clove garlic, crushed
4 tsp soy sauce
2 tsp sweet chili
   dipping sauce
2 tsp toasted sesame oil

1 Mix together all the ingredients for the marinade. Add the salmon and spoon the marinade over until coated. Let marinate in the refrigerator for at least 1 hour.
2 Put the stock, soy sauce, garlic, chili, and ginger in a saucepan and bring to a boil. Reduce the heat and simmer for 10 minutes, then stir in the tahini.
3 Meanwhile, preheat the broiler to high and line the broiler pan with foil. Broil the salmon for 3-4 minutes each side, occasionally spooning over the marinade.
4 Put the cooked noodles in two shallow bowls. Pour the broth over, and place the salmon on top. Sprinkle with the scallion and carrot, then serve.

SERVES 2
27G CARBOHYDRATE PER SERVING

056 SMOKED HADDOCK CHOWDER

10oz undyed smoked
   haddock fillets
¼ cup split red
   lentils, rinsed
1 bay leaf
1 leek, sliced
1 carrot, sliced

1 stick celery, sliced
3¾ cups vegetable stock
   (see page 30)
⅓ cup (drained weight)
   canned
no-sugar-or-salt corn
   kernels, rinsed

3 tbsp reduced-fat
   crème fraîche
salt and freshly
   ground black pepper
1 tbsp snipped fresh
   chives, to serve

1 Place the haddock in a sauté pan and cover with water. Poach for 8 minutes or until cooked. Remove the fish from the poaching liquid using a fish slice, and let cool. Remove the skin and any bones, and flake the flesh into large pieces; set aside.
2 Place the lentils, bay leaf, leek, carrot, celery, and stock in a large saucepan. Bring to a boil, skim off any scum that rises to the surface and reduce the heat. Simmer for 25 minutes, half-covered, until the lentils and vegetables are tender, adding the corn 5 minutes before the end of the cooking time.
3 Remove the bay leaf, and transfer the soup to a blender. Mix until half-puréed but still chunky. Return the soup to the pan, and stir in the crème fraîche. Gently stir in the haddock, making sure you don't break up the chunks, and season to taste. Heat gently, then serve sprinkled with the chives.

SERVES 2
15G CARBOHYDRATE PER SERVING

chapter 3

SALADS

Salads don't have to be sidelined as an accompaniment but can make a nutritious complete meal in themselves. Many of the recipes that follow contain a protein element, such as lean meat, poultry, seafood, nuts, seeds, cheese, or eggs, helping satiate the appetite. However, if you are looking for a side salad to go with a main dish or a light snack, there are plenty of recipes to choose from that make the most of the wide variety of salad leaves now available. It's well worth taking the time to make your own dressings; not only can you make them to suit your own taste but you can control what goes into them. Many store-bought dressings contain added sugar and carbohydrate-based fillers, which add bulk but are unnecessary. All of the salad recipes come with their own dressing, but feel free to experiment by mixing and matching. Generally speaking, chunky salads and those based on robust lettuce leaves can stand up to stronger dressings such as those that are mayo- or cheese-based. Reserve light vinaigrettes for those salads that contain mild-tasting leaves or experiment with the wonderful array of different flavored oils such as toasted sesame, or walnut—a little goes a long way.

057 WATERCRESS, WALNUT, & ROQUEFORT SALAD

½ cup walnut halves
1 small red William pear,
  cored and sliced
1 tsp lemon juice
1⅔ bunches watercress,
  tough stalks removed
1 cup cubed Roquefort
  cheese

DRESSING:
2 tbsp extra-virgin
  olive oil
1 tbsp lemon juice
½ tsp Dijon mustard
salt and freshly
  ground black pepper

1 Toast the walnuts in a dry skillet for 2 minutes.
2 To make the dressing, whisk together the oil, lemon
   juice, and mustard, then season.
3 Toss the pear slices in the lemon juice to prevent them browning.
   Arrange the watercress in a bowl and top with the pear slices,
   Roquefort, and walnuts. Pour over the dressing, toss well, and serve.

SERVES 2
11G CARBOHYDRATE PER SERVING

058 BEAN SPROUT, RADISH, & ONION SALAD

1 cup bean sprouts
6 radishes, sliced
½ small red onion,
  sliced into rings

DRESSING:
2 tsp extra-virgin olive oil
2 tsp toasted sesame oil
2 tsp lemon juice

2 tsp rice wine vinegar
1 tsp grated fresh
  ginger
salt and freshly
  ground black pepper

1 Mix together the ingredients for the dressing and season.
2 Put the bean sprouts, radishes, and red onion in a serving dish.
   Pour the dressing over and toss to coat the salad.

SERVES 2
5.5G CARBOHYDRATE PER SERVING

059 SIMPLE CAULIFLOWER SALAD

1½ cups cauliflower
  florets

DRESSING:
2 tbsp extra-virgin
  olive oil
1 tsp English mustard
½ tsp white wine
  vinegar

1 small clove
  garlic, crushed
salt and freshly
  ground black pepper

1 Steam the cauliflower for 10-12 minutes until just tender. Let cool slightly.
2 Mix together the ingredients for the dressing, then season to taste. Pour the
   dressing over the cauliflower, and toss until combined. Serve slightly warm or at
   room temperature.

SERVES 2
2.5G CARBOHYDRATE PER SERVING

060 WARM MUSHROOM SALAD WITH WALNUT DRESSING

2 large flat mushrooms,
  sliced and quartered
2 small handfuls small
  spinach leaves

DRESSING:
2 tbsp extra-virgin
  olive oil
1 tbsp walnut oil

1 tsp red wine vinegar
½ tsp Dijon mustard
salt and freshly ground
  black pepper

1 Heat half of the olive oil, and fry the mushrooms for about 5 minutes until softened. Add a little water if the mushrooms become too dry. Let cool slightly.
2 Whisk together the ingredients for the dressing, then season.
3 Put the spinach in a bowl, top with the mushrooms. and spoon the dressing over.

SERVES 2
3G CARBOHYDRATE PER SERVING

061 FENNEL & ORANGE SALAD

1 fennel bulb, trimmed
  and finely sliced
½ orange, peeled and
  thinly sliced into rounds
1 tbsp chopped fresh mint

DRESSING:
2 tbsp extra-virgin
  olive oil
2 tsp white wine vinegar
salt and freshly ground
  black pepper

1 Arrange the fennel and orange on a serving platter.
2 Mix together the ingredients for the dressing in a small bowl; season to taste.
3 Pour the dressing over the salad and sprinkle with mint.

SERVES 2
7G CARBOHYDRATE PER SERVING

062 SPICY CAULIFLOWER SALAD

1½ cups cauliflower
  florets
2 tbsp extra-virgin
  olive oil

1 clove garlic, crushed
1 tsp garam masala
1 tsp cumin seeds
2 tsp lemon juice

salt
1 tbsp flaked almonds,
  toasted
1 tbsp chopped fresh
  cilantro

1 Steam the cauliflower for 10-12 minutes until just tender. Let cool slightly.
2 Heat the oil in a skillet and add the garlic and spices and cook for 1 minute over a gentle heat, stirring frequently. Add the cauliflower and lemon juice. Turn the cauliflower until it is coated in the spice mixture, then season with salt.
3 Transfer the cauliflower to a bowl and let cool slightly. Sprinkle with the almonds and cilantro before serving.

SERVES 2
2.5G CARBOHYDRATE PER SERVING

ROASTED BELL PEPPER SALAD WITH POACHED EGG

1 red bell pepper,
    seeded and sliced
1 yellow bell pepper,
    seeded and sliced
3oz chorizo sausage,
    peeled and cut into
    bite-sized pieces

2 handfuls mixed
    salad leaves
⅓ cup black olives
2 eggs
salt and freshly
    ground black
    pepper

DRESSING:
2 tbsp extra-virgin
    olive oil, plus extra
    for brushing
1 tsp balsamic vinegar

1 Preheat the broiler to high and line the broiler pan with foil. Brush the bell peppers with oil and broil for about 10 minutes, turning occasionally, until tender and slightly blackened around the edges. Let cool slightly, then peel.

2 Meanwhile, heat a skillet and dry-fry the chorizo for 2 minutes until golden. Let cool slightly.

3 Arrange the salad leaves in 2 shallow bowls. Add the bell peppers, chorizo, and olives.

4 Half-fill a skillet with water and bring to a boil, then reduce the heat to low. Break the eggs into the pan and cook them at a gentle simmer for about 3 minutes, then remove using a slotted spoon, and drain well.

5 Beat together the oil and vinegar, and pour over the salad. Place the eggs on top of the salad, and season.

SERVES 2
9G CARBOHYDRATE PER SERVING

064 WARM SALAD WITH SATAY DRESSING

1 cup broccoli florets
1 cup green beans
1 small carrot,
   cut into thin ribbons
½ red bell pepper,
   cut into strips
½ cup bean sprouts
2 scallions, sliced

SATAY DRESSING:
3 tbsp no-sugar crunchy
   peanut butter
1 tsp extra-virgin olive oil
1 tsp soy sauce
2 tsp hot water
2 tbsp reduced-fat
   coconut milk

¼ tsp crushed
   dried chili flakes
1 small clove garlic,
   crushed
1 tsp grated
   fresh root ginger

1 Put the ingredients for the satay dressing in a bowl and beat until combined.
2 Steam the broccoli and beans for 5 minutes until just tender.
   Add the carrots 2 minutes before the end of the cooking time.
3 Arrange the cooked vegetables on a serving platter with the bell pepper,
   bean sprouts, and scallions. Serve with the satay dressing.

SERVES 2

11.5G CARBOHYDRATE PER SERVING

065 MARINATED ARTICHOKE SALAD

16-oz can artichokes,
   drained and rinsed
1 tbsp snipped
   fresh chives
1 tbsp chopped
   fresh oregano

1 tbsp fresh thyme

DRESSING:
2 tbsp extra-virgin
   olive oil
1 tbsp lemon juice

1 small clove
   garlic, crushed
salt and freshly
   ground black pepper

1 Mix together the ingredients for the dressing, then season to taste.
2 Put the artichokes and herbs in a serving bowl. Pour the dressing over and turn
   the salad until coated in the dressing. Let marinate for at least 1 hour. Serve at
   room temperature.

SERVES 2

11.5G CARBOHYDRATE PER SERVING

066 BEAN & ROASTED RED BELL PEPPER SALAD

1 red bell pepper, seeded
   and quartered
2½ tbsp extra-virgin
   olive oil
1 clove garlic, crushed
3 tbsp fresh oregano

2 tsp balsamic vinegar
1 cup canned lima beans,
   drained and rinsed
salt and freshly
   ground black pepper

1 Preheat the oven to 200°C/400°F/Gas 6. Place the bell pepper on a baking
   tray, brush with some of the oil and roast for 20-25 minutes until tender and
   blackened around the edges. Set aside until cool enough to handle.
2 Peel the red bell pepper then cut into small bite-sized pieces.
3 Gently heat the remaining oil in a saucepan and cook the garlic for 1 minute.
   Remove from the heat and stir in the oregano, vinegar, and the red bell pepper.
4 Put the beans in a serving bowl, and pour the red bell pepper mixture over.
   Season well, and stir until the beans are coated in the dressing.

SERVES 2

13G CARBOHYDRATE PER SERVING

067 **WILD RICE SALAD**

3 tbsp wild rice,
rinsed
4-inch piece
cucumber, seeded and
finely chopped
3 vine-ripened tomatoes,
seeded and chopped

½ red onion, finely diced
2 tbsp chopped fresh
flat-leaf parsley
2 tbsp chopped
fresh oregano
2 tbsp chopped
fresh mint

DRESSING:
2 tbsp extra-virgin
olive oil
2 tsp balsamic vinegar
½ tsp Dijon mustard
1 small clove garlic,
crushed
salt and freshly
ground black pepper

1 Cook the wild rice in boiling salted water following the package instructions,
   then drain. Let cool slightly.
2 Put the rice in a serving bowl with the cucumber, tomatoes, onion, and herbs.
3 Whisk together the ingredients for the dressing; season, then pour over
   the salad. Toss the salad to coat it in the dressing.

SERVES 2
20G CARBOHYDRATE PER SERVING

068 **QUINOA TABBOULEH**

2oz quinoa
3 vine-ripened small
tomatoes, seeded
and chopped
2-inch piece
cucumber, diced

2 scallions,
finely chopped
2 tbsp lemon juice
1 tbsp extra-virgin
olive oil
2 tbsp chopped
fresh mint

2 tbsp chopped
fresh cilantro
2 tbsp chopped
fresh parsley
salt and freshly
ground black
pepper

1 Cover the quinoa with 1 cup water and bring to a boil.
   Reduce the heat, cover, and simmer over a low heat for about
   10-15 minutes until tender. Drain if necessary.
2 Let the quinoa cool slightly before combining with the rest of
   the ingredients. Season well before serving at room temperature.

SERVES 2
24G CARBOHYDRATE PER SERVING

069 **WARM ORIENTAL SALAD**

¼lb fine green beans
6 spears asparagus,
trimmed
½ cup snow peas

DRESSING:
1 tbsp extra-virgin olive oil
1 tbsp toasted sesame oil
1 tsp grated fresh
root ginger

1 tsp soy sauce
1 small clove
garlic, crushed

1 Steam the green beans and asparagus for 4 minutes, then add the snow peas
   and cook for a further 2 minutes until the vegetables are just tender.
   Refresh under cold running water and drain well.
2 Meanwhile, heat the oils in a saucepan. Add the ginger, soy sauce, and garlic,
   then cook for 1 minute until heated through. Pour the warm dressing over
   the vegetables and leave for a few minutes to let the flavors mingle.

SERVES 2
5.5G CARBOHYDRATE PER SERVING

070 MIMOSA SALAD

1½ cups small
   spinach leaves
2 scallions, sliced on
   the diagonal
2-inch piece cucumber,
   seeded and cut into
   matchsticks

2 free-range eggs, beaten
1 tbsp sesame seeds,
   toasted

DRESSING:
1 tbsp sunflower oil,
   plus extra for frying

1 tbsp toasted sesame oil
1 tsp each grated
   lemon zest and juice
salt and freshly
   ground black pepper

1   Mix together the ingredients for the dressing, and season.
2   Put the spinach, scallions, and cucumber in a serving dish.
     Spoon over the dressing.
3   Heat a little oil in a skillet, season the beaten eggs, and pour them into the pan.
     Swirl the egg so it covers the base of the pan. Cook until just set. Remove from
     the pan, and cut into thin slices. Arrange the omelet strips on the salad.
4   Serve the salad sprinkled with sesame seeds.

SERVES 2
4G CARBOHYDRATE PER SERVING

071 SESAME NOODLE SALAD

2oz medium
   egg noodles
½ cup snow peas
3-inch piece cucumber,
   seeded and cut into
   matchsticks
1 carrot, cut
   into thin strips

2 tomatoes
2 scallions, shredded
3 tbsp chopped
   fresh cilantro
1 tbsp sesame
   seeds, toasted

DRESSING:
1 tbsp sunflower oil
1 tbsp toasted sesame oil
1 tsp soy sauce
1 tsp grated fresh root
   ginger
1 small clove garlic,
   crushed

1   Cook the noodles following the package instructions, and refresh under cold
     running water. Meanwhile, mix together the ingredients for the dressing.
2   Steam the snow peas for 2 minutes until tender but still crisp.
3   Put the noodles and snow peas into a serving bowl with the
     cucumber, carrot, tomatoes, and scallions.
4   Spoon the dressing over and toss with your hands to combine.
     Sprinkle with the cilantro and sesame seeds before serving.

SERVES 2
26G CARBOHYDRATE PER SERVING

072 BEET SALAD WITH HORSERADISH DRESSING

⅔ cup cooked beets in
   natural juice, cubed
4-inch piece cucumber,
   seeded and roughly
   chopped
¼ red onion, sliced

DRESSING:
1 tbsp extra-virgin
   olive oil
1 tbsp fat-reduced
   crème fraîche

1 tbsp creamed
   horseradish
salt and freshly
   ground black pepper

1   Whisk together the ingredients for the dressing; season.
2   Put the beets, cucumber, and red onion in a bowl.
3   Spoon the dressing over, and serve.

SERVES 2
10G CARBOHYDRATE PER SERVING

073 GOAT'S CHEESE SALAD

4 slices baguette,
  preferably whole wheat
4 slices round goat's
  cheese
large handful mixed
  salad leaves

1 tbsp each fresh mint,
  chives, and basil

DRESSING:
1 tbsp extra-virgin
  olive oil

1 tbsp walnut oil
1 tsp red wine vinegar
1 small clove garlic,
  crushed
salt and freshly
  ground black pepper

1 Preheat the broiler to medium. Whisk together the ingredients
  for the dressing, and season to taste.
2 Broil one side of each baguette slice until golden. Place a round of
  goat's cheese on the untoasted side, then return to the broiler and
  cook for 2-3 minutes until melted.
3 Meanwhile, put the salad leaves and herbs in a serving bowl.
  Pour the dressing over and toss to coat the leaves. Divide between
  two plates, and top each serving with two slices of toasted cheese.

SERVES 2
12.5G CARBOHYDRATE PER SERVING

074 JAPANESE-STYLE SMOKED TOFU SALAD

2oz buckwheat
  noodles
½lb smoked tofu
1 cup white cabbage,
  finely shredded
1 small carrot,
  finely shredded

2 scallions, sliced
1 green chili, seeded and
  finely sliced into rounds
1 tbsp sesame seeds,
  toasted
salt and freshly
  ground black pepper

DRESSING:
1 tsp grated fresh ginger
1 clove garlic, crushed
2 tbsp silken tofu
2 tsp soy sauce
1 tbsp sesame oil
2 tbsp hot water

1 Cook the noodles in plenty of boiling salted water following the package
  instructions. Drain, and refresh under cold running water.
2 Blend all the ingredients for the dressing until smooth and creamy; season.
3 Drain the tofu, and steam for 5 minutes, then cut into long, thin slices.
4 Mix together the cabbage, carrot, onions, and chili. To serve, arrange
  the noodles on two plates, then top with the salad and slices of tofu.
  Spoon over the dressing, and sprinkle with sesame seeds.

SERVES 2
24.5G CARBOHYDRATE PER SERVING

075 ZUCCHINI & HALOUMI SALAD

5 small zucchini, sliced
  lengthwise
6 slices haloumi cheese

DRESSING:
2 tbsp extra-virgin olive oil
1 tbsp lemon juice

1 tbsp chopped fresh
  flat-leaf parsley
1 tbsp capers, rinsed

1 Steam the zucchini for 1-2 minutes until just tender. Refresh under cold
  running water and drain well.
2 Blend together the ingredients for the dressing. Arrange the zucchini
  in a shallow dish, and pour the dressing over.
3 Heat a griddle pan until hot. Place the haloumi in the pan and cook for
  about 2 minutes each side until golden. Arrange on top of the zucchini.

SERVES 2
6G CARBOHYDRATE PER SERVING

076 MELON & FETA SALAD

2 wedges melon,
  preferably Charentais
  or Cantaloupe, peeled
  and cut into cubes
¾ cup feta cheese,
  cubed
mint leaves, to garnish

DRESSING:
1 tbsp fresh lemon juice
1½ tbsp extra-virgin
  olive oil
freshly ground
  black pepper

1   Arrange the melon and feta on a platter. Whisk together the lemon juice and oil
    and pour over the melon and feta. Season with pepper, and garnish with mint.

SERVES 2
8G CARBOHYDRATE PER SERVING

077 BABY MOZZARELLA SALAD

6oz baby
  mozzarella balls
5 small plum tomatoes,
  seeded and sliced
2 tbsp torn basil leaves
1 tbsp chopped fresh mint

DRESSING:
2 tbsp extra-virgin
  olive oil
2 tsp balsamic vinegar
salt and freshly
  ground black pepper

1   Mix together the ingredients for the dressing, then season to taste.
2   Put the mozzarella and tomatoes in a serving bowl, then pour the dressing over.
    Sprinkle with the herbs before serving at room temperature.

SERVES 2
3.5G CARBOHYDRATE PER SERVING

078 GREEK SALAD

¾ cup cubed Greek feta
    cheese
3 vine-ripened tomatoes,
    seeded and cut
    into chunks
4-inch piece
    cucumber, cut
    into chunks
⅓ cup black olives

1 tsp dried oregano
freshly ground
    black pepper

DRESSING:
2 tbsp extra-virgin
    olive oil
1 tbsp lemon juice

1   Place the feta, tomatoes, cucumber, and black olives in a serving bowl.
2   Whisk together the olive oil and lemon juice, and pour the dressing
    over the salad. Toss with your hands to coat the salad in the dressing.
3   Sprinkle with the oregano, and season with black pepper before serving.

SERVES 2
9G CARBOHYDRATE PER SERVING

079 THAI CUCUMBER & MANGO SALAD

½ small mango, sliced
1 small cucumber,
  seeded and sliced
  into half-moons

2 tbsp roasted
  peanuts, crushed

DRESSING:
1 tbsp fish sauce

2 tbsp lime juice
1 small clove
  garlic, crushed
¼ tsp dried
  crushed chilies

1 Mix together all the ingredients for the dressing.
2 Arrange the mango and cucumber on a serving platter.
3 Spoon over the dressing, and sprinkle with the peanuts.

SERVES 2
12.5G CARBOHYDRATE PER SERVING

080 TOMATO & BASIL SALAD

1 red scallion,
  finely chopped
1 beefsteak tomato,
  thinly sliced

2 tbsp extra-virgin
  olive oil
handful of fresh basil

salt and freshly ground
  black pepper
¼ cup Parmesan
  shavings

1 Arrange the scallion and tomato on a serving platter.
2 Pour over the oil, season well, and sprinkle with the basil and Parmesan.

SERVES 2
4G CARBOHYDRATE PER SERVING

081 ORIENTAL COLESLAW

1 cup white cabbage,
  grated
1 carrot, grated
3 scallions,
  finely sliced

1 tbsp toasted sesame
  seeds, to serve

DRESSING:
1 tbsp extra-virgin olive oil

1 tbsp toasted
  sesame oil
1 tbsp rice vinegar
salt and freshly
  ground black pepper

1 Whisk together the ingredients for the dressing in a small bowl.
2 Put the cabbage, carrot, and scallions in a salad bowl. Spoon the dressing over
   the salad and toss to coat. Season, and sprinkle with the sesame seeds before
   serving.

SERVES 2
6G CARBOHYDRATE PER SERVING

082 NUTTY COLESLAW

1 cup grated or finely
  shredded white
  cabbage
1 carrot, grated
2 scallions,
  finely sliced

2 tbsp chopped
  walnuts, toasted

DRESSING:
1 tbsp extra-virgin
  olive oil

2 tsp white wine vinegar
2-3 tbsp reduced-fat
  mayo
salt and freshly
  ground black pepper

1 Whisk together the ingredients for the dressing in a small bowl.
2 Place the cabbage, carrot, and scallions in a salad bowl.
   Spoon over the dressing and toss to coat the salad.
3 Season, and sprinkle over the walnuts before serving.

SERVES 2
5.5G CARBOHYDRATE PER SERVING

083 SIMPLE BELL PEPPER SALAD

2 orange bell peppers,
seeded and quartered
10 black olives

DRESSING:
2 tbsp extra-virgin olive
oil, plus extra for
brushing

2 tsp lemon juice
salt and freshly
ground black pepper

1   Preheat the oven to 200°C/400°F/Gas 6. Place the bell peppers on a baking
    tray, brush with some of the oil and roast for 20-25 minutes until tender
    and blackened around the edges. Set aside until cool enough to handle.
2   Peel the skin off the bell peppers, and thickly slice the flesh. Put the bell
    peppers in a shallow dish with the olives.
3   Mix together the oil and lemon juice, season to taste, then pour the dressing
    over the bell peppers.

SERVES 2
7G CARBOHYDRATE PER SERVING

084 GRILLED EGGPLANT SALAD

1 eggplant, sliced
2 tbsp extra-virgin
olive oil

DRESSING:
2 tbsp extra-virgin
olive oil
1 tbsp lemon juice

2 tbsp chopped
fresh mint
salt and freshly
ground black pepper

1   Steam the eggplant for 6 minutes, then drain well and pat dry with
    paper towels.
2   Preheat the broiler to medium and line the broiler pan with foil. Place the
    eggplant in the broiler pan and brush the top with oil. Broil for 2-3 minutes,
    then turn over, brush with more oil and return to the broiler for 2-3 minutes
    until tender and golden.
3   Meanwhile, mix together the ingredients for the dressing; season.
4   Put the eggplant in a shallow dish, pour over the dressing, and serve warm.

SERVES 2
3G CARBOHYDRATE PER SERVING

085 MIXED LEAF SALAD
WITH TOASTED SEEDS

2 handfuls mixed salad
leaves, including
watercress and spinach
1¾ cups fresh herbs,
including parsley,
arugula, and basil
1 tbsp sunflower seeds
1 tbsp pumpkin seeds

DRESSING:
2 tbsp extra-virgin
olive oil
1-2 tsp lemon juice
½ tsp Dijon mustard
salt and freshly ground
black pepper

1   Arrange the salad leaves and herbs in a salad bowl.
    Lightly toast the seeds in a dry skillet until just colored.
    Let them cool slightly before sprinkling them over the salad.
2   Whisk together the olive oil, lemon juice, and mustard.
    Season to taste, and drizzle the dressing over the salad.

SERVES 2
2G CARBOHYDRATE PER SERVING

086 HERB & ALFALFA SALAD

1¼ cups small
  spinach leaves
1¼ cups arugula
4 heaped tbsp alfalfa
¼ cup Parmesan
  shavings

DRESSING:
2 tbsp extra-virgin
  olive oil
2 tsp white wine
  vinegar
½ tsp Dijon mustard

2 tbsp chopped
  fresh basil
2 tbsp snipped
  fresh chives
salt and freshly
  ground black pepper

1 Whisk together the oil, vinegar, and mustard, then stir in the herbs; season.
2 Put the spinach, arugula, and alfalfa in a salad bowl. Spoon over the dressing,
   then sprinkle with the Parmesan.

SERVES 2
2G CARBOHYDRATE PER SERVING

087 ENDIVE & RED ONION SALAD

2 heads Belgian endive,
  leaves separated
½ red onion, sliced

DRESSING:
2 tbsp extra-virgin
  olive oil

2 tsp lemon juice
salt and freshly
  ground black pepper

1 Arrange the Belgian endive and onion in a shallow dish.
2 Mix together the oil and lemon juice, then season. Pour the dressing over
   the salad, and serve.

SERVES 2
3G CARBOHYDRATE PER SERVING

088 RED LEAF SALAD WITH
ROMESCO DRESSING

2 handfuls mixed red
  salad leaves, such as
  oak leaf, radicchio, and
  lollo rosso
⅓ cup cubed Greek
  feta cheese
10 pitted black
  olives, sliced
salt and freshly
  ground black pepper

DRESSING:
1 tbsp almonds, chopped
2 tomatoes, peeled,
  seeded, and diced
2 tbsp olive oil
1 small clove garlic, sliced
2 tsp red wine vinegar
handful of fresh
  flat-leaf parsley
¼ tsp paprika

1 To make the dressing, lightly toast the almonds in a dry skillet until golden.
   Put the nuts in a food processor or blender with the rest of the sauce
   ingredients and 1 tablespoon water, then mix until very finely
   chopped and a sauce consistency; season.
2 Put the salad leaves in a serving bowl and spoon the dressing over.
   Sprinkle the feta and olives on top.

SERVES 2
5G CARBOHYDRATE PER SERVING

089 **AVOCADO, RED ONION, & SPINACH SALAD**

1 red onion,	**DRESSING:**
cut into wedges	2 tbsp extra-virgin
2 tsp extra-virgin olive oil	olive oil, plus extra
1³/₄ cups small	for greasing
spinach leaves	1-2 tsp balsamic vinegar
1 avocado, peeled,	salt and freshly
pitted, and sliced	ground black pepper
little fresh lemon juice	

1 Preheat the oven to 200°C/400°F/Gas 6. Pour the olive oil into a baking dish, and add the onion wedges. Bake for 25 minutes, turning occasionally, until the onion is tender. Let cool.
2 To make the dressing, whisk together the oil and vinegar, then season.
3 Arrange the spinach in a serving bowl. Toss the avocado in lemon juice, and add to the bowl with the onion. Pour over the dressing, and toss gently.

SERVES 2
6G CARBOHYDRATE PER SERVING

090 JAPANESE SALAD

½oz arame seaweed
¼lb radishes,
  thinly sliced into
  rounds
½ small cucumber,
  cut into thin sticks

¾ cup bean sprouts,
  rinsed
toasted sesame
  seeds, for sprinkling

DRESSING:
1 tbsp sunflower oil
1 tsp toasted sesame oil
2 tsp white wine
  vinegar
1 tsp soy sauce

1 Rinse the arame in a sieve under cold running water. Place in a bowl
   and cover with more cold water. Let soak for 5 minutes–the
   arame should double in volume. Drain, and place in a saucepan.
2 Cover the arame with cold water and bring to a boil. Reduce the
   heat and simmer for 20 minutes until tender, then drain.
3 Meanwhile, mix the sunflower oil, sesame oil, vinegar, and soy
   sauce together in a bowl to make the dressing.
4 In a serving dish, gently combine the arame with the radishes, cucumber,
   and bean sprouts. Spoon over the dressing and sprinkle with sesame seeds
   before serving.

SERVES 2
6G CARBOHYDRATE PER SERVING

SALADS

091 SMOKED TROUT SALAD WITH DILL DRESSING

1¼ cups spinach, arugula, and watercress salad
1 shallot, diced
2-inch cucumber chunk, coarsely grated
2 cooked beets in natural juice, diced

½ avocado, pitted, peeled, and sliced
2 smoked trout fillets

DRESSING:
1 tbsp extra-virgin olive oil

1 tbsp reduced-fat mayo
1½ tbsp dill sauce
1 tbsp warm water
freshly ground black pepper

1 Mix together all the ingredients for the dressing, then season with pepper.
2 Place the salad leaves on 2 serving plates, then arrange the shallot, cucumber, beets, and avocado on top.
3 Place the trout on top of the salad, and drizzle over the dressing.

SERVES 2

8G CARBOHYDRATE PER SERVING

092 SALMON & NECTARINE SALAD

2 salmon fillets, about ¼lb each
1 tbsp lemon juice
3½ cups arugula leaves

1 fresh nectarine, sliced
½ avocado, pitted, peeled, and cubed
salt and freshly ground black pepper

DRESSING:
1 tbsp extra-virgin olive oil
1 tbsp reduced-fat mayo
2 tsp lime juice

1 Preheat the oven to 200°/400°F/Gas 6. Put the salmon on a piece of foil. Pour the lemon juice over the salmon and season. Fold up the foil to make a parcel, then place on a baking tray and cook for about 12-15 minutes. Leave to cool.
2 Meanwhile, mix together the ingredients for the dressing; season.
3 Divide the arugula between two plates. Place the nectarine and avocado on top.
4 Remove the skin from the salmon and break into large flakes. Add to the salad and spoon over the dressing.

SERVES 2

6.5G CARBOHYDRATE PER SERVING

093 HOT-SMOKED SALMON SALAD

½ fennel bulb
4-inch piece cucumber, seeded
½ cup canned flageolet beans, drained and rinsed

1 avocado, pitted, peeled, and finely sliced
6oz hot-smoked salmon
2 tbsp snipped fresh chives

DRESSING:
2 tbsp reduced-fat mayo
1 tbsp extra-virgin olive oil
2 tsp lemon juice
salt and freshly ground black pepper

1 Whisk together the ingredients for the dressing, and season. Add 1 tablespoon warm water if it appears too thick.
2 Thinly slice the fennel and cucumber using a mandolin. Put them in a serving bowl with the beans and avocado. Spoon over the dressing, and turn the salad using a spoon until coated.
3 Top with the fish, and sprinkle with chives before serving.

SERVES 2

11.5G CARBOHYDRATE PER SERVING

094 TERIYAKI SALMON SALAD

1½ tbsp soy sauce
4 tbsp fresh orange juice
2 tbsp sherry vinegar
2 tbsp white wine

2 salmon fillets, about
  5oz each
salt and freshly ground
  black pepper

1 tsp sesame seeds, to
  serve, optional

1   Preheat the broiler to high and line the broiler pan with foil. Put the soy sauce,
    orange juice, sherry vinegar, and white wine into a saucepan.
    Bring to a boil and cook for 2-3 minutes until reduced and thickened.

2   Spoon the sauce over the salmon and broil, occasionally basting the fish
    with the sauce, for 7-10 minutes, depending on the thickness of the fillets,
    until just cooked and caramelized on top.

SERVES 2
5G CARBOHYDRATE PER SERVING.
SERVE WITH SESAME NOODLE SALAD (SEE PAGE 51).

095 FRESH TUNA NIÇOISE

1 tbsp extra-virgin olive oil
1 tbsp fresh lemon juice
2 tuna steaks, 5oz each
3oz fine green
  beans, cooked
2 handfuls mixed
  salad leaves

6 cherry tomatoes,
  halved
½ small red onion, sliced
1 hard-cooked
  free-range egg
handful of pitted black
  olives
salt and freshly ground
  black pepper

DRESSING:
1 tbsp extra-virgin
  olive oil
½ tsp white
  wine vinegar
1 small clove
  garlic, crushed
3 tsp mayo

1 Mix together the oil and lemon juice, and season well. Place the tuna in a shallow
  dish and pour over the marinade. Chill for 30 minutes, turning occasionally.
2 Put the green beans, salad leaves, tomatoes, onion, egg, and olives in a bowl.
3 Whisk together the ingredients for the dressing, then pour over the salad
  and toss well using your hands.
4 Heat a griddle or skillet until hot. Place the tuna steaks in the pan,
  brush with the marinade and cook for 5 minutes, turning once, until cooked
  on the outside and pink in the center. Brush with the marinade when needed.
5 Arrange the salad on serving plates, and top each one with a tuna steak.

SERVES 2
7G CARBOHYDRATE PER SERVING

SALADS

62

096 SMOKED HADDOCK SALAD

¾lb traditionally smoked
  haddock fillet
2 handfuls spinach and
  watercress leaves
2 scallions, chopped
2 free-range eggs
freshly ground black
  pepper

DRESSING:
2 tbsp reduced-fat
  mayo
1 tbsp white wine vinegar
2 tsp horseradish sauce
1 tbsp extra-virgin
  olive oil
1 tbsp warm water

1 Preheat the oven to 200°C/400°F/Gas 6. Put the haddock on a piece
of lightly oiled foil, large enough to make a parcel. Season with pepper
and fold up the foil, crimping the edges together to seal.
2 Bake the haddock for about 15 minutes until cooked. Remove the skin
and any bones from the fish, and slice in half; let cool slightly.
3 Meanwhile, whisk together the ingredients for the dressing, and season
with pepper. Put the salad leaves and scallions in a salad bowl and
spoon over three-quarters of the dressing. Toss to coat the leaves.
4 Poach the eggs in a sauté pan of barely simmering water, then remove
using a slotted spoon.
5 Divide the salad between two plates, top with the haddock and egg,
and spoon over the remaining dressing.

SERVES 2
3.5G CARBOHYDRATE PER SERVING

097 CRAB SALAD WITH HERB MAYO

8 spears asparagus,
  trimmed
2 handfuls mixed salad
  leaves
2 dressed crabs

HERB MAYO:
1 tbsp extra-virgin
  olive oil
2 tbsp reduced-fat
  mayo

1 tbsp fresh basil
1 tbsp fresh oregano
1 tbsp fresh chives
salt and freshly ground
  black pepper

1 Put the ingredients for the herb mayo in a
blender and mix until smooth and creamy. Season.
2 Steam the asparagus for about 5 minutes or until tender.
3 Divide the salad leaves between two plates, then scoop out
the crabmeat and place on top of the leaves. Top with the
asparagus. Serve with the herb mayo.

SERVES 2
2G CARBOHYDRATE PER SERVING

098 AVOCADO & PRAWN SALAD WITH CHILI SALSA

1 cup cooked
   king prawns
½ cup Cantaloupe melon,
   cubed
1 avocado, pitted,
   peeled, and sliced

2 tbsp torn basil
   leaves, to sprinkle

CHILI SALSA:
2 tbsp extra-virgin
   olive oil

juice of ½ lemon
2 tbsp diced red onion
¼–½ tsp dried
   crushed chili flakes
salt and freshly
   ground black pepper

1   Mix together the ingredients for the salsa in a small bowl;
    season to taste and set aside.
2   Put the prawns, melon, and avocado on a serving platter.
    Spoon over the salsa, and serve sprinkled with the basil.

SERVES 2
8G CARBOHYDRATE PER SERVING

099 MIXED SEAFOOD SALAD

1¾ cups mixed cooked
   seafood, such as
   shrimp, scallops, squid,
   and mussels
10 vine-ripened cherry
   tomatoes, halved

salt and freshly ground
   black pepper
¾ cup basil leaves, torn,
   to garnish

DRESSING:
juice of 1 small lemon
2 tbsp extra-virgin
   olive oil
½ red chili, seeded and
   finely chopped
1 clove garlic, crushed

1   Put all of the mixed cooked seafood in a shallow serving bowl and add
    the tomatoes.
2   Mix together the lemon juice, oil, chili, and garlic and pour over the seafood.
    Season well and sprinkle with basil before serving.

SERVES 2
10G CARBOHYDRATE PER SERVING

100 SQUID SALAD WITH HERB DRESSING

9oz fresh prepared squid,
   cleaned and each one
   cut into 3
3¾ cups arugula
3 tomatoes, seeded
   and chopped

DRESSING:
2 tbsp fresh basil
1 tbsp fresh oregano
1 tbsp fresh chives
2 tbsp extra-virgin
   olive oil

2 tsp lemon juice
1 clove garlic, crushed
salt and freshly ground
   black pepper

1   Mix the ingredients for the dressing in a food processor or blender.
    Season to taste and set aside.
2   Brush a griddle pan with oil and cook the squid over a medium-high
    heat for 1½ minutes, turning halfway.
3   Put the arugula and tomatoes in a shallow dish. Add the squid, and
    spoon over the dressing. Toss until the salad is coated in the dressing.

SERVES 2
3G CARBOHYDRATE PER SERVING

101 FAVA BEAN, PRAWN, & AVOCADO SALAD

²⁄₃ cup shelled
  fava beans
2 handfuls mixed
  salad leaves
1 avocado, peeled,
  pitted, and sliced
1 tsp lemon juice
1 cup shelled
  cooked king prawns
1 tbsp chopped chives

DRESSING:
1 tbsp extra-virgin
  olive oil
2 tsp lemon juice
1 tbsp creamed
  horseradish sauce
1 tbsp fat-reduced
  crème fraîche
salt and freshly
  ground black pepper

1   Steam the fava beans for 3-4 minutes until tender. Let cool slightly,
    then remove the tough outer shell from each bean.
2   To make the dressing, whisk together the oil, lemon juice,
    creamed horseradish, and crème fraîche. Season well.
3   Arrange the salad leaves in 2 shallow bowls. Toss the avocado in the
    lemon juice and add to the bowls with the fava beans and prawns.
    Pour over the dressing, toss gently, and sprinkle with chives before serving.

SERVES 2
7G CARBOHYDRATE PER SERVING

SALADS

102 CHICKEN SALAD WITH SPICY AVOCADO DRESSING

2 skinless chicken
  breast halves, 6oz each
1 tbsp extra-virgin
  olive oil
1 small yellow bell pepper,
  seeded and sliced
2 handfuls mixed
  arugula, spinach, and

watercress leaves
12 cherry tomatoes, halved
2 scallions,
  sliced diagonally
1 tbsp fresh cilantro
  leaves, to garnish
salt and freshly
  ground black pepper

DRESSING:
1 avocado, peeled,
  pitted, and chopped
juice and zest of 1 lime
3 tbsp fromage frais
1 tbsp chopped cilantro
¼ tsp dried crushed chili

1. Put the chicken breasts between 2 sheets of plastic wrap and flatten with the end of rolling pin. Heat a griddle pan and brush with the oil. Season the chicken and griddle for about 2–4 minutes each side, depending on the thickness of the fillets, until cooked through. Remove from the pan and add the bell pepper and cook for about 5 minutes until tender.
2. Blend together the ingredients for the dressing and season well.
3. Peel the bell pepper slices. Arrange the salad leaves on 2 plates, then add the bell peppers, tomatoes, and scallions. Spoon over the dressing. Slice the chicken and place on top of the salad, then sprinkle with cilantro.

SERVES 2
10G CARBOHYDRATE PER SERVING

SALADS

66

103 WARM CHICKEN SALAD WITH THAI-STYLE DRESSING

2 skinless chicken breast
halves, about ¼lb each,
cut into wide strips
1 tbsp extra-virgin
olive oil, for brushing
1¾ cups small spinach
leaves
1 red bell pepper, thinly
sliced

2-inch piece cucumber,
seeded and cut
into matchsticks
2 cherry tomatoes,
quartered
2 scallions, cut
lengthwise into
strips
basil leaves, to garnish

DRESSING:
½ cup reduced-fat
coconut milk
2 scallions, chopped
1 clove garlic, chopped
handful of fresh cilantro
handful of fresh basil
juice and finely grated
zest of 1 lime
salt and freshly ground
black pepper

1 Put the ingredients for the dressing in a blender and mix until
smooth and creamy; season. Spoon half of the dressing over the
chicken strips and let marinate in the refrigerator for about 1 hour.
2 Preheat the broiler to high, line the broiler pan with foil, and brush with oil.
Remove the chicken from the marinade and broil for about 3-4 minutes
each side or until cooked through. Let cool slightly.
3 Put the spinach, red bell pepper, cucumber, tomatoes, and scallions
in a serving bowl. Spoon over the dressing, and toss to coat the leaves.
Top with the chicken strips.

SERVES 2
11G CARBOHYDRATE PER SERVING

104 CHICKEN & WALNUT SALAD

2 skinless chicken breast
halves, ¼lb each, cut
into strips
1 tbsp extra-virgin
olive oil
1 head Belgian endive,
leaves separated
1 Little Gem lettuce,
leaves separated
½ cup walnut halves,
toasted

DRESSING:
2 tbsp extra-virgin
olive oil
2 tbsp fat-reduced crème
fraîche
2 tsp white wine vinegar
1 tsp Dijon mustard
1 tbsp chopped fresh mint
salt and freshly ground
black pepper

1 Whisk together the ingredients for the dressing, then season well.
2 Preheat the broiler to high and line the broiler pan with foil.
3 Brush the chicken with a little oil, season, and broil for about 3-4
minutes each side until cooked through. Let cool slightly.
4 Put the Belgian endive and lettuce in a serving bowl. Sprinkle over the walnuts.
Top with the chicken, and spoon over the dressing.

SERVES 2
3.5G CARBOHYDRATE PER SERVING

105 CHICKEN CAESAR SALAD

2 skinless chicken breast halves, ¼lb each, cut into strips
2 handfuls Cos lettuce, leaves torn into bite-sized pieces
Parmesan shavings, to serve

DRESSING:
2 anchovy fillets
1½ tbsp extra-virgin olive oil, plus extra for brushing
1 tbsp reduced-fat mayonnaise
½ clove garlic

2 tsp lemon juice
¼ tsp Dijon mustard
¼ tsp Worcestershire sauce
2 tbsp finely grated Parmesan
salt and freshly ground black pepper

1   Blend the dressing ingredients until smooth and creamy. Season to taste.
2   Heat a griddle pan until hot. Brush the pan with oil and griddle the chicken for 3-4 minutes each side until cooked through. Let cool slightly.
3   Put the lettuce leaves in a bowl, and spoon over the dressing. Toss to coat the leaves. Put the chicken on top, and sprinkle with Parmesan shavings.

SERVES 2
2.5G CARBOHYDRATE PER SERVING

106 ITALIAN SALAD

2 portobello mushrooms, sliced
2 slices prosciutto
1 avocado
1 tsp lemon juice
1¼ cups small spinach leaves

2 tbsp Parmesan shavings

DRESSING:
1 tbsp extra-virgin olive oil, plus extra for brushing

2 tbsp reduced-fat mayo
2 anchovy fillets
1 tsp Dijon mustard
1 tsp lemon juice
salt and freshly ground black pepper

1   Preheat the broiler to medium-high and line with foil. Brush the mushrooms with oil and broil for about 5 minutes until starting to turn crisp. Broil the prosciutto at the same time until crisp. Let both cool slightly.
2   Peel, pit, and slice the avocado and drizzle with the lemon juice to prevent it browning, and put it in a bowl with the spinach. Slice and add the mushrooms.
3   Blend together the ingredients for the dressing and season to taste. Pour the dressing over the salad, and toss to coat. Top with the prosciutto and Parmesan.

SERVES 2
4.5G CARBOHYDRATE PER SERVING

107 TOMATO, BACON, & EGG SALAD

5 vine-ripened tomatoes
2 slices unsmoked bacon
2 handfuls soft lettuce leaves
2 hard-cooked eggs, quartered
2 tbsp snipped chives

DRESSING:
2 tbsp extra-virgin olive oil
2 tsp lemon juice
½ tsp Dijon mustard
salt and freshly ground black pepper

1   Seed and finely chop one of the tomatoes and cut the remaining into eighths. Whisk together the dressing ingredients, and mix in the chopped tomato.
2   Preheat the broiler to high and cook the bacon for 3-4 minutes until crisp. Let cool slightly, then break into bite-sized pieces.
3   Put the lettuce in a serving bowl, followed by the tomatoes, bacon, and eggs. Season the dressing to taste, spoon it over the salad, and sprinkle with chives.

SERVES 2
5G CARBOHYDRATE PER SERVING

108 CHICKEN SALAD WITH PINE NUTS & PESTO DRESSING

2 skinless chicken breast
  halves, ¼lb each, sliced
  into strips
2 Little Gem lettuces
½ avocado flesh, cubed
2 tbsp pine nuts, toasted

DRESSING:
1 tbsp extra-virgin
  olive oil
1 tbsp red or green pesto
¼ tsp dried chili flakes
2 tsp white wine vinegar

salt and freshly
  ground black pepper

1 Brush a griddle pan with oil and heat. Griddle the chicken strips for about
   3-4 minutes each side until cooked through. Let cool slightly.
2 Meanwhile, mix together the ingredients for the dressing.
3 Separate the lettuce leaves and put them in a salad bowl along with the
   avocado and chicken and spoon over the dressing. Sprinkle with the
   pine nuts before serving.

SERVES 2
5G CARBOHYDRATE PER SERVING

109 PROSCIUTTO & MOZZARELLA SALAD

2 yellow bell peppers,
  seeded and quartered
2 tbsp extra-virgin
  olive oil

1½ cups mozzarella
  cheese chunks, drained
4 slices prosciutto, cut
  into 1-inch pieces

1 clove garlic, crushed
2 tsp balsamic vinegar
salt and freshly
  ground black pepper

1 Preheat the oven to 200°C/400°F/Gas 6. Brush the bell peppers with half of
   the oil. Place them on a baking sheet and roast for 25-30 minutes until tender
   and blackened around the edges. Let cool slightly, then peel off the skin.
2 Slice the bell peppers. Place them in a bowl with the mozzarella and prosciutto.
3 Mix the garlic and vinegar with the remaining oil. Season to taste and pour over
   the salad. Toss the salad in the dressing and serve.

SERVES 2
7G CARBOHYDRATE PER SERVING

110 MIXED SALAD LEAVES WITH BACON CRISPS

2 slices unsmoked bacon
1 avocado, pitted,
  peeled, and sliced
1 tsp lemon juice

2 handfuls mixed salad
  leaves of your choice,
  such as endive, spinach,
  watercress, lollo rosso
1½ cups arugula leaves
⅓ cup cubed mozzarella
  cheese

DRESSING:
2 tbsp extra-virgin
  olive oil
2 tsp white wine vinegar
1 clove garlic, crushed
salt and freshly
  ground black pepper

1 Preheat the broiler to high and cook the bacon for 3-4 minutes until crisp.
   Let cool slightly.
2 Meanwhile, mix together the ingredients for the dressing; season.
3 Toss the avocado in the lemon juice. Put the salad leaves and
   arugula in a salad bowl. Top with the avocado and mozzarella.
   Spoon over the dressing and place the bacon slices on top.

SERVES 2
5G CARBOHYDRATE PER SERVING

111 DUCK & ORANGE SALAD WITH WATERCRESS

5oz skinless
  duck breast
1 bunch watercress
¼ fennel bulb, sliced
½ orange, peeled and
  sliced into rounds

DRESSING:
2 tbsp extra-virgin
  olive oil, plus extra
  for brushing
2 tbsp fresh orange juice
1 tbsp fresh lemon juice
salt and freshly
  ground black pepper

1 Preheat the broiler to high and line the broiler pan with foil. Brush the duck with a little oil and season, then broil for 4-5 minutes each side until cooked. Let rest for 3 minutes, then thinly slice.
2 Mix together the ingredients for the dressing, then season.
3 Arrange the watercress and sliced fennel on a serving plate, then top with the orange slices. Place the duck on top, and then gently spoon the dressing over.

SERVES 2
7.5G CARBOHYDRATE PER SERVING

112 VIETNAMESE PORK & CUCUMBER SALAD

2 lean pork medallions,
  about ¼lb each, sliced
  into strips
1 tbsp sunflower oil
1 cup bean sprouts
1 small cucumber,
  seeded and sliced with
  a mandolin
2 scallions, sliced on
  the diagonal

DRESSING:
2 tbsp fish sauce
2 tbsp rice vinegar
1 clove garlic, chopped
2 tbsp fresh apple juice
1 chili, seeded and finely
  chopped
2 tbsp lime juice

1 Mix together the ingredients for the dressing. Pour half of the dressing into a shallow dish, and add the pork. Spoon the dressing over and marinate for at least 1 hour.
2 Preheat the broiler to high and line the broiler pan with foil. Remove the pork from the marinade. Brush the pork with oil and broil for about 5 minutes until cooked, turning halfway.
3 Meanwhile, divide the bean sprouts, cucumber, and scallions between two serving plates. Top with the pork, and spoon over the remaining dressing.

SERVES 2
10G CARBOHYDRATE PER SERVING

113   THAI-STYLE BEEF SALAD

10oz rump steak, cut into
  ½-inch strips
1 tbsp olive oil
2 Little Gem lettuces,
  leaves separated
2 shallots, finely sliced
1 large vine-ripened
  tomato, quartered

1 bird's eye chili, seeded
  and finely sliced
2 tbsp chopped fresh
  cilantro
1 tbsp torn fresh basil
salt and freshly ground
  black pepper

DRESSING:
juice of 1 lime
½ tsp fructose
1 tbsp extra-virgin
  olive oil
1 clove garlic, crushed
1 tbsp Thai fish sauce
2 tsp soy sauce

1 Put the beef in a bowl with the oil and season well. Heat a skillet
   and fry the beef for 4-5 minutes. Let cool slightly.
2 Arrange the salad leaves in 2 shallow dishes and top with the beef.
   Scatter over the shallots, tomato, and chili.
3 To make the dressing, mix the lime juice with the fructose until it
   has dissolved, then stir in the oil, garlic, fish sauce, and soy sauce.
   Pour the dressing over the salad. Season, and sprinkle with the fresh herbs.

SERVES 2
9G CARBOHYDRATE PER SERVING

chapter 4

SNACKS & LIGHT MEALS

This chapter features a range of recipes that suit a number of different eating occasions, whether you are looking for a quick, yet healthy snack, to tame a rumbling tummy, or a light meal that could be served at lunchtime, or a simple supper dish. It can be tricky to find snacks that are not carbohydrate-based, healthy or not. It's all too easy to grab a slice of white bread, or a cookie, handful of crisps, pastry, or croissant when feeling hungry and time is short, but eating these can lead to peaks and troughs in blood sugar levels, and doesn't satisfy the appetite for long. When it comes to snacking, look at foods that perhaps you wouldn't necessarily regard as a typical snack, such as dips, a hard-cooked egg, an omelet, a slice of ham, canned fish, a handful of nuts or seeds, or vegetable crudités. If opting for bread or crackers, choose unrefined, whole wheat types and eat in moderation: An open sandwich piled high with filling, rather than the usual two-slice version with a small amount of filling. Many of the following light meals can be made in advance, or can form the base of a larger main meal when paired with a moderate amount of noodles, brown rice, or a salad.

114 GREEN OLIVE TAPENADE

1¼ cups green pitted
   olives, rinsed if in brine
2 cloves garlic, crushed

2 tbsp capers, rinsed
2 tbsp extra-virgin
   olive oil

freshly ground
   black pepper

1   Put the olives, garlic, capers, and oil in a food processor
    and mix until finely chopped. Season to taste with pepper.

SERVES 6
3G CARBOHYDRATE PER PORTION

115 RED BELL PEPPER HOUMOUS

1 small red bell pepper,
   seeded and quartered
3 tbsp extra-virgin
   olive oil

1⅓ cups canned no-salt-
   or-sugar garbanzos,
   drained and rinsed
2 cloves garlic, crushed

1 tbsp light tahini
1 tbsp warm water
juice of ½ lemon
salt and freshly
   ground black pepper

1   Preheat the oven to 200°C/400°F/Gas 6. Place the bell pepper in a roasting
    pan with 1 tablespoon of the oil. Roast the bell pepper for 30-35 minutes until
    tender and the skin begins to blister. Let cool slightly, then peel off the skin.
2   Place the bell pepper, garbanzos, garlic, tahini, water, lemon juice, and the rest
    of the oil in a food processor or blender and purée until smooth. Season.

SERVES 5
11G CARBOHYDRATE PER SERVING

116 SMOKED MACKEREL PÂTÉ

6oz smoked mackerel
   fillets, skinned

juice of ½ lemon
2 tbsp cream cheese

½ tsp paprika
freshly ground
   black pepper

1   Cut the smoked mackerel into pieces and place in a blender or food processor
    with the lemon juice, cream cheese, and paprika. Mix until smooth
    and creamy, and season with pepper to taste.

SERVES 5
2G CARBOHYDRATE PER SERVING

117 RICOTTA & HERB DIP

½ cup ricotta cheese
6 tbsp chopped
   fresh mint

6 tbsp chopped
   fresh basil
juice of ½ lemon

3 tbsp extra-virgin
   olive oil
salt and freshly
   ground black pepper
paprika, to garnish

1   Blend together the ricotta, herbs, lemon juice, olive oil, and seasoning
    until smooth and creamy. Sprinkle with paprika before serving.

SERVES 3
2G CARBOHYDRATE PER SERVING

118 GUACAMOLE

1 avocado, pitted
1 small clove garlic,
   crushed

1 tbsp fresh lemon juice
salt and freshly ground
   black pepper

1 Scoop out the avocado flesh using a spoon. Roughly mash with the
   garlic and lemon juice until fairly smooth and creamy. Season to taste.

SERVES 2
2G CARBOHYDRATE PER SERVING

119 BABA GANOUSH

1 large eggplant,
   pricked all over
   with a fork

3 large cloves
   garlic, unpeeled
1 tsp ground coriander
1 tsp ground cumin
1 tbsp light tahini

2 tbsp extra-virgin
   olive oil
juice of ½ lemon
salt and freshly
   ground black pepper

1 Preheat the oven to 200°C/400°F/Gas 6. Place the eggplant in a roasting pan
   and roast for 25 minutes. Add the garlic and cook for a further 15 minutes until
   the eggplant and garlic are very tender.
2 Halve the eggplant lengthwise and scoop out the flesh with a spoon into a food
   processor. Peel the garlic cloves and put them in the processor with
   the spices, tahini, oil, and lemon juice. Mix until smooth. Season well.

SERVES 4
4G CARBOHYDRATE PER SERVING

120 TAHINI DIP

⅔ cup thick
   natural bio yogurt
2 tbsp light tahini

1 tsp cayenne, plus
   extra for sprinkling
1 tbsp chopped fresh mint

1 scallion,
   finely sliced
salt

1 Mix together the yogurt, tahini, cayenne, mint, and scallion. Season with salt and
   chill for at least 30 minutes. Sprinkle with extra cayenne before serving.

SERVES 3
4G CARBOHYDRATE PER SERVING

121 GARLIC DIP

1 large bulb garlic,
   top sliced off
1 tbsp lemon juice

1 tbsp extra-virgin olive oil
3 tbsp reduced-fat
   mayo

1 tbsp chopped
   fresh parsley
salt and freshly
   ground black pepper

1 Preheat the oven to 190°C/375°F/Gas 5. Put the garlic bulb in a roasting
   pan and roast for about 20 minutes until the garlic pulp has softened.
2 Squeeze the garlic pulp into a food processor with the lemon juice, oil,
   mayo, and parsley. Mix until smooth and creamy. Season to taste.

SERVES 3
3.5G CARBOHYDRATE PER SERVING

122 BLACK OLIVE TAPENADE

1 cup pitted black olives, rinsed
2 cloves garlic, crushed

2 tbsp extra-virgin olive oil
salt and freshly ground black pepper

1   Put the olives, garlic, and oil in a food processor and mix until finely chopped. Season to taste.

SERVES 4
1.5G CARBOHYDRATE PER SERVING

123 TUNA & AVOCADO SPREAD

½ cup canned tuna in spring water, drained

1 avocado, pitted, peeled, and flesh chopped
1 tbsp lemon juice

1 tbsp reduced-fat mayo
salt and freshly ground black pepper

1   Put the tuna, avocado, lemon juice, and mayo in a food processor. Mix until smooth and creamy. Season well.

SERVES 2
2G CARBOHYDRATE PER SERVING

124 EGG & TUNA PÂTÉ

7-oz can tuna in spring water, drained
2 free-range eggs, hard-cooked

2 tbsp snipped fresh chives
2 tbsp reduced-fat mayo

½ tsp paprika
salt and freshly ground black pepper
2 large round lettuce leaves

1   Mash the tuna and eggs in a bowl, then mix in the chives, mayo, and paprika. Season and served spooned into lettuce leaves.

SERVES 4
1.5G CARBOHYDRATE PER SERVING

125 ANCHOÏDE

8 anchovy fillets
2 tbsp olive oil
1 large clove garlic, chopped

2 sun-blush tomatoes in oil, drained and chopped
1 tbsp tomato paste

1 tbsp lemon juice
freshly ground black pepper

1   Put all the ingredients in a blender or food processor and mix until smooth. Use as a dip with vegetable sticks, as a topping on hard-cooked eggs, or spread on whole wheat toast.

SERVES 8
1G CARBOHYDRATE PER SERVING

126   ORIENTAL OMELET PARCEL

1 cup broccoli,
  cut into small florets
½-inch piece fresh
  root ginger, peeled
  and finely grated
1 large clove garlic,
  crushed

2 red chilies, seeded
  and thinly sliced
2 tbsp sunflower oil
4 scallions,
  sliced on the
  diagonal
1¾ cups bean sprouts

1 large head pak choi,
  shredded
2 tbsp chopped
  fresh cilantro
3 tbsp black bean sauce
3 free-range eggs, beaten
salt and freshly
  ground black pepper

1   Blanch the broccoli in boiling water for 2 minutes, drain, then refresh under
    cold running water.
2   Meanwhile, stir-fry the ginger, garlic, and half of the chili in 1 tablespoon of the
    oil for 1 minute. Add the scallions, broccoli, bean sprouts, and pak choi and
    stir-fry for 2 minutes, tossing the vegetables continuously. Add the black bean
    sauce and half of the cilantro and heat through. Set aside and keep warm.
3   Heat a little of the remaining oil in a skillet and add a third of the beaten egg.
    Swirl the egg until it covers the base of the pan. Cook the eggs until set, then
    turn out onto a plate and keep warm while you make two further omelets,
    adding more oil when necessary.
4   To serve, spoon a quarter of the vegetable stir-fry down the middle of each
    omelet and roll up loosely. Cut in half crosswise on the diagonal so that the
    filling is visible. Garnish with cilantro leaves and a few slices of chili.

SERVES 2
8G CARBOHYDRATE PER SERVING

127 SPINACH, OLIVE, & FETA FRITTATA

3½ cups spinach leaves,
   tough stalks removed
½ tbsp extra-virgin
   olive oil

1 onion, sliced
¼ cup black olives, pitted
   and halved
6 free-range eggs, beaten

1 cup feta, cubed
salt and freshly
   ground black pepper

1   Wash the spinach well and place in a saucepan. Cook, covered,
for about 3 minutes until wilted. Drain well, and squeeze out any
excess water. Roughly chop, and set aside.
2   Heat the oil in a medium-sized skillet. Add the onion and
sauté for 8 minutes, stirring occasionally, until softened.
3   Preheat the broiler to high. Spread the spinach over the base of the
skillet and scatter over the olives. Season the eggs and pour over
the spinach mixture. Scatter the feta on top. Cook over a moderate
heat for 5-6 minutes until the base is set.
4   Place the pan under the broiler (protect the handle with a double
layer of foil, if necessary) and cook the top of the frittata for about
3 minutes until set and lightly golden. Cut into wedges to serve.

SERVES 4
3G CARBOHYDRATE PER SERVING

128 PARMESAN CRISPS

**1 tbsp Parmesan, finely
  grated**

1   Preheat the oven to 190°C/375°F/Gas 5. Sprinkle the Parmesan into 6 mounds
    on a baking tray, leaving space between each one to allow them to spread. Cook
    for about 5 minutes until light golden and slightly crisp.
    Remove using a spatula and let cool and crisp further.

MAKES 6 CRISPS
NEGLIGIBLE CARBOHYDRATE

129 TUNA & LEEK TORTILLA

**1 tbsp extra-virgin
  olive oil
1 large leek, finely sliced**

**7-oz can tuna
  in spring water,
  drained**

**6 free-range eggs, beaten
salt and freshly
  ground black pepper**

1   Heat the oil in a medium-sized, ovenproof skillet, then fry the leek for
    5 minutes until softened. Stir in the tuna, retaining some chunks and making
    sure that the leek and tuna are evenly spread over the base of the pan.
2   Preheat the broiler to medium. Season the beaten eggs and pour them
    carefully over the tuna and leek mixture. Cook over a medium heat for
    5 minutes until the eggs are just set and the base of the tortilla is golden.
3   Place the pan under the broiler and cook the top of the tortilla for 3 minutes
    until set and lightly golden. Serve cut into wedges.

SERVES 4
1G CARBOHYDRATE PER SERVING

130 ASPARAGUS & RICOTTA FRITTATA

**1 tbsp extra-virgin
  olive oil
1 onion, thinly sliced**

**8 fine spears
  asparagus, trimmed
6 free-range eggs,
  lightly beaten**

**⅓ cup ricotta cheese
salt and freshly
  ground black pepper**

1   Heat the oil in a medium-sized, ovenproof skillet. Add the onion and fry for 8
    minutes, stirring occasionally, until softened. Add the asparagus and cook for
    a further 5 minutes until just tender.
2   Spread the onion evenly over the base of the pan and arrange the asparagus
    on top. Preheat the broiler to medium.
3   Season the eggs, and carefully pour them over the vegetables. Teaspoon the
    ricotta into the egg. Cook over a medium heat for 5-6 minutes until the eggs
    are just set and the base of the frittata is set and golden.
4   Place the pan under the preheated broiler (protect the pan handle with foil if
    necessary) and cook the top for 2-3 minutes until it is just set and risen. Serve
    cut into wedges.

SERVES 4
2G CARBOHYDRATE PER SERVING

131 OMELET FINES HERBES WITH PARMESAN

1 tbsp butter
2 free-range eggs,
  lightly beaten
salt and freshly
  ground black pepper

1 tbsp snipped
  fresh chives
1 tbsp fresh oregano
¼ cup Parmesan
  shavings

1   Melt the butter in a medium-sized skillet. Season the eggs and pour them into
    the pan. Swirl the eggs until they cover the base and cook until semi-set, then
    sprinkle the herbs and Parmesan over; serve flat.

SERVES 1
1G CARBOHYDRATE

132 GRIDDLED ASPARAGUS WITH PROSCIUTTO

12 spears asparagus,
  trimmed

4 slices prosciutto
1 tsp extra-virgin
  olive oil

1 tbsp balsamic vinegar
salt and freshly ground
  black pepper

1   Wrap 3 asparagus spears in a slice of prosciutto to give you 4 bundles.
2   Brush the griddle pan with the oil and heat. Add the asparagus bundles
    and griddle for 4 minutes, turning occasionally.
3   Add the balsamic vinegar and cook over a medium-high heat for
    about 1 minute until lightly golden. Season to taste.

SERVES 2
2.5G CARBOHYDRATE PER SERVING

133 SIMPLE HAM & EGG PIES

sunflower oil,
  for greasing
4 slices good quality
  lean cured ham

2 free-range
  eggs, beaten
½ cup semi-skimmed
  milk

salt and freshly
  ground black pepper
¼ cup grated mature
  Cheddar
1 tomato, sliced

1   Preheat the oven to 180°C/350°F/Gas 4. Lightly oil 4 cups of a deep muffin
    pan. Line the base and sides of each cup with a slice of ham, folding the ham
    where necessary to make a cup shape. Trim the top if necessary.
2   Mix together the eggs and milk; season. Sprinkle the cheese into each
    ham-lined muffin cup, then pour the egg mixture over the top.
    Place a slice of tomato on top of each "pie."
3   Bake the pies for 15-20 minutes until the egg filling has risen and set.
    Let cool slightly before transferring to a wire rack.

MAKES 4
2.5G CARBOHYDRATE PER PIE

134 MEDITERRANEAN TORTILLA WRAP

1 small soft whole wheat tortilla	2 slices mozzarella 2 slices tomato	1 tsp ready-made pesto 1 tsp extra-virgin olive oil

1 Lay the tortilla on a counter and place the mozzarella in the center. Top with the tomato and pesto. Fold in the sides of the tortilla to make a package.
2 Heat the oil in a skillet. Place the package seam-side down in the skillet. Cook over a low heat for 2-3 minutes, turning once, until golden.

SERVES 1
16G CARBOHYDRATE

135 ROASTED ASPARAGUS WITH FETA & MINT

2 tsp extra-virgin olive oil 10 spears asparagus, trimmed	½ cup cubed feta cheese 1 tbsp mint leaves 1 tbsp lemon juice	freshly ground black pepper

1 Preheat the oven to 190°C/375°F/Gas 5. Put the oil in a roasting pan and add the asparagus, turning the spears to coat them in the oil. Roast for 15-20 minutes until slightly golden and tender.
2 Arrange the asparagus in a shallow dish, and add the feta and mint. Pour the lemon juice over, and season.

SERVES 2
1.5G CARBOHYDRATE PER SERVING

136 FAVA BEAN FALAFEL

1 cup shelled fava beans	2 scallions, finely sliced	1 tbsp each fresh mint and parsley
¾ cup (drained weight) canned garbanzos, rinsed	1 tsp ground cumin ½ tsp dried crushed chili flakes	½ free-range egg, beaten salt and freshly ground black pepper
2 cloves garlic, crushed	1 tsp ground coriander 1 tsp lemon juice	soy flour, for dusting sunflower oil, for frying

1 Steam the fava beans for 2 minutes, then refresh under cold running water until cool.
2 Pop the beans out of their tough outer shell and put them in a food processor with the garbanzos, garlic, scallions, spices, lemon juice, herbs, and egg. Season well and mix until the mixture forms a coarse paste. Chill for 1 hour to let the mixture firm up.
3 Form the mixture into 12 walnut-sized balls using floured hands, then roll in flour until lightly coated. Shake to remove any excess flour.
4 Heat 1 tablespoon of oil in a skillet and cook the falafel in batches (adding more oil if necessary) for 6 minutes, turning occasionally, until golden. Drain on paper towels.

SERVES 4
9G CARBOHYDRATE PER SERVING

137 MUSHROOM MELT

1 tsp extra-virgin olive oil
2 large, flat mushrooms,
  stalks removed

2 tbsp dry white wine
salt and freshly
  ground black pepper

4 tsp ready-made
  pesto
2 slices mozzarella

1   Preheat the oven to 180°C/350°F/Gas 4. Lightly oil a large piece of foil and
    place the mushrooms on top. Spoon over the wine, season, and fold over
    the foil to make a package. Place on a baking sheet and cook for 10 minutes.
2   Open up the package and place 2 teaspoonfuls of pesto on each mushroom
    and top with a slice of mozzarella. Return the mushrooms to the oven
    for 8-10 minutes until the cheese has melted.

SERVES 2
3G CARBOHYDRATE PER SERVING

138 ROASTED BLACK BEAN TOFU

2 cloves garlic, crushed
1-inch piece fresh root
  ginger, peeled and
  grated

3 tbsp black bean sauce
1 tbsp soy sauce
2 tsp sesame oil
2 tbsp fresh apple juice

5-oz block firm tofu,
  patted dry and cubed

1   Mix together the garlic, ginger, black bean sauce, soy sauce,
    sesame oil, and apple juice in a shallow dish. Add the tofu and turn it
    to coat it in the marinade. Marinate in the refrigerator for at least 1 hour,
    preferably more, turning the tofu occasionally.
2   Preheat the oven to 180°C/350°F/Gas 4. Arrange the tofu on a lightly
    oiled baking tray. Spoon some of the marinade over the tofu and roast
    for 20 minutes, turning halfway, until golden and crisp on the outside.

SERVES 2
8G CARBOHYDRATE PER SERVING

139 SPICY TOFU CAKES

9-oz block firm tofu,
  patted dry and grated
1 tbsp curry paste
  of your choice
1 large clove
  garlic, crushed

1 tbsp grated
  fresh root ginger
½ tsp dried
  crushed chili flakes
2 tbsp chopped
  fresh cilantro

2 scallions,
  finely chopped
1½ tbsp soy flour
salt
1 tbsp sunflower
  oil, for frying

1   Mix the tofu with the curry paste, garlic, ginger, chili, cilantro, and scallions
    in a bowl. Stir in the flour and salt to make a coarse, sticky paste. Refrigerate,
    covered, for 1 hour to let the mixture firm up slightly.
2   Take large walnut-sized balls of the mixture and, using floured
    hands, flatten into rounds until you have 6 patties.
3   Heat the oil in a skillet and cook the tofu cakes for 4-6 minutes,
    turning once, until golden. Drain on paper towels, and serve warm.

SERVES 3
3G CARBOHYDRATE PER SERVING

140 THAI TEMPEH CAKES WITH CHILI MAYO

6oz tempeh
(fermented soy
beans), chopped
1 stalk lemon grass,
outer layer removed
and finely chopped
1 large clove garlic,
chopped

1 tbsp grated
fresh root ginger
2 shallots, finely chopped
1 bird's eye chili, seeded
and finely chopped
2 tbsp chopped
fresh cilantro
2 tsp lime juice
½ free-range egg, beaten

1½ tbsp soy flour,
plus extra for dusting
salt
1 tbsp sunflower oil

CHILI MAYO:
2 tbsp reduced-fat
mayo
1 tbsp sweet chili sauce

1   To make the chili mayo, mix together the mayo and chili sauce in a small bowl,
    and set aside.
2   Put the tempeh, lemon grass, garlic, ginger, shallots, chili, cilantro, and
    lime juice in a food processor. Mix until a coarse paste, then add the
    egg, flour, and seasoning and mix again until coarse and sticky.
    Refrigerate, covered, for 1 hour to let the mixture firm up slightly.
3   Take large walnut-sized balls of the mixture and, using floured hands,
    flatten into rounds until you have 4 patties. Heat the oil in a skillet and cook
    the patties for 5-6 minutes, turning once, until golden.
    Drain on paper towels and serve warm with the chili mayo.

SERVES 2
8G CARBOHYDRATE

141 BELL PEPPER & TOFU KEBABS

2 tbsp no-sugar
smooth peanut butter
1 tbsp olive oil
1 clove garlic, crushed

1 tbsp soy sauce
1 tbsp fresh apple juice
½ orange bell pepper,
seeded and cut into

8 chunks
½ x 9-oz block firm tofu,
patted dry and cut into
12 cubes

1   Mix together the peanut butter, oil, garlic, soy sauce, and apple juice in a
    shallow dish. Add the bell pepper and tofu and turn to coat them in the
    marinade. Marinate in the refrigerator for at least 1 hour.
2   Preheat the broiler to medium and line the broiler pan with foil. Thread the tofu
    and bell pepper onto 4 skewers and broil for 8-10 minutes, turning occasionally
    and spooning over some of the marinade, until golden.

SERVES 2
5.5G CARBOHYDRATE PER SERVING

142 HERBY SARDINES ON TOAST

1 slice whole wheat bread
2 canned sardines
in olive oil,
spines removed

1 tomato, seeded
and chopped
sprinkling dried crushed
chili flakes

1 tbsp chopped
fresh parsley
salt and freshly
ground black pepper

1   Preheat the broiler to high. Toast the bread on one side.
2   Drain the sardines and place them on top of the untoasted side of the bread.
    Top with the chopped tomato and a few dried chili flakes. Season to taste.
    Broil for 3 minutes, then sprinkle with parsley before serving.

SERVES 1
12.5G CARBOHYDRATE

143 **SMOKED SALMON RILLETTES**

9oz smoked salmon,
 sliced into fine strips
5-inch piece cucumber,
 seeded and
 coarsely grated

¼ fennel bulb,
 coarsely grated
2 tbsp crème fraîche
2 tbsp creamed
 horseradish

2 tbsp lemon juice
2 tbsp chopped fresh dill
salt and freshly ground
 black pepper
arugula leaves, to garnish

1　Mix together all the ingredients except the arugula in a bowl. Season with
　a little salt and plenty of black pepper. Chill for 30 minutes.
2　Spoon the salmon mixture into 2 x 3½-inch ring molds, or in neat mounds
　in the center of 2 plates. Garnish with arugula leaves before serving.

SERVES 2
5G CARBOHYDRATE PER SERVING

144 GLAZED SALMON STICKS

5oz salmon fillet,
  skinned and
  cut into 16 cubes

MARINADE:
2 tbsp fresh orange juice
1 tbsp soy sauce
1 tsp extra-virgin olive oil

1 tsp toasted sesame oil
1 clove garlic, sliced
½ tsp dried crushed chili
  flakes, optional

1 Mix together the ingredients for the marinade in a shallow dish.
   Add the cubes of salmon and turn until the fish is coated in the marinade.
   Let marinate in the refrigerator for 1 hour, turning the fish occasionally.
2 Preheat the broiler to high and line the broiler pan with foil. Thread the cubes
   of salmon onto 4 skewers and brush with the marinade. Broil the kebabs for
   3-5 minutes, turning halfway and brushing with the marinade, until cooked.

SERVES 2
3G CARBOHYDRATE PER SERVING

145 HERBY SALMON SKEWERS

5oz salmon fillet,
  skinned and
  cut into 16 cubes
2 scallions,
  each sliced into 6
4 bay leaves

MARINADE:
1 tbsp extra-virgin
  olive oil
1 large clove garlic, sliced
1 tbsp fresh oregano

1 tbsp fresh thyme
handful of fresh basil
salt and freshly
  ground black pepper

1 Mix together the ingredients for the marinade. Add the cubes of salmon
   and turn until the fish is coated in the marinade. Let marinate in
   the refrigerator for 1 hour, turning the fish occasionally.
2 Preheat the broiler to high and line the broiler pan with foil. Divide the
   salmon and scallions among 4 skewers, placing a bay leaf
   at the center of each kebab. Broil the kebabs for 3-5 minutes,
   turning halfway and brushing with the marinade, until cooked.

SERVES 2
2G CARBOHYDRATE PER SERVING

146 THAI SALMON ROLLS

1 stalk lemon grass, peeled
  and finely chopped
½ cup cooked peeled
  shrimp, chopped
2 tbsp chopped
  fresh cilantro
2 tbsp chopped
  fresh basil

2 tsp finely chopped,
  peeled fresh root
  ginger
juice of 1 lime and
  zest of ½ lime
2-inch piece cucumber,
  peeled, seeded, and cut
  into fine strips

1 scallion,
  finely chopped
1 tsp soy sauce
½ tsp dried
  crushed chili flakes
¼lb smoked salmon,
  cut into 6 strips

1 Mix together the lemon grass, shrimp, herbs, ginger, half the lime juice
   and all the lime zest, cucumber, scallions, soy sauce, and chili in a bowl.
2 Arrange the salmon strips on a chopping board. Divide the shrimp mixture
   between the salmon strips, and carefully fold up to encase the filling.
   Squeeze over the remaining lime juice before serving.

SERVES 3
4G CARBOHYDRATE PER SERVING

147   **GRAVADLAX OPEN SANDWICH**

2 slices rye bread
2 large lettuce
  leaves
4 wafer-thin slices
  cucumber
2 slices gravadlax

1 tbsp dill sauce
1 tbsp mayo
1 tsp lemon juice
1 hard-cooked egg,
  quartered

freshly ground
  black pepper
a little chopped
  fresh dill, to garnish

1   Place the rye bread on a serving plate. Arrange a lettuce leaf and two
    slices of cucumber on top of each slice. Arrange the gravadlax on top.
2   Mix together the dill sauce, mayo, and lemon juice and spoon the mixture over
    the gravadlax. Top with the egg, season with pepper, and garnish with the dill.

SERVES 2
18G CARBOHYDRATE PER SERVING

148   CRAB CAKES WITH CHILI DIP

⅔ cup fresh or
  canned white crab meat
¼ lb cod fillet, skinned and
  chopped
2 cloves garlic, chopped
¼ tsp dried
  crushed chilies

1 stalk lemon grass, peeled
  and finely chopped
1 tbsp finely grated
  fresh ginger
2 tbsp chopped fresh
  cilantro, plus
  extra to garnish
1 tbsp egg white

salt and freshly
  ground black pepper
sunflower oil, for frying

CHILI DIP:
2 tbsp sweet chili sauce
1 tbsp reduced-fat crème
  fraîche

1   Mix the crab, cod, garlic, chili, lemon grass, ginger, cilantro, egg white, and
seasoning in a food processor or blender until it forms a rough paste. Cover
and chill for 30 minutes.
2   To make the dip, mix together the chili sauce and crème fraîche.
3   Heat a little oil in a non-stick skillet and place 3 heaped tablespoons
in the pan, flattening the tops with a spatula. Fry for 3–4 minutes on
each side until golden. Drain on paper towels and keep warm while you
cook a further three cakes.
4   Serve three cakes per person with a spoonful of chili dip.
Garnish with cilantro.

SERVES 2
14G CARBOHYDRATE PER SERVING

149 TUNA BURGERS

7-oz can tuna
in spring water,
drained well
1 onion, grated

1 tsp dried oregano
2 slices day-old
whole wheat bread,
crusts removed

½ free-range egg, beaten
salt and freshly
ground black pepper
soy flour, for dusting
1 tbsp sunflower oil

1 Mash the tuna in a bowl and mix in the onion and oregano.
2 Process the bread into bread crumbs and stir them into the tuna
   mixture with the egg. Season well, and chill for about 1 hour to firm up.
3 Cover a plate with the flour, and divide the tuna mixture into 4.
   Dust your hands and form each portion into a burger shape, then dust
   with more flour—the mixture is quite loose but will firm up when cooked.
4 Heat the oil in a large skillet and cook the burgers for about
   6 minutes, turning once, until golden.

MAKES 4
7.5G CARBOHYDRATE PER BURGER

150 GARLIC & LEMON SQUID

10oz prepared
fresh squid, each
sliced into 3,
tentacles reserved

2 tbsp extra-virgin
olive oil
2 cloves garlic,
chopped
juice and grated
zest of 1 lemon

1 bird's eye chili,
seeded and chopped
1 tbsp chopped
fresh parsley
salt and freshly
ground black pepper

1 Rinse and pat dry the squid. Heat the oil in a sauté pan and fry the garlic,
   lemon zest, and chili for 1 minute.
2 Add the squid, including the tentacles, and cook for another 1-2 minutes.
   Pour the lemon juice over, season, and sprinkle with parsley.

SERVES 2
4G CARBOHYDRATE PER SERVING

151 SCALLOPS WITH PEACH SALSA

6 scallops
salt and freshly
ground black pepper

SALSA:
1 tbsp lemon juice
1 peach, stoned,
pitted, and diced

1 tbsp torn basil leaves
1 shallot, diced
1 tbsp extra-virgin
olive oil, plus extra
for brushing

1 Mix together the ingredients for the salsa and set aside to let the
   flavors merge.
2 Heat a griddle pan until hot. Brush the scallops with a little oil and season.
   Griddle the scallops for 1 minute each side. Serve with the salsa.

SERVES 2
6G CARBOHYDRATE PER SERVING

152 BACON-WRAPPED SCALLOPS ON SKEWERS

1 tbsp olive oil
6 scallops
½ tsp lemon juice

freshly ground
black pepper

6 slices lean bacon,
  rind removed
arugula leaves, to garnish

1   Preheat the broiler to medium-hot. Line the broiler pan with foil
    and brush with oil.
2   Pat the scallops with paper towels, squeeze over the lemon juice,
    and season with pepper. Wrap each scallop in a slice of bacon.
3   Thread 3 scallops onto each skewer and broil for about 4 minutes,
    turning once until the bacon is cooked.
    Garnish with arugula leaves to serve.

SERVES 2
3G CARBOHYDRATE PER SERVING

SNACKS & LIGHT M

153 AVOCADO WITH CRAB

½ cup fresh
  white crab meat
1 tbsp snipped
  fresh chives

1 tbsp reduced-fat
  mayo
1 tbsp lemon juice,
  plus extra to
  squeeze over

salt and freshly
  ground black pepper
1 large avocado,
  halved and pitted
¼ tsp cayenne pepper

1   Mix together the crab, chives, mayo, and lemon juice, then season.
2   Spoon the mixture on top of each avocado half. Squeeze over
    extra lemon juice, if liked, and sprinkle with cayenne.

SERVES 2
4G CARBOHYDRATE PER SERVING

154 PAN-FRIED PRAWNS IN GARLIC

6 large raw tiger prawns,
  peeled, deveined and
  tail left on

1 tbsp extra-virgin
  olive oil
1 tsp cayenne pepper
2 cloves garlic, chopped

1 tbsp chopped
  fresh parsley
salt and freshly
  ground black pepper

1   Put the prawns and half of the oil on a plate and sprinkle over the cayenne.
    Turn the prawns to coat them in the spiced oil.
2   Heat a skillet and add the prawns, spiced oil, and garlic, then fry for
    about 3 minutes, turning once, until cooked. Season and sprinkle with parsley.

SERVES 2
1G CARBOHYDRATE PER SERVING

155 SPICY SHRIMP FAJITAS

1 clove garlic, chopped
½ red bell pepper, seeded
  and cut into strips
1 tbsp extra-virgin olive oil
⅔ cup passata

½ tsp dried crushed chili
  flakes
½ tsp ground cumin
1 tbsp tomato paste
juice of ½ lime
packed 1 cup cooked
  medium shrimp

2 small soft
  whole wheat tortillas
½ small avocado,
  pitted, peeled,
  and diced
1 tbsp reduced-fat
  crème fraîche

1   Fry the garlic and red bell pepper in the olive oil over a medium-low heat for
    3 minutes until softened. Add the passata, chili, cumin, and tomato paste
    and cook for 8 minutes over a medium heat until reduced and thickened.
    Add the lime juice, and stir in the shrimp, then heat through.
2   Warm the tortillas, place on 2 plates, and spoon over the shrimp mixture.
    Arrange the avocado and crème fraîche on top.

SERVES 2
16G CARBOHYDRATE PER SERVING

156 REAL SHRIMP COCKTAIL

2½ tbsp reduced-fat
  mayo
½ tbsp tomato catsup
few drops Tabasco

packed 1 cup large
  cooked peeled shrimp
salt and freshly
  ground black pepper

Romaine lettuce
  leaves, shredded
¼ tsp paprika
lemon wedges, to serve

1 Mix together the mayo, catsup, and Tabasco in a bowl. Add the shrimp and turn them to coat them in the sauce; season to taste.
2 Arrange the lettuce leaves on 2 plates. Spoon the shrimp cocktail on top of the lettuce. Sprinkle with paprika and serve with lemon wedges.

SERVES 2
3G CARBOHYDRATE PER SERVING

157 COCONUT CHILI SHRIMP

2 shallots,
  finely chopped
1 bird's eye chili,
  finely chopped
3 tbsp torn
  fresh basil

3 tbsp chopped
  fresh cilantro
2 tsp fish sauce
2 tbsp reduced-fat
  coconut milk
juice and finely
  grated zest of 1 lime

½ stalk lemon grass,
  peeled and
  finely chopped
1 cup cooked peeled
  shrimp
2 tbsp unsalted roasted
  peanuts, chopped

1 Mix together the shallots, chili, herbs, fish sauce, coconut milk, lime juice and zest, and lemon grass. Add the shrimp and turn to coat them in the sauce. Let marinate in the refrigerator for 30 minutes, then serve sprinkled with peanuts.

SERVES 2
6.5G CARBOHYDRATE PER SERVING

158 SHRIMP WITH TOMATO SALSA

1 Little Gem lettuce,
  shredded
packed 1 cup medium
  cooked peeled
  shrimp

TOMATO SALSA:
2 tomatoes,
  seeded and diced
½ avocado, pitted, peeled,
  and diced
½ red onion, diced

1 tbsp lime juice
¼ tsp crushed
  dried chilies
1 tbsp chopped
  fresh cilantro
salt

1 Gently mix together the ingredients for the salsa in a bowl.
2 Divide the lettuce between 2 serving plates and top with the shrimp, then the salsa.

SERVES 2
4.5G CARBOHYDRATE PER SERVING

159 FISH TIKKA BROCHETTES

	MARINADE:	
1²⁄₃ cups skinless firm white fish, cut into 1-inch cubes sunflower oil, for brushing lemon wedges, to serve	1 tsp ground cumin 2 tsp garam masala 1 green chili, finely chopped	2 cloves garlic, chopped ½ tsp cayenne pepper 4 tbsp natural bio yogurt salt

1 Mix together all of the ingredients for the marinade in a shallow dish. Season with salt.
2 Add the fish cubes, turning them carefully until coated in the marinade. Cover with plastic wrap and let marinate for at least 1 hour.
3 Preheat the broiler to medium-high and line the broiler pan with foil. Brush the foil with oil.
4 Thread the fish cubes onto 4 skewers, brush with a little oil, then broil for about 5-7 minutes, turning occasionally, until cooked. Serve garnished with lemon wedges.

SERVES 2
3G CARBOHYDRATE PER SERVING

160 CHICKEN TIKKA

	MARINADE:	
2 chicken breast halves about ¼lb each, sliced into strips 2 large crisp salad leaves, and lemon wedges, to serve	1 clove garlic, crushed 2 tsp grated ginger 1 tbsp lemon juice 2 tsp garam masala ½ tsp hot chili powder	1 tsp paprika 1 tsp ground cumin 6 tbsp thick natural bio yogurt salt

1 Mix together all the ingredients for the marinade in a shallow dish. Add the chicken and turn to coat. Let marinate in the refrigerator for at least an hour or overnight.
2 Preheat the broiler and line the broiler pan with foil. Place the tikka-coated chicken in the broiler pan and cook for about 3-4 minutes each side until cooked through. Serve on a bed of lettuce leaves with lemon wedges.

SERVES 2
6G CARBOHYDRATE PER SERVING

161 CHICKEN FAJITAS

2 chicken breast halves,
    about ¼lb each, cut
    into strips
1 small red onion,
    sliced
½ red bell pepper,
    seeded and sliced
2 small soft
    whole wheat tortillas
2 tsp sour cream

MARINADE:
1 tbsp extra-virgin
    olive oil, plus
    extra for brushing
1 hot green chili, seeded
    and finely chopped

1 clove garlic, crushed
juice of 1 lime
½ tsp ground cumin
3 tbsp chopped
    fresh cilantro
salt

1   Mix together the ingredients for the marinade, reserving half of the
    cilantro. Add the chicken and marinate for at least 1 hour or overnight.
2   Heat a griddle pan, brush with oil, and add the chicken. Cook for 6-8 minutes,
    turning once, until cooked through. Add the onion and bell pepper after 3
    minutes and griddle until softened. Meanwhile, heat the marinade in a pan.
3   Warm the tortillas, place the chicken and vegetables on top.
    Spoon the marinade over, sprinkle with the reserved cilantro
    and add a spoonful of sour cream before serving.

SERVES 2
18G CARBOHYDRATE PER SERVING

162 CHICKEN, AVOCADO, & ARUGULA WRAP

½ avocado, pitted,
    peeled and flesh
    scooped out
1 small clove
    garlic, crushed
squeeze fresh lemon juice

1 tsp reduced-fat
    mayo
1 small soft whole wheat
    tortilla
1 small cooked,
    preferably roasted,

chicken breast half,
    sliced on the diagonal
handful of wild
    arugula leaves
salt and freshly
    ground black pepper

1   Roughly mash the avocado with the garlic, lemon juice, and mayo.
    Gently warm the tortilla and spread with the avocado mixture.
2   Arrange the chicken and arugula leaves on top. Season and roll
    up before serving.

SERVES 1
18G CARBOHYDRATE

CHICKEN SATAY

2 skinless chicken breast halves, about 5oz each
1 tbsp extra-virgin olive oil
1 tbsp lemon juice
salt and freshly ground black pepper

chopped fresh cilantro, to garnish

SATAY SAUCE:
5 tbsp no-sugar smooth peanut butter
1 tbsp olive oil
1 tbsp hot water

1 tbsp soy sauce
1 tbsp fresh apple juice
2 tbsp reduced-fat coconut milk
1 red chili, seeded and chopped

1 To make the satay sauce, mix together all the ingredients in a bowl.
2 Soak 8 wooden skewers in water to prevent them burning. Cut each breast into 4 strips lengthwise and thread each one onto a skewer.
3 Combine the olive oil, lemon juice, and seasoning in a small bowl, then brush the chicken with the marinade.
4 Heat a griddle pan or broiler to medium-hot. Cook the chicken skewers for 3 minutes on each side until golden and cooked through, making sure there is no trace of pink inside. Serve the skewers with the satay sauce, and sprinkled with cilantro.

MAKES 8 KEBABS
6G CARBOHYDRATE PER KEBAB

164 OPEN CLUB SANDWICH

1 slice whole wheat bread,
 toasted on one side
1 tsp reduced-fat
 mayo

salt and freshly
 ground black pepper
1 large crisp lettuce leaf
⅓ cup cooked sliced
 chicken breast

1 tomato, sliced
1 slice rindless bacon,
 broiled until crisp

1 To make the sandwich, place the bread toasted-side down on a plate. Spread
 the untoasted side with the mayo. Season, then cover this with the
 lettuce leaf and sliced chicken. Place the tomato on top, and finish with
 the bacon.

SERVES 1
12.5G CARBOHYDRATE

165 BACON & GOAT'S CHEESE PITTA

1 small whole wheat pitta
2 tbsp soft
 goat's cheese

small plum tomato, sliced
1 slice rindless bacon,
 broiled until crisp

1 tbsp alfalfa sprouts
freshly ground
 black pepper

1 Warm the pitta, then spread over the goat's cheese.
2 Top with the tomato. Cut the bacon slice in half and place on top,
 then finish with the alfalfa. Season with pepper.

SERVES 1
18G CARBOHYDRATE

166 MEXICAN TURKEY BURGER

1¼ cups lean
 ground turkey

1 tsp paprika
½ tsp hot chili powder
½ tsp ground cumin
½ tsp dried oregano

juice of ½ lime
salt and freshly
 ground black pepper
1 tbsp sunflower oil

1 Mix all the ingredients, except the oil, together in a bowl. Season, then
 form the mixture into 2 burgers about ½-inch thick. Chill for 30 minutes.
2 Heat the oil in a skillet over a medium heat, then cook the burgers
 for 3 minutes each side until golden.

MAKES 2 BURGERS
1G CARBOHYDRATE PER BURGER

167 CRISPY DUCK WRAP

2 duck breast halves,
  about ¼lb each
2 small soft
  whole wheat tortillas
1 tbsp hoisin sauce

1 scallion, sliced into
  thin strips
2-inch chunk cucumber,
  seeded and cut into
  thin strips

MARINADE:
½ tsp Chinese five spice
powder
½ tsp Sichuan
peppercorns, ground
1 tbsp groundnut oil
salt

1   Slash the duck breasts with a small sharp knife and put them in a dish.
    Mix together the ingredients for the marinade, and rub it into the duck.
    Let marinate for at least 1 hour or overnight.
2   Preheat the oven to 190°C/375°F/Gas 5. Place the duck in a roasting pan,
    spoon over the marinade, then roast for 35 minutes, turning once, until
    cooked through. Set aside for 5 minutes, then cut into very thin strips.
3   Warm the tortillas and spread with the hoisin sauce. Arrange the duck down
    the center, then top with the scallion and cucumber. Roll up and serve.

SERVES 2
18G CARBOHYDRATE PER SERVING

168 GLAZED PORK IN LETTUCE WRAP

2 pork fillets, about 5oz
  each, trimmed of fat
  and thinly sliced
2 large Iceberg
  lettuce leaves
2 tbsp finely
  chopped
  scallions

2 tbsp finely chopped
  fresh cilantro
2-inch piece
  cucumber, seeded
  and thinly sliced
2 tbsp mayo
½ tsp sesame oil
freshly ground
  black pepper

MARINADE:
4 tsp soy sauce
2 tbsp fresh
  orange juice
4 tbsp dry sherry
2 tsp Sichuan
  peppercorns, ground
2 cloves garlic,
  chopped

1   Mix together the ingredients for the marinade in a shallow dish and
    add the pork. Cover and marinate for at least 1 hour.
2   Heat a large skillet over a high heat and add the pork and the
    marinade. Fry for about 3 minutes, turning frequently.
3   Open out each lettuce leaf, and divide the pork and any remaining
    marinade between each one. Top with the scallions, cilantro,
    cucumber, mayo, and sesame oil. Season with pepper. Serve as
    is or roll up each lettuce leaf to enclose the filling.

SERVES 2
5G CARBOHYDRATE PER SERVING

169   **LAMB & FETA BURGER**

1 cup lean ground lamb
⅓ cup small pieces
   chopped feta cheese
1 clove garlic, crushed

1 tbsp fresh oregano
   or 1 tsp dried
5 pitted black olives,
   finely chopped

salt and freshly ground
   black pepper
sunflower oil, for frying

1   Mix together all the ingredients, except the oil, in a bowl.
    Season well, cover and chill in the refrigerator for about
    30 minutes until the mixture is fairly firm.
2   With your hands, form the mixture into 2 burgers.
    Heat enough oil to cover the base of a skillet
    and cook the burgers for 3 minutes on each side.

MAKES 2
1G CARBOHYDRATE PER BURGER

170 LAMB & TOMATO BRUSCHETTA

1 lamb fillet,
  about ¼lb
1 tbsp extra-virgin
  olive oil
2 tsp lemon juice
1 clove garlic, crushed

1 tsp dried oregano
1 slice seeded whole
  wheat bread, toasted
1 tsp Dijon mustard
1 tsp reduced-fat
  mayo

handful of
  arugula leaves
1 vine-ripened
  tomato, sliced
salt and freshly
  ground black pepper

1 Flatten the lamb with the top of a rolling pin or meat mallet. Put the oil, lemon juice, garlic, and oregano in a dish and add the lamb. Marinate for about 1 hour.
2 Preheat the broiler to medium-high and line the broiler pan with foil. Add the lamb, and spoon over some of the marinade. Broil for 1–2 minutes each side.
3 Spread the toast with the mustard and mayo. Place the arugula leaves on top, then the lamb, and finally the tomato. Season well.

SERVES 1
16.5G CARBOHYDRATE

171 SESAME BEEF SKEWERS

¼lb lean fillet
  steak, cut into
  1-inch cubes
1 zucchini, cut into
  ¼-inch slices
½ red bell pepper, seeded
  and cut into
  6 large chunks
1 tbsp sesame seeds,
  toasted

MARINADE:
1 tsp extra-virgin olive oil
1 tbsp sesame oil
juice of ½ lime
½ tsp cayenne pepper
salt and freshly
  ground black pepper

1 Mix together the ingredients for the marinade. Add the steak, zucchini, and red bell pepper and marinate in the refrigerator for 1 hour.
2 Divide the steak, zucchini, and bell pepper between 2 metal skewers.
3 Heat a griddle pan. Brush the skewers with the marinade and griddle for about 3 minutes each side until the vegetables are tender. Sprinkle with the sesame seeds, and serve.

SERVES 2
4G CARBOHYDRATE PER SERVING

172　BEEF CARPACCIO

2 tbsp ground black pepper	½lb thick lean beef fillet, trimmed
2 tbsp chopped fresh thyme	1 tbsp extra-virgin olive oil salt

1　Mix together the pepper, thyme, and salt on a plate.
　Roll the beef in the flavorings until covered.
2　Heat the oil until hot, then sear the beef until
　golden around the edges but still red in the center.
3　Set aside, let cool, and then chill, wrapped in plastic wrap.
　To serve, slice the beef as thinly as possible.

SERVES 2
0.5G CARBOHYDRATE PER SERVING

173　CHILI BEEF FAJITAS

1 tbsp extra-virgin olive oil	½ tsp ground cumin	1 tbsp chopped fresh cilantro
½ onion, thinly sliced	¼lb lean beef fillet, cut into thin strips	juice of ½ lime
½ red bell pepper, seeded and sliced	salt and freshly ground black pepper	2 crisp lettuce leaves, shredded
¼ tsp dried crushed chili flakes	2 small soft whole wheat tortillas	2 tsp sour cream
½ tsp paprika		

1　Heat the oil in a skillet and fry the onion for 5 minutes, then the bell pepper
　and cook for another 3 minutes.
2　Add the spices and cook for 1 minute, before adding the beef. Season and
　cook, stirring frequently, for another 2 minutes.
3　Warm the tortillas, place the lettuce leaves on top, then the beef mixture.
　Squeeze the lemon juice over and serve with a spoonful of sour cream
　and garnish with the cilantro.

SERVES 2
18G CARBOHYDRATE PER SERVING

chapter 5

MAIN MEALS

Thailand, India, Spain, Italy, France, and the Caribbean are just a few of the countries that have influenced the recipes in this chapter. This diversity of culinary ideas goes to show that low-carb cooking needn't be restrictive or dull. A richly spiced Indonesian beef curry, light crisp sea bass with Japanese pickled vegetables, and comforting stuffed eggplant are just a taste of things to come. This chapter is broken down into sections on meat, poultry, seafood, and vegetarian recipes. Many dishes come with a serving suggestion of, for example, a complex carbohydrate-based food, salad, or vegetable depending on the level of carbohydrates in the main meal and the range of ingredients it includes. The complex carbohydrate-based accompaniments include brown rice, whole wheat pasta, couscous, and buckwheat or soba noodles, and have been chosen because they are unrefined, do not upset blood sugar levels, and provide valuable fiber as well as vitamins and minerals. This does not mean you can over-indulge—2oz of each type is recommended. While you don't have to include this element when making the recipe, it gives an idea of how to prepare a balanced and nutritious meal.

MEAT

When buying meat, always go for quality cuts, preferably organic, and keep it lean. The following recipes have been created to cater for all manner of eating occasions, whether you are looking for a quick and simple supper, such as Pork and Apple Pan-fry or Pasta with Lamb and Arugula, or a more leisurely meal. The slow-cooked Fall Beef Stew, or Roast Mediterranean Lamb are perfect Sunday lunch dishes.

174 LAMB KOFTAS WITH GARBANZO MASH

packed 1 cup lean
ground lamb
1 onion, finely chopped

1 tbsp chopped
fresh cilantro, plus
extra to garnish
1 tbsp chopped
fresh parsley

½ tsp ground coriander
¼ tsp chili powder
salt and freshly ground
black pepper
1 tbsp olive oil

1 Place the lamb, onion, fresh herbs, cilantro, chili, and seasoning in a food
   processor. Mix until thoroughly combined.
2 Divide the mixture into 6 portions, and, using wet hands, shape each one into
   a sausage shape around a skewer. Refrigerate the skewers for 30 minutes.
3 To cook, preheat a griddle pan and add the oil. Cook the skewers in two
   batches for 10 minutes, turning occasionally until browned on all
   sides and cooked through.
4 Serve the koftas with the Garbanzo Mash (see page 195),
   sprinkled with chopped cilantro.

SERVES 2
2G CARBOHYDRATE PER SERVING.
SERVE WITH SIMPLE BELL PEPPER SALAD (SEE PAGE 56).

175 MOROCCAN LAMB STUFFED BELL PEPPERS

1 tbsp olive oil
1 onion, finely chopped
1 large clove
garlic, chopped
1 cup mushrooms,
chopped
¾ cup lean
ground lamb

1 tsp ground cumin
1 tsp ground cinnamon
1 tsp ground coriander
1¼ cups passata
⅔ cup beef
or vegetable stock
1 tbsp tomato paste

1 large yellow bell pepper,
halved lengthwise
and seeded
salt and freshly
ground black pepper

1 Preheat the oven to 180°C/350°F/Gas 4.
2 Heat the oil in a saucepan, add the onion and cook, covered, stirring
   occasionally, over a medium heat for 7 minutes until softened. Add the
   garlic and mushrooms and cook, stirring frequently, for a further 3 minutes.
3 Push the contents of the pan to one side and add the lamb. Cook, stirring
   frequently, until browned. Stir in the spices, and cook for another minute.
4 Pour in the passata and stock, then add the tomato paste. Cook for
   20 minutes until the sauce has reduced and thickened.
5 Meanwhile, blanch the bell pepper halves in a pan of boiling water for
   3 minutes, then drain well. Place in a baking dish and fill with the lamb mixture.
   Cover the dish with foil and bake for 20 minutes, then remove the foil
   and cook for a further 10 minutes until the bell peppers begin to color.

SERVES 2
15.5G CARBOHYDRATE PER SERVING.
SERVE WITH CHARGRILLED THYME ZUCCHINI (SEE PAGE 194).

176 PASTA WITH LAMB & ARUGULA

1 tbsp olive oil
2 lean lamb steaks,
   about 5oz each
2 bay leaves

2 shallots, peeled
   and halved
2 cloves garlic, peeled
2oz whole wheat
   spaghetti

2 large handfuls of
   fresh arugula leaves
12 fresh basil leaves
salt and freshly
   ground black pepper

1 Preheat the oven to 190°C/375°F/Gas 5. Pour the oil into a roasting pan,
   add the lamb and turn to coat in the oil. Put the bay leaves under the
   lamb and surround with the shallots and garlic. Roast for about 15 minutes.
2 Meanwhile, cook the pasta in plenty of boiling salted water according to
   the package instructions. Drain, reserving 2 tablespoons of the cooking water.
3 Remove the lamb and garlic from the dish, and thinly slice. Toss the pasta
   with the lamb, garlic, cooking water, shallots, and any juices in the roasting pan.
4 Add the arugula, basil, and seasoning. Toss with your hands before serving.

SERVES 2
21.5G CARBOHYDRATE PER SERVING.
SERVE WITH A MIXED LEAF SALAD WITH TOASTED SEEDS (SEE PAGE 56).

177 LAMB STEAKS WITH MINT SALSA

2 lean lamb steaks,
   about 5oz each
2 tsp olive oil
freshly ground black
   pepper

MINT SALSA:
large handful of
   fresh mint leaves
2 tbsp extra-virgin
   olive oil

1 tbsp capers, rinsed
1 tbsp reduced-fat
   mayo
2 scallions,
   finely chopped

1 To make the salsa, put the mint, oil, capers, mayo, and scallions
   in a food processor or blender, then mix until finely chopped.
   Season with pepper, and set aside.
2 Put the lamb between 2 sheets of plastic wrap and flatten with the top
   of a rolling pin. Heat the oil in a skillet and cook the lamb for 1 minute
   each side. Serve the lamb with a large spoonful of the salsa.

SERVES 2
2G CARBOHYDRATE PER SERVING.
SERVE WITH CANNELLINI BEAN PURÉE (SEE PAGE 197) AND A SALAD.

178 SPICE-CRUSTED LAMB

2 lean lamb steaks,
   about 5oz each
salt and freshly ground
   black pepper

SPICE MIX:
1 tbsp fresh mint leaves
1 shallot, peeled
   and halved
1 handful fresh
   cilantro leaves

2 tbsp olive oil
½ tsp ground cumin
2 tsp lemon juice
1 large red chili,
   seeded and sliced

1 Put all the ingredients for the spice mix in a food processor or blender
   and mix until finely chopped. Season, and spoon the mixture over
   the lamb. Marinate for 1 hour in the refrigerator.
2 Preheat the broiler to high and line the broiler pan with foil. Broil the lamb
   for 3-4 minutes each side.

SERVES 2
1.5G CARBOHYDRATE PER SERVING.
SERVE WITH SPICY COUSCOUS (SEE PAGE 194) AND STEAMED BROCCOLI.

ROAST MEDITERRANEAN LAMB

1¼lb boneless leg
  of lamb
1 clove garlic, sliced
2 tbsp chopped
  fresh oregano

2 tbsp chopped
  fresh rosemary
4 bay leaves
2 tbsp olive oil

salt and freshly
  ground black pepper
8 small plum tomatoes
2 tbsp pine nuts,
  toasted (optional)

1. Stuff the garlic and herbs into the joint cavity and tuck the bay leaves under the string wrapped round the lamb. Rub half of the oil into the joint, season and leave, covered, in the refrigerator for 1-2 hours.
2. Preheat the oven to 190°C/375°F/Gas 5. Heat the remaining oil in a skillet, add the lamb, and brown the meat all over to seal in the juices. Transfer the lamb to a roasting pan, and cover with foil. Roast for 20 minutes, then remove the foil. Add ½ cup of water to the pan to keep the lamb moist, and cook for a further 35 minutes, occasionally basting the meat in the juices.
3. Arrange the tomatoes around the lamb 15 minutes before the end of the cooking time. Let the meat rest for 10 minutes, then carve into slices, and serve with the tomatoes and pine nuts.

SERVES 4

7G CARBOHYDRATE PER SERVING.

SERVE WITH PURÉE OF ROASTED VEGETABLES
(SEE PAGE 198) AND STEAMED GREEN BEANS.

180 MARINATED LAMB WITH SPINACH

2 lean lamb steaks,
  about 5oz each
2 large flat mushrooms
¾lb fresh spinach, tough
  stalks removed
1 tsp lemon juice
salt and freshly ground
  black pepper

MARINADE:
2 tbsp olive oil
1 tbsp lemon juice
2 tbsp chopped
  fresh oregano
1 tbsp chopped
  fresh rosemary

1 Mix together the ingredients for the marinade in a shallow dish.
   Season and add the lamb and mushrooms. Turn to coat the lamb and
   mushrooms in the marinade, and marinate in the refrigerator for at least 1 hour.
2 Preheat the broiler to high and line the broiler pan with foil. Broil the lamb
   and mushrooms for 2-3 minutes each side, occasionally brushing them with
   the marinade.
3 Meanwhile, steam the spinach for about 2-3 minutes until wilted. Squeeze the
   spinach dry with your hands, then roughly chop. Season the spinach, and pour
   the lemon juice over.
4 Place a mushroom on each plate, then top with the spinach, then the lamb.
   Drizzle over any remaining marinade.

SERVES 2
5.5G CARBOHYDRATE PER SERVING.
SERVE WITH PURÉE OF ROASTED VEGETABLES (SEE PAGE 198).

181 OLIVE & LAMB CASSEROLE

4 lean lamb chops,
  trimmed
soy flour, for dusting
1 tsp olive oil
2 cloves garlic, chopped

¾ cup dry
  white wine
1¼ cups
  chicken stock
1 tbsp thyme leaves

½ cup pitted
  green olives, rinsed
1 tsp grated lemon zest
salt and freshly
  ground black pepper

1 Lightly dust the lamb in the flour and shake to remove any excess.
2 Heat the oil in a casserole dish and fry the lamb for about 3 minutes each
   side until browned and sealed. Add the garlic and cook for another minute.
3 Add the wine, stock, and thyme to the pan. Bring to a boil, then reduce
   the heat, cover, and simmer for 45 minutes, turning the lamb once.
4 Remove the lid, add the olives and lemon zest and cook for another
   15-20 minutes until the lamb is tender and the sauce has thickened.
   Season to taste before serving.

SERVES 2
7.5G CARBOHYDRATE PER SERVING.
SERVE WITH ROASTED FENNEL (SEE PAGE 195).

182 PEPPERED STEAK WITH MUSTARD MAYO

1 tbsp crushed
  black peppercorns
2 sirloin steaks,
  about 5oz each
1 tbsp olive oil
salt

MUSTARD MAYO:
2 tbsp reduced-fat
  mayo
1 tbsp extra-virgin
  olive oil
1 tsp Dijon mustard

1   First make the mustard mayo by mixing together all of the ingredients for
    it in a small bowl. Season and set aside.
2   Put the crushed black peppercorns on a large plate. Coat both sides of each
    steak by placing it on the plate, and using your fingers to press it down
    firmly onto the peppercorns until they become embedded in the surface
    of the meat.
3   Heat the oil in a skillet, add the steaks, season with salt, and cook for
    about 2 minutes each side, until cooked to your liking.
4   Serve the steaks with a spoonful of the mustard mayo.

SERVES 2
1G CARBOHYDRATE PER SERVING.
SERVE WITH CAULIFLOWER MASH (SEE PAGE 129) AND A GREEN VEGETABLE.

183 PROVENÇAL STEAK

2 tbsp olive oil
1 shallot, sliced
2 cloves garlic,
  crushed

2 tsp herbes de Provence
½ cup canned chopped
  tomatoes
1 bay leaf

2 sirloin steaks,
  about 5oz each
salt and freshly
  ground black pepper

1   Heat half of the oil in a saucepan and fry the shallot for 3 minutes until
    softened, stirring frequently. Add the garlic and herbs and cook for
    1 minute, stirring.
2   Stir in the tomatoes and bay leaf and simmer over a low heat for
    5-6 minutes until reduced and thickened. Season to taste.
3   Meanwhile, heat the remaining oil in a skillet. Season the steaks and
    cook for about 2 minutes each side until cooked to your liking.
4   Serve the steaks with the sauce spooned over the top.

SERVES 2
4G CARBOHYDRATE PER SERVING.
SERVE WITH CELERY ROOT MASH (SEE PAGE 200) AND STEAMED VEGETABLES.

184 MEATBALLS IN RED CURRY SAUCE

1 shallot, chopped
1 clove garlic, chopped
1 tbsp finely chopped
   fresh ginger root
½ tsp ground cumin
1 tbsp lemon juice
1 tbsp chopped fresh
   cilantro

1 free-range egg, beaten
⅔ cup lean
   ground beef
1 tbsp olive oil
salt and freshly
   ground black pepper

RED CURRY SAUCE:
1 tbsp olive oil
1 onion, finely chopped
1 tbsp tandoori
   curry powder
1 cup canned chopped
   tomatoes
⅔ cup reduced-fat
   coconut milk

1   Place all of the ingredients, except those for the sauce, in a food processor
    and mix to a coarse paste. Form the mixture into walnut-sized balls.
    Place the meatballs on a plate, and chill for around 30 minutes.
2   To make the sauce, heat the oil in a sauté pan and fry the onion for
    8 minutes until softened. Add the curry powder, and cook for 1 minute, stirring.
3   Stir in the chopped tomatoes, coconut milk, and 2 tablespoons of water.
    Bring to a boil, then reduce the heat. Add the meatballs and simmer,
    covered, for 20 minutes until cooked. Carefully turn the meatballs
    occasionally during cooking.

SERVES 2
12G CARBOHYDRATE PER SERVING.
SERVE WITH BROWN RICE AND STEAMED VEGETABLES.

185 SPICY GROUND BEEF

1 tbsp olive oil
1 onion, chopped
1¼ lean
   ground beef
1 large clove garlic,
   chopped
1 tsp ground cumin
1-2 tsp hot chili powder

1 bay leaf
1¼ cups passata
2 tsp sun-dried
   tomato paste
⅔ cup canned
   borlotti beans,
   drained and rinsed

½ cup vegetable stock
   (see page 30)
salt and freshly
   ground black pepper

1   Heat the oil in a sauté pan and fry the onion for 8 minutes, stirring
    occasionally. Add the beef, break it up with a spatula, and cook for
    3-4 minutes until browned. Stir in the garlic, spices, and bay leaf,
    then cook for another 1 minute.
2   Add the passata, tomato paste, beans, and stock, then cook, half-covered,
    for 25-30 minutes until the sauce has reduced and thickened. Remove the
    lid if the sauce appears too watery. Season to taste.

SERVES 2
16G CARBOHYDRATE PER SERVING.
SERVE WITH A GREEN SALAD.

HOMEMADE BEEF BURGER ON MUSHROOM MUFFIN

1 cup lean
   ground beef
1 large clove garlic,
   crushed
1 tsp dried oregano
2 large portobello
   mushrooms

2 tbsp olive oil
2 tbsp white wine
salt and freshly
   ground black pepper
2 thick slices
   beefsteak tomato
2 lettuce leaves

**BLUE CHEESE
   DRESSING:**
1 tbsp extra-virgin olive oil
1 tbsp reduced-fat
   mayo
¼ cup Roquefort Cheese,
   crumbled

1 Mix together the beef, garlic, and oregano in a bowl. Season well and shape the mixture into 2 burgers. Cover with plastic wrap and chill for 30 minutes.

2 To make the blue cheese dressing, mix together the ingredients in a bowl.

3 Preheat the oven to 200°C/400°F/Gas 6. Put the mushrooms on a piece of foil large enough to make a package. Drizzle over half of the oil and the wine. Season and fold up the foil to make a package. Put the package on a baking sheet and cook for 20 minutes until softened.

4 Meanwhile, heat the remaining oil and fry the burgers over a medium heat for 4 minutes on each side.

5 To serve, place a mushroom on each plate, top with a slice of tomato, a lettuce leaf, then the burger. Add a drizzle of blue cheese dressing before serving.

SERVES 2
2G CARBOHYDRATE PER SERVING.
SERVE WITH NUTTY COLESLAW (SEE PAGE 55) AND SEEDED WHOLE WHEAT BREAD.

MAIN MEALS

187 FALL BEEF STEW

2 tbsp soy flour
salt and freshly
  ground black pepper
1¾lb casserole beef,
  cubed
3 tbsp olive oil

12 shallots, peeled
  and halved,
  or quartered if large
1 carrot, cut into batons
1 cup brown cap
  mushrooms, halved

2 bay leaves
1 tbsp chopped
  fresh rosemary
2 cups red wine
1 cup beef stock
1 tbsp soy sauce

1 Preheat the oven to 170°C/325°F/Gas 3. Put the flour in a clean plastic food bag and season generously. Toss the beef in the flour until coated. Heat 1 tablespoon of the oil in a large casserole dish. Cook the beef in batches of about a third for 5–6 minutes, turning occasionally, until browned all over. Add another tablespoon of oil as necessary. Set aside.

2 Add the remaining oil to the pan with the shallots, carrot, mushrooms, and herbs, and cook for 3 minutes, stirring occasionally.

3 Pour in the wine and bring to a boil. Cook over a high heat until the alcohol has evaporated and the liquid reduced. Add the stock and soy sauce, then cook for another 3 minutes.

4 Stir in the beef, cover with a lid, and transfer to the oven. Cook for 2 hours until the stock has formed a thick, rich gravy and the meat is tender. Season to taste before serving.

SERVES 4
17G CARBOHYDRATE PER SERVING.
SERVE WITH CELERY ROOT MASH (SEE PAGE 200), STEAMED SAVOY CABBAGE, AND PEAS.

188 SLOW-COOKED INDONESIAN BEEF

1 tbsp groundnut oil
½ onion, finely chopped
1¼ cups chuck
  steak, cut into
  1½-inch cubes
3 cloves garlic, chopped
½-inch piece fresh root
  ginger, peeled and
  finely chopped

2 stalks lemon grass,
  peeled, and crushed
  with the back of a knife
2 small red chilies,
  seeded and finely
  chopped
2 cardamom pods, split
2 tsp ground turmeric
½ tsp ground coriander

½ tsp chili powder
½ tsp ground cumin
1 cup reduced-fat coconut
  milk
1 tbsp ground almonds
salt
2 tbsp unsweetened
  shredded coconut,
  toasted

1 Heat the oil in a saucepan and fry the onion for 8 minutes, stirring occasionally, until softened. Add the meat and cook for 2–3 minutes each side until browned and sealed.

2 Add the garlic, ginger, lemon grass, chilies, and spices and cook, stirring, for 1 minute.

3 Pour in the coconut milk and ½ cup water. Bring to a boil, then reduce the heat, cover, and simmer over a low heat for 2 hours. Add a little extra water if the curry seems too dry.

4 Uncover, add the almonds, and cook for 5–10 minutes. Season to taste and serve sprinkled with the toasted coconut.

SERVES 2
9.5G CARBOHYDRATE PER SERVING.
SERVE WITH BROWN RICE AND STEAMED PAK CHOI.

189 THAI-STYLE BEEF WITH BROCCOLI

1 cup broccoli
  florets
2 tbsp sunflower oil
1 tsp sesame oil
packed 1 cup lean beef
  steak, cut into
  thin strips
2 kaffir lime leaves

1 stick lemon grass,
  peeled, and crushed
  using the back of
  a knife
2 cloves garlic, chopped
1-inch piece fresh root
  ginger, peeled
  and finely chopped

½ red bell pepper,
  seeded and sliced
2 scallions, sliced on
  the diagonal
½ tsp dried crushed
  chili flakes
2 tbsp light soy sauce

1   Steam the broccoli for 2–3 minutes until half-cooked, then rinse under
    cold running water and drain well.
2   Heat both types of oil in a wok or large skillet. Add the beef and
    stir-fry over a medium heat for 2 minutes until browned all over.
    Add the kaffir lime, lemon grass, garlic, and ginger, and stir-fry for
    1 minute, stirring continuously.
3   Add the red bell pepper, scallions, chili, and broccoli, then stir-fry for
    2–3 minutes. Add the soy sauce and cook for another 1–2 minutes.
    Remove the lemon grass and kaffir lime leaves before serving.

SERVES 2
7.5G CARBOHYDRATE PER SERVING.
SERVE WITH BROWN RICE.

190 BEEF & MUSHROOM STIR-FRY

1 tbsp sunflower oil
packed 1 cup lean beef
  steak, cut into
  thin strips
2 cloves garlic,
  finely chopped

1-inch piece fresh root
  ginger, peeled
  and finely chopped
1 tsp Sichuan
  peppercorns, crushed
1¼ cups mushrooms,
  sliced

½ red bell pepper,
  seeded and sliced
2 scallions, sliced on
  the diagonal
2 tbsp soy sauce

1   Heat the oil in a wok or large skillet. Add the beef and stir-fry over a medium
    heat for 2 minutes until browned all over. Add the garlic, ginger, and Sichuan
    peppercorns, then stir-fry for 1 minute, stirring continuously.
2   Add the mushrooms, red bell pepper, and 1 scallion, then stir-fry for
    2–3 minutes. Pour in the soy sauce and 2 tablespoons of water, and stir-fry
    for 2 minutes until the vegetables are just tender and the liquid has reduced.
3   Serve sprinkled with the remaining scallion.

SERVES 2
7G CARBOHYDRATE PER SERVING.
SERVE WITH BROWN RICE.

191 GRIDDLED VENISON WITH BERRY SAUCE

1 tbsp olive oil
2 venison steaks,
  about 5oz each
salt and freshly
  ground black pepper

BERRY SAUCE:
$\frac{2}{3}$ cup frozen
  mixed berries
1 small apple, peeled,
  cored, and diced

1 star anise
2 tbsp water

1   To make the sauce, put the berries, apple, star anise, and water in
    a saucepan. Bring to a boil, then reduce the heat and simmer, covered,
    for 8 minutes until the apple is soft. Remove the star anise and transfer
    to a blender and purée, then sieve to remove any seeds. Set aside.
2   Brush a griddle pan with oil and heat until smoking. Season the venison,
    and griddle for 4-5 minutes each side. Serve with the berry sauce.

SERVES 2

11G CARBOHYDRATE PER SERVING.

SERVE WITH CELERY ROOT MASH (SEE PAGE 200) AND STEAMED GREEN BEANS.

192 GAMMON STEAKS WITH PINEAPPLE SALSA

2 lean gammon steaks, about 5oz each
oil, for brushing
salt and freshly ground black pepper

PINEAPPLE SALSA:
¾ cup peeled, cored, and diced fresh pineapple
1 tbsp chopped fresh cilantro

1 tsp lemon juice
½ hot red chili, finely chopped
1 tbsp extra-virgin olive oil

1   Preheat the broiler to medium-high and line the broiler pan with foil. To make the salsa, mix together the pineapple, cilantro, lemon juice, chili, and oil; season to taste.
2   Brush the foil with oil and broil the gammon for 3–5 minutes each side, depending on the thickness of the steaks. Serve with a large spoonful of salsa.

SERVES 2
4G CARBOHYDRATE PER SERVING.
SERVE WITH CANNELLINI BEAN PURÉE (SEE PAGE 197) AND A GREEN SALAD.

193 PORK WITH COCONUT RELISH

2 lean pork fillets, about ¼lb each
sunflower oil, for brushing
salt and freshly ground black pepper

COCONUT RELISH:
2 tbsp unsweetened shredded coconut
1 green chili, finely chopped

1 cup fresh cilantro
⅓ cup natural bio yogurt
juice of ½ lemon

1   Mix together the ingredients for the relish in a food processor. Transfer to a bowl and season well with salt. Leave in the refrigerator for 1 hour to let the relish thicken.
2   Heat a griddle pan to high. Brush the pork fillets with oil, and griddle for 3–5 minutes each side, depending on the thickness of the fillets. Season, and serve with the coconut relish.

SERVES 2
3G CARBOHYDRATE PER SERVING.
SERVE WITH SESAME SPINACH (SEE PAGE 197).

194 SPANISH PAPRIKA PORK

1 tbsp olive oil
2 pork fillets, about ¼lb each, cut into strips
2 gluten-free pork sausages, cut into 1-inch pieces

1 onion, sliced
1 clove garlic, chopped
1 yellow bell pepper, seeded and roughly chopped
2 tsp smoked sweet paprika

14-oz can chopped tomatoes
salt and freshly ground black pepper

1   Heat the oil in a large saucepan, and add the pork and sausages and cook for 3–5 minutes until browned all over. Add the onion and cook, stirring frequently, for 5 minutes until softened.
2   Add the garlic and bell pepper and cook for 3 minutes, then stir in the paprika and tomatoes. Cook, half-covered, for 10 minutes until the sauce has thickened. Season to taste.

SERVES 2
15G CARBOHYDRATE PER SERVING.
SERVE WITH BRAISED LEEKS (SEE PAGE 202).

195 PORK STIR-FRY WITH MIXED BELL PEPPERS

1 tbsp groundnut oil
2 tsp sesame oil
2 lean pork fillets,
 about 5oz each,
 cut into strips
½ red bell pepper,
 seeded and sliced

½ yellow bell pepper,
 seeded and sliced
2 cloves garlic, sliced
½-inch piece fresh root
 ginger, peeled and finely
 sliced into matchsticks
3 tbsp fresh apple juice

1 tbsp soy sauce
salt and freshly
 ground black pepper

1 Heat a wok or large skillet. Add the oils and stir-fry the pork for
 3-5 minutes until browned all over.
2 Add the bell peppers, garlic, and ginger and stir-fry for 2 minutes, then
 pour in the apple juice and soy sauce, and stir-fry for another 2 minutes.
 Season and serve.

SERVES 2
8.5G CARBOHYDRATE PER SERVING.
SERVE WITH BROWN RICE.

196 BAKED PORK WITH CIDER

2 tbsp olive oil
1 red onion, sliced
1¾ cups dry apple cider

2 tbsp chopped fresh
 marjoram or oregano
1 tsp butter

salt and freshly
 ground black pepper
2 lean pork fillets,
 about 5oz each

1 Preheat the oven to 190°C/375°F/Gas 5. Heat half of the oil in a skillet.
 Add the onion and cook for 4 minutes, season with salt and cook for
 another minute until golden.
2 Pour in the cider. Bring to a boil, then reduce the heat and simmer until
 reduced by half. Stir in the marjoram, then add the butter and cook,
 stirring, until melted; season to taste.
3 Pour the remaining oil in a roasting pan. Coat the pork in the oil,
 then spoon over the sauce. Cover with foil and bake for 15 minutes.

SERVES 2
7.5G CARBOHYDRATE PER SERVING.
SERVE WITH BAKED CARAWAY CABBAGE (SEE PAGE 200).

197 MARINATED GINGER PORK

2 lean pork fillets,
 about 5oz each
1 tbsp olive oil

MARINADE:
1 tbsp olive oil
1 tbsp soy sauce
1 tsp sesame oil

1½ tsp grated
 fresh root ginger
1 tbsp chopped
 fresh cilantro

1 Mix together the ingredients for the marinade in a shallow dish. Add the pork
 and turn it so that it is completely coated in the marinade. Cover the dish with
 plastic wrap, and marinate in the refrigerator for at least 1 hour or overnight.
2 Heat the oil in a skillet and cook the pork for 4 minutes, then turn,
 add the marinade, and cook for a further 4-5 minutes.

SERVES 2
1G CARBOHYDRATE PER SERVING.
SERVE WITH WHOLE WHEAT NOODLES AND SESAME SPINACH (SEE PAGE 197).

198 PAN-FRIED PORK WITH MINTY PEA PURÉE

	MINTY PEA PURÉE:	
1 tbsp olive oil	1¼ cups frozen peas	2 tbsp reduced-fat
2 pork fillets, about	2 tbsp chopped	crème fraîche
5oz each	fresh mint	2 tbsp hot water
chopped fresh parsley,	1 tbsp olive oil	salt and freshly
to garnish		ground black pepper

1 To make the pea purée, boil the peas until cooked. Drain and transfer
   to a blender with the mint, olive oil, crème fraîche, and hot water and
   purée until smooth. Season to taste and keep warm.
2 Heat the oil in a skillet. Cook the pork for 4–5 minutes each side,
   then season well. Place the pea purée in a mound in the center of
   each plate, and top with the pork, then garnish with parsley.

SERVES 2
10G CARBOHYDRATE PER SERVING.
SERVE WITH GARLIC & LEMON CHARD (SEE PAGE 202).

199 SPICED PORK WITH CILANTRO HOUMOUS

2 tbsp olive oil
1 tsp sweet paprika
1 tbsp chopped
   fresh rosemary

2 pork chops,
   about 6oz each,
   fat trimmed
salt and freshly
   ground black pepper

CILANTRO HOUMOUS:
6 tbsp houmous
2 tbsp reduced-fat
   crème fraîche
2 tbsp chopped
   fresh cilantro

1 Mix together the oil, paprika, and rosemary in a shallow dish. Season well. Add the pork and turn to coat in the marinade. Cover with plastic wrap and let marinate in the refrigerator for at least 1 hour.
2 Preheat the broiler to its highest setting and line the broiler pan with foil. Broil the chops for 5-7 minutes each side until cooked through.
3 Meanwhile, mix together the houmous, crème fraîche, and cilantro. Season, and serve with the pork chops.

SERVES 2
7.5G CARBOHYDRATE PER SERVING.
SERVE WITH STEAMED ZUCCHINI.

200 ROSEMARY & GARLIC ROASTED PORK FILLETS

3 tbsp chopped
   fresh rosemary
3 tbsp chopped
   fresh flat-leaf parsley
3 tbsp extra-virgin
   olive oil

2 cloves garlic, chopped
juice of ½ lemon
2 lean pork fillets,
   about 5oz each
4 shallots, peeled
   and halved

salt and freshly
   ground black pepper

1 Preheat the oven to 200°C/400°F/Gas 6. Purée the herbs, 2 tablespoons of the olive oil, the garlic, and the lemon juice in a food processor.
2 Heat the remaining oil in a skillet, and cook the pork for 3 minutes until browned all over.
3 Lay the pork on a piece of foil, large enough to make a package, and top with the herb mixture.
4 Place the shallots next to the pork, season, and fold the foil to make a package. Place on a baking sheet and roast in the oven for 20-25 minutes, depending on the thickness of the pork.

SERVES 2
4.5G CARBOHYDRATE PER SERVING.
SERVE WITH CANNELLINI BEAN PURÉE (SEE PAGE 197) AND STEAMED BROCCOLI.

201 PORK & APPLE PAN-FRY

2 tsp soy flour
1 tsp paprika
packed 1 cup pork
   tenderloin, trimmed
   and cut into
   bite-sized pieces
1 tbsp olive oil
1 onion, finely chopped

½ dessert apple, cored,
   peeled, and cut into
   bite-sized pieces
1 tbsp chopped
   fresh rosemary
⅔ cup vegetable stock
   (see page 30)

2 tomatoes, seeded
   and roughly chopped
⅔ cup canned
   flageolet beans,
   drained and rinsed
2 tbsp reduced-fat
   crème fraîche
salt and freshly
   ground black pepper

1 Mix together the flour and paprika in a small plastic food bag and add
   the pork pieces. Shake the bag to toss the pork in the seasoned flour.
   Turn out the pork onto a plate and shake off any excess flour.
2 Heat the oil in a sauté pan, add the pork and cook for 5 minutes,
   turning the meat, until browned all over. Add the onion and cook
   for a further 7 minutes until softened.
3 Mix in the apple and rosemary, then cook for 3-4 minutes until
   the apple begins to break down.
4 Pour in the stock, bring to a boil, then reduce the heat and simmer for
   15 minutes until reduced and thickened. Stir in the tomatoes and beans,
   then cook, half-covered, for another 10 minutes over a low heat. Stir in
   the crème fraîche and heat through before serving. Season to taste.

SERVES 2
16G CARBOHYDRATE PER SERVING.
SERVE WITH GARLIC & LEMON CHARD (SEE PAGE 202).

202 CHEAT'S CASSOULET

1 tbsp extra-virgin olive oil
1 onion, finely chopped
1 stick celery,
   finely chopped
1 large clove
   garlic, chopped

packed 1 cup cubed lean
   pork fillet
½ tsp cayenne pepper
½ tsp ground cumin
1 cup canned chopped
   tomatoes

⅔ cup canned
   flageolet beans,
   drained and rinsed
salt and freshly
   ground black pepper

1 Preheat the oven to 190°C/375°F/Gas 5.
2 Heat the oil in a medium-sized ovenproof saucepan with a lid and fry
   the onion and celery for 4 minutes until softened. Add the garlic and pork,
   and cook for 2 minutes, turning occasionally until browned on all sides.
3 Stir in the spices and cook for another 1 minute. Add the tomatoes
   and beans, and cook for 5 minutes, stirring occasionally.
4 Cover with a lid and transfer the pan to the oven and cook for
   15 minutes, then remove the lid and cook for another 5 minutes.

SERVES 2
15.5G CARBOHYDRATE PER SERVING.
SERVE WITH STEAMED GREEN VEGETABLES.

203 SPICY MEATBALLS IN TOMATO SAUCE

1¼ cups lean ground pork
1 onion, grated
1 tsp ground cumin
1 tsp paprika
1 large clove
   garlic, crushed
1 small free-range egg,
   beaten

salt and freshly ground
   black pepper

TOMATO SAUCE:
1 tbsp extra-virgin
   olive oil
2 cloves garlic, chopped

½ tsp dried
   crushed chilies
⅔ cup dry white wine
1¼ cups passata
1 bay leaf
2 tsp tomato paste
2 tsp chopped fresh
   cilantro, to serve

1 Put the ground pork, onion, ground cumin, paprika, garlic, and egg in
a bowl and mix well until combined. Season with salt and pepper, and
refrigerate for 30 minutes.

2 Meanwhile, make the tomato sauce. Heat the olive oil in a large skillet
and fry the garlic and chilies for 1 minute, then pour in the white wine.
Cook over a high heat until the wine has almost evaporated.

3 Add the passata, bay leaf, and tomato paste, stir well, and cook over
a medium-low heat, half-covered, for 5 minutes.

4 Remove the meatball mixture from the refrigerator and form into
walnut-sized balls. Place them in the sauce and cook, half-covered,
over a medium-low heat for 15-20 minutes until they are cooked through.
Sprinkle with cilantro before serving.

SERVES 2
11G CARBOHYDRATE PER SERVING.
SERVE WITH WHOLE WHEAT PITTA BREAD AND A MIXED LEAF SALAD.

MAIN MEALS

POULTRY

Low in fat and packed with protein, any variety of poultry lends itself to a whole range of dishes that fit very comfortably into a low-carb lifestyle. Some of the recipes in this section contain a carbohydrate element, such as Chili Chicken with Butternut Squash Mash, Chicken with Lemon Quinoa, or Polenta-crusted Chicken with Beans. These are, however, a source of good complex carbs and provide a range of nutrients and fiber. Simply serve them with a side vegetable or salad.

204 ROASTED CHICKEN WITH SUN-BLUSH TOMATO PESTO

2 skinless chicken breast halves, about 5oz each
1 tsp extra-virgin olive oil

RED PESTO
⅓ cup sun-blush tomatoes in oil (drained weight), chopped
1 clove garlic, crushed

3 tbsp pine nuts, lightly toasted
⅓ cup olive oil
salt and freshly ground black pepper

1 Preheat the oven to 200°C/400°F/Gas 6. To make the red pesto, put the sun-blush tomatoes, garlic, 2 tablespoons of the pine nuts, and the oil in a food processor and blend until they form a coarse paste. Season to taste.
2 Arrange the chicken in a baking dish. Brush each breast with the oil then place a tablespoon of red pesto over each one. Spread the pesto using the back of a spoon so it covers the top of the chicken breast. Any left over pesto can be stored in an airtight container in the refrigerator for up to a week.
3 Roast the chicken for 30 minutes until the juices run clear when the breast is pierced with a skewer and there is no sign of any pink in the middle. Sprinkle with the reserved toasted pine nuts before serving.

SERVES 2
10G CARBOHYDRATE PER SERVING.
SERVE WITH BEAN & ROASTED RED BELL PEPPER SALAD (SEE PAGE 49)
AND A GREEN SALAD.

205 POLENTA-CRUSTED CHICKEN WITH BEANS

2 skinless chicken breast halves, about 5oz each
1 tbsp polenta or cornmeal
4 tsp sun-dried tomato paste

½ tsp dried oregano
2½ tbsp olive oil
8 small plum tomatoes
5 cloves garlic, unpeeled
1¼ cups canned cannellini beans, drained and rinsed

2 tsp chopped fresh rosemary
salt and freshly ground black pepper

1 Preheat the oven to 200°C/400°F/Gas 6. Mix together the polenta, tomato paste, oregano, and ½ tablespoon of the oil. Season and press the mixture over each chicken breast.
2 Pour 1 tablespoon of the oil into a roasting pan and add the chicken. Roast for 10 minutes, then add the tomatoes and garlic to the pan. Cook for a further 8-10 minutes. Keep the chicken warm, and peel the tomatoes and garlic, then chop the latter.
3 Heat the remaining oil in a saucepan and add the beans and rosemary, and cook over a medium-low heat for 5 minutes. Stir in the roasted tomatoes and garlic, season, then heat through.
4 Divide the beans and tomatoes between two plates and top with the chicken.

SERVES 2
18G CARBOHYDRATE PER SERVING.
SERVE WITH MINTY ZUCCHINI (SEE PAGE 194).

206 SPANISH CHICKEN CASSEROLE

4 chicken thighs
soy flour, for dusting
salt and freshly
  ground black pepper
1½ tbsp olive oil
1 large red onion, sliced
1 small orange bell pepper,
  seeded and sliced

2 large cloves garlic,
  chopped
½ cup chicken stock
  (see page 30)
½ cup dry sherry
1 bay leaf
zest and juice of
  ½ orange

½ tsp smoked paprika
1 tsp Worcestershire
  sauce
¼ cup black olives

1   Dust the chicken in seasoned flour. Heat ½ tbsp of the oil in a casserole dish, add the chicken and cook for 7 minutes, turning halfway, until golden. Remove from the pan and keep warm.
2   Pour away any oil in the pan and heat the remaining oil. Add the onion and fry, covered, for 5 minutes. Add the bell pepper and garlic and cook, covered, for another 5 minutes. Return the chicken to the pan.
3   Pour in the stock, sherry, bay leaf, orange juice and zest, paprika, Worcestershire sauce, and olives, then bring to a boil. Reduce the heat and simmer, half-covered, for 30-35 minutes until the chicken is cooked through and the sauce has reduced.

SERVES 2
11G CARBOHYDRATE PER SERVING.
SERVE WITH BUCKWHEAT AND BRAISED LEEKS (SEE PAGE 202).

207 BEST EVER ROAST CHICKEN

1 lemon, sliced into
  quarters
2¼lb free-range chicken,
  giblets removed

1 bulb garlic, halved
  horizontally
1 tbsp thyme leaves,
  plus 10 sprigs

¼ cup butter,
  softened
salt and freshly
  ground black pepper

1   Preheat the oven to 200°C/400°F/Gas 6. Insert the lemon wedges into the chicken cavity with the garlic and thyme sprigs.
2   Mix together 3 tablespoons of the butter with the thyme leaves until combined. Insert the thyme-flavored butter under the skin of the breast with your fingers, and spread until evenly coated.
3   Spread the remaining butter over the top of the chicken, and season well. Put the chicken on top of a rack in a roasting pan and pour ½-inch of water into the pan. Cover with foil.
4   Roast the chicken for 30 minutes, remove the foil and baste the chicken with the juices. Return the chicken to the oven for about 50 minutes until cooked through and there is no sign of pink when a skewer is inserted into the thickest part of the thigh. Baste the chicken every 20 minutes.
5   Let the chicken rest for 5 minutes before carving.

SERVES 3
1G CARBOHYDRATE PER SERVING.
SERVE WITH CAULIFLOWER MASH (SEE PAGE 129) AND STEAMED VEGETABLES.

MAIN MEALS

208 ROAST LEMON & SAGE ROCK CORNISH HENS

8 cloves garlic
2 rock Cornish hens
8 shallots, peeled

2 tbsp lemon juice
  and grated zest
  of ½ lemon
1 tbsp olive oil

salt and freshly
  ground black pepper
8 sage leaves

1 Preheat the oven to 200°C/400°F/Gas 6. Arrange the garlic in the bottom
   of a roasting pan and place the birds on top and the shallots around.
2 Drizzle the lemon juice over the birds, rubbing it in with your fingers,
   then rub in the oil. Sprinkle over the lemon zest and season well.
   Place 4 sage leaves on each bird.
3 Roast the birds for 15 minutes, baste with any juices, then return to the oven
   for another 20 minutes. Baste again and cook for a final 10 minutes until
   cooked through and there is no sign of pink when a skewer is inserted
   into the thickest part of the thigh.
4 Remove from the oven, discard the garlic, and let rest for 5 minutes before
   serving with the shallots.

SERVES 2
5G CARBOHYDRATE PER SERVING.
SERVE WITH PURÉE OF ROASTED VEGETABLES (SEE PAGE 198)
AND A SELECTION OF STEAMED VEGETABLES.

209 CHICKEN WITH PICO DE GALLO

2 skinless chicken
  breast halves,
  about 5oz each
olive oil, for brushing
½ tsp ground cumin

PICO DE GALLO:
4 radishes, finely chopped
3 vine-ripened tomatoes,
  seeded and chopped
¼ red onion,
  finely chopped

1 green chili, seeded
  and finely chopped
juice of ½ lime
2 tbsp chopped
  fresh cilantro
salt and freshly
  ground black pepper

1 Mix together all the ingredients for the pico de gallo in a bowl. Season, then
   chill until ready to serve.
2 Preheat the broiler to high and line the broiler pan with foil. Brush the chicken
   breasts with oil, then rub in the cumin. Broil for 5-6 minutes each side until
   cooked through. Serve with the pico de gallo.

SERVES 2
3G CARBOHYDRATE PER SERVING.
SERVE WITH ROASTED CUMIN PUMPKIN (SEE PAGE 195).

210 STUFFED CHICKEN POCKETS

½ cup chestnut
mushrooms, diced
1½ tbsp olive oil, plus
extra for greasing
2 tbsp prosciutto or lean
bacon, chopped

¼ cup fresh whole wheat
bread crumbs
1 tsp finely chopped
fresh thyme
1 tbsp lemon juice

2 skinless chicken breast
halves, about 5oz each
small knob of butter
salt and freshly
ground black pepper

1   Preheat the oven to 200°C/400°F/Gas 6. Fry the mushrooms in 1 tablespoon
    of the oil for 3 minutes. Mix the mushrooms in a food processor with the
    prosciutto or bacon, bread crumbs, thyme, lemon juice, and the rest of the oil.
2   Make a deep incision down the middle of each chicken breast using a sharp
    knife to form a pocket. Stuff the mushroom mixture into each breast and
    close the pocket to encase the filling. Place in a lightly oiled roasting pan.
3   Spread the butter over the chicken with your fingers, season, and cover the
    pan with foil. Roast for 10 minutes, then remove the foil and roast for another
    6-8 minutes until cooked through and there is no sign of pink in the middle.

SERVES 2
6.5G CARBOHYDRATE PER SERVING.
SERVE WITH CELERY ROOT MASH (SEE PAGE 200) AND STEAMED GREEN VEGETABLES.

211 TAPENADE CHICKEN

2 skinless chicken
breast halves,
about 5oz each
a little oil for roasting

TAPENADE:
⅔ cup pitted green olives,
rinsed if in brine
1 clove garlic, crushed
1 tbsp capers, rinsed

1 tbsp extra-virgin
olive oil
salt and freshly ground
black pepper

1   To make the tapenade, put the olives, garlic, capers, and oil in a food
    processor and mix until finely chopped. Season to taste with pepper.
2   Preheat the oven to 200°C/400°F/Gas 6. Lightly oil a roasting pan. Arrange
    the chicken in the pan and cover each one with a decent amount of tapenade.
3   Cover the dish with foil and roast for 10 minutes, then remove the foil and
    cook for another 10 minutes until the chicken is cooked through and
    there is no trace of pink.

SERVES 2
5.5G CARBOHYDRATE PER SERVING.
SERVE WITH GARLIC & LEMON CHARD (SEE PAGE 202).

212 CHICKEN WITH LEMON QUINOA

**2 skinless chicken
breast halves,
about 5oz each
olive oil,
for brushing**

**2 tsp crushed coriander
seeds
salt and freshly ground
black pepper**

**LEMON QUINOA:
2oz quinoa
hot vegetable stock
(see page 30), to cover
juice and finely grated
zest of ½ lemon
2 tbsp fresh thyme**

1   Put the quinoa in a saucepan and cover with stock until it is about ½ inch
    above the level of the quinoa. Bring to a boil, reduce the heat, cover, and
    simmer for about 10 minutes until the stock has been absorbed and the grains
    are tender. Let stand, covered, for 5 minutes, then fluff up with a fork.
2   Preheat the broiler to high and line the broil pan with foil. Put the quinoa
    in a bowl and stir in the lemon juice, zest, and thyme. Stir well to combine,
    and season to taste.
3   Arrange the chicken in the broiler pan, brush with oil, sprinkle with the
    coriander seeds, and season. Broil for 5-6 minutes each side until cooked
    through and there is no trace of pink in the center.
4   Divide the quinoa between two plates, and top with the chicken breasts.

SERVES 2
19G CARBOHYDRATE.
SERVE WITH ROASTED FENNEL (SEE PAGE 195).

MAIN MEALS

213 CHICKEN BALLS IN CRÉME FRAÎCHE SAUCE

**⅔ cup cubed skinless
chicken breast
1 tbsp grated Parmesan
1 tbsp olive oil
2 tbsp fresh whole wheat
bread crumbs**

**salt and freshly
ground black pepper**

**CRÉME FRAÎCHE SAUCE:
1¼ cups chicken stock
(see page 30)**

**1 tbsp wholegrain
mustard
2 tbsp reduced-fat
crème fraîche
2 scallions,
finely sliced**

1   Place the chicken, Parmesan, oil, and bread crumbs in a food processor
    and mix until a coarse paste. Season well and form the paste into
    6 walnut-sized balls. Put the balls on a plate and chill for 30 minutes to firm.
2   Bring a saucepan of water to a boil. Reduce the heat, drop the balls
    into the water, 5 at a time, and simmer for 2-3 minutes. Remove with
    a slotted spoon and drain carefully, then set aside.
3   Put the stock and mustard into a sauté pan. Bring to a boil and cook
    for 5 minutes until reduced, adding the chicken balls 2 minutes before
    the end of the cooking time. Stir in the crème fraîche and scallions,
    and heat through gently for 2-3 minutes. Season to taste before serving.

SERVES 2
8G CARBOHYDRATE PER SERVING.
SERVE WITH BRAISED LEEKS (SEE PAGE 202).

214 PROSCIUTTO-WRAPPED CHICKEN WITH MOZZARELLA

6 slices prosciutto
2 skinless chicken
  breast halves,
  about 5oz each

¼lb mozzarella, cut
  into 6 slices
4 basil leaves
1 tbsp olive oil

salt and freshly
  ground black pepper
½ tsp lemon juice

1 Preheat the oven to 200°C/400°F/Gas 6. Arrange 2 slices of prosciutto
   slightly overlapping on a plate. Place a chicken breast in the center of the
   prosciutto slices, and top with 3 slices mozzarella. Place 2 basil leaves on
   the mozzarella, and sprinkle with a little olive oil. Season well.
2 Wrap the prosciutto around the chicken and filling, then place a third slice
   of prosciutto over the top of the package lengthwise and tuck the ends in
   underneath. Repeat to make another package.
3 Brush a roasting pan with oil, place the chicken packages in the pan and
   cover with foil. Roast for 10 minutes, remove the foil and cook for another
   15 minutes until the chicken is cooked through and there is no trace of pink.
4 Squeeze over a little lemon juice before serving.

SERVES 2
1G CARBOHYDRATE PER SERVING.
SERVE WITH QUINOA TABBOULEH (SEE PAGE 50).

215 POACHED CHICKEN WITH SPRING VEGETABLES

2 skinless chicken
  breast halves,
  about 5oz each
⅓ cup dry white wine
1 unpeeled onion,
  coarsely chopped
2 bay leaves

1 sprig fresh rosemary
6oz fine green beans
6 stalks asparagus,
  trimmed
1 zucchini, sliced
  lengthwise
3 tbsp ready-made pesto

1 tbsp reduced-fat
  mayo
salt and freshly
  ground black pepper

1 Put the chicken in a saucepan with the wine, onion, bay leaves, and rosemary.
   Add enough water to just cover the chicken. Bring to a boil, then reduce
   the heat and simmer, half-covered, for about 15-20 minutes until cooked.
2 Meanwhile, steam the green beans, asparagus, and zucchini until just tender.
3 Mix together the pesto and mayo in a small bowl.
4 Remove the chicken from the cooking liquid, and slice. Arrange the vegetables
   on two serving plates, top with the chicken and spoon over the pesto sauce.
   Season to taste.

SERVES 2
6G CARBOHYDRATE PER SERVING.
SERVE WITH SMALL POTATOES IN THEIR SKINS.

CHICKEN ESCALOPE WITH MANGO SALSA

2 skinless chicken breast
    halves, about
    5oz each
½ tsp lemon juice
salt and freshly
    ground black pepper
olive oil, for brushing

MANGO SALSA:
small mango, diced
¼ red onion, finely diced
juice of ½ lime
½ red chili, seeded
    and finely chopped
2 tbsp torn basil leaves

1   To make the salsa, mix together the mango, red onion, lime juice,
    red chili, and basil leaves. Season with salt and stir to combine.
2   Put the chicken breasts between two sheets of plastic wrap and flatten
    with the end of a rolling pin. Squeeze over a little lemon juice, and season.
3   Heat a griddle pan and brush with oil. Griddle the chicken for about
    3-4 minutes on each side, depending on the thickness of the fillet,
    until cooked through. Serve with the mango salsa.

SERVES 2
8G CARBOHYDRATE PER SERVING.
SERVE WITH WARM WHOLE WHEAT PITTA BREAD
AND MARINATED ARTICHOKE SALAD (SEE PAGE 49).

217 BROILED CHICKEN WITH CAULIFLOWER MASH

2 skinless chicken breast
  halves, about 5oz each
olive oil,
  for brushing
salt and freshly
  ground black pepper

CAULIFLOWER MASH:
½lb cauliflower
  florets
1 tbsp olive oil
2 shallots, finely chopped
1 clove garlic, crushed

1 cup hot vegetable
  stock (see page 30)
2 tbsp reduced fat
  crème fraîche

1 Preheat the broiler to high and line the broiler pan with foil. Brush the chicken breasts with oil and season. Broil for about 5-6 minutes each side or until cooked through.
2 Meanwhile, steam the cauliflower until tender. Heat the olive oil in a skillet and cook the shallots and garlic for 3-4 minutes until softened.
3 Put the cauliflower, shallots, garlic, hot vegetable stock, and crème fraîche in a food processor or blender, then purée. Season well with salt and pepper.
4 To serve, divide the cauliflower mash between two plates, and top with the chicken breasts.

SERVES 2
5.5G CARBOHYDRATE PER SERVING.
SERVE WITH MINTY ZUCCHINI (SEE PAGE 194).

218 GINGER CHICKEN WITH SAUTÉED SPINACH

2 tbsp olive oil
1¼ cups bite-sized
  pieces chicken
3 tomatoes, seeded
  and diced

1 clove garlic, chopped
½-inch piece fresh
  root ginger, peeled
  and grated
1 tsp toasted sesame oil

2½ cups small
  spinach leaves
1 tbsp lemon juice
salt and freshly
  ground black pepper

1 Heat half the olive oil in a sauté pan. Add the chicken and fry for 5 minutes until sealed and golden on all sides. Stir in the tomatoes, garlic, and ginger and cook for 3 minutes.
2 Add 2 tablespoons of water and cook over a medium-low heat until reduced and the chicken is cooked through. Season to taste, remove from the pan and keep warm.
3 Wipe the pan, and add the remaining olive oil and the sesame oil. Heat the oils, then add the spinach, lemon juice, and seasoning. Cook the spinach, stirring continuously, for 2-3 minutes until wilted.
4 Divide the spinach between 2 serving plates and top with the chicken mixture.

SERVES 2
4.5G CARBOHYDRATE PER SERVING.
SERVE WITH GARBANZO MASH (SEE PAGE 195).

MAIN MEALS

219 FLORENTINE CHICKEN

1 tbsp olive oil
1 onion, finely chopped
1¼ cups skinless chicken
  pieces

1 clove garlic,
  chopped
1 tsp paprika
½ tsp caraway seeds
½ cup dry white wine

2 tbsp reduced-fat
  crème fraîche
1½ cups fresh spinach
salt and freshly
  ground black pepper

1 Heat the oil in a sauté pan and cook the onions over a medium heat
  for 5 minutes until softened. Add the chicken pieces and cook
  for 3-5 minutes until sealed and golden on all sides.
2 Stir in the garlic, paprika, and the caraway seeds and cook for 2 minutes,
  stirring continuously. Add the wine and cook for 3-4 minutes until the
  liquid has reduced, then stir in the crème fraîche.
3 Add the spinach, mix well, then cover with a lid and cook for 2 minutes
  until softened. Season to taste.

SERVES 2
5G CARBOHYDRATE PER SERVING.
SERVE WITH CELERY ROOT MASH (SEE PAGE 200).

220 GRIDDLED CHICKEN WITH CARAMELIZED ONIONS & FAVA BEANS

1 cup shelled
  fava beans
2 tbsp olive oil
1 onion, chopped

salt and freshly
  ground black pepper
1 tsp lemon juice

2 skinless chicken
  breast halves,
  about 5oz each

1 Blanch the fava beans for 2 minutes, then rinse under cold running water
  until cool enough to handle. Remove the tough outer casing and set aside.
2 Heat 1½ tablespoons of the oil in a skillet and fry the onion for 10 minutes until
  softened. Add the beans and enough water to cover. Simmer for about
  8 minutes until the water has evaporated. Season, and add the lemon juice.
3 Meanwhile, brush the chicken breasts with the remaining oil, then season.
  Heat a griddle pan, add the chicken and cook for 5-6 minutes each side
  until cooked through and there is no trace of pink in the center.
4 Serve the onion and beans with the chicken.

SERVES 2
7.5G CARBOHYDRATE PER SERVING.
SERVE WITH BAKED CARAWAY CABBAGE (SEE PAGE 200).

221 THAI CHICKEN CURRY

½lb skinless chicken
  breast, cubed
1 tbsp sunflower oil
1 quantity Spice Paste
  (see page 185)
1 bird's eye chili,
  seeded and chopped

⅔ cup reduced-fat
  coconut milk
⅔ cup chicken stock
  (see page 30)
1 small red bell pepper,
  seeded and sliced
¼lb green beans

1 cup spinach
  leaves, shredded
salt and freshly
  ground black pepper
1 tbsp chopped fresh
  cilantro, to garnish

1 Heat the oil in a large saucepan and cook the chicken for 5 minutes until
   it is golden all over, stirring occasionally. Add the spice paste and chili
   and cook for 1 minute, stirring.
2 Add the coconut milk and stock and bring to a boil. Reduce the heat
   and simmer, half-covered, for 10 minutes until reduced.
3 Add the green beans and red bell pepper and cook for 5 minutes, then stir in
   the spinach and cook for another 2 minutes until the vegetables are just tender.
4 Season to taste and sprinkle with cilantro before serving.

SERVES 2
9.5G CARBOHYDRATE PER SERVING.
SERVE WITH BROWN RICE.

222 MALAY CHICKEN CURRY

1 tbsp olive oil
1 onion, grated
4 chicken thighs
2 tsp grated fresh ginger
2 large cloves garlic,
  crushed
1 stick lemon grass,
  peeled, and crushed
  with the back of a knife

2 tsp ground cumin
2 tsp ground coriander
1 tsp ground turmeric
1 cinnamon stick
2 cloves
2 cardamom pods, split
½ tsp hot chili powder
1 bird's eye chili,
  finely chopped

⅔ cup reduced-fat
  coconut milk
⅔ cup vegetable
  stock (see page 30)
salt
juice of ½ lime
2 tbsp chopped
  fresh cilantro

1 Heat the oil in a large saucepan. Add the onion and fry, half-covered,
   for 5 minutes. Add the chicken thighs and brown for about 5 minutes,
   turning until golden all over. Remove the chicken from the pan.
2 Add the ginger, garlic, lemon grass, spices, and fresh chili and cook for
   2 minutes, stirring continuously. Add 3 tablespoons of water, and cook
   for a further 2 minutes.
3 Return the chicken to the pan with the coconut milk, stock, and a little
   salt. Bring to a boil, then reduce the heat and simmer, half-covered, for
   40 minutes, stirring occasionally, until the chicken is cooked through and
   the sauce has reduced and thickened.
4 Stir in the lime juice and heat through, then serve sprinkled with cilantro.

SERVES 2
8G CARBOHYDRATE PER SERVING.
SERVE WITH BROWN RICE.

223 CAJUN CHICKEN BREASTS

2 skinless chicken
  breast halves,
  about 5oz each
5 tbsp natural
  bio yogurt
1 tbsp chopped fresh mint
salt

CAJUN MARINADE:
2 tbsp olive oil
1 tbsp lemon juice
½ tsp cayenne pepper
½ tsp paprika
½ tsp ground cumin

1   To make the marinade, mix together the oil, lemon juice, cayenne pepper,
    paprika, and cumin in a shallow dish. Season with salt.
2   Place the chicken breasts in the dish and spoon over the marinade.
    Marinate in the refrigerator for at least 1 hour or leave overnight.
3   Mix together the yogurt and mint, then season. Set aside.
4   Heat the broiler until very hot, then reduce the heat to medium and cook
    the chicken for about 5-6 minutes each side until slightly blackened
    on the outside and cooked inside. Serve with the mint yogurt.

SERVES 2

4G CARBOHYDRATE PER SERVING.

SERVE WITH CANNELLINI BEAN PURÉE (SEE PAGE 197) AND A GREEN SALAD.

224 SPICED CHICKEN & LEMON KEBABS

10oz skinless chicken
  breast, cut into
  16 large cubes
1 lemon, quartered
  lengthwise, then halved
  again to make 8 wedges

8 bay leaves
½ red bell pepper, seeded
  and cut into 8 pieces
salt and freshly
  ground black pepper

MARINADE:
2 tbsp natural
  bio yogurt
1 clove garlic, crushed
1 tsp ground cumin
1 tsp ground coriander
½ tsp cayenne pepper

1   Mix together the ingredients for the marinade in a shallow dish. Season
    and add the chicken pieces, turning to coat them in the marinade. Marinate
    in the refrigerator for 1 hour or overnight.
2   Preheat the broiler to high and line the broiler pan with foil. To make each
    kebab, place a lemon wedge on the skewer followed by a piece of chicken, a bay
    leaf, chicken, red bell pepper, chicken, bay leaf, red bell pepper, chicken, and
    lemon wedge. Repeat to make 3 more kebabs.
3   Broil the kebabs for about 8-10 minutes, turning occasionally, until the
    chicken is cooked through.

SERVES 2

6G CARBOHYDRATE PER SERVING.

SERVE WITH GARBANZO MASH (SEE PAGE 195) AND A GREEN SALAD.

225 CHILI CHICKEN WITH BUTTERNUT SQUASH MASH

2 skinless chicken
breast halves,
about 5oz each
2 tbsp olive oil
4 tsp harissa (chili)
paste

2 cups peeled and cubed
butternut squash
(about 1lb 10oz
unpeeled squash)
2 cloves garlic,
left whole but peeled

1 tbsp reduced-fat
mayo
salt and freshly
ground black pepper
1 tbsp chopped fresh
cilantro, to garnish

1 Preheat the oven to 220°C/425°F/Gas 7. Make shallow cuts in each chicken
   breast, brush with half of the oil, and coat both sides in the harissa paste.
   Season well and chill, covered, for 30 minutes.
2 Put the chicken in a roasting pan and roast for about 30 minutes.
3 Meanwhile, put the squash and garlic in a saucepan, cover with water,
   and bring to a boil. Cook for 10 minutes, drain well, and add the mayo
   and the remaining olive oil. Season well, and mash until smooth.
4 Divide the squash between two plates and top with the chicken.
   Sprinkle with cilantro before serving.

SERVES 2
17G CARBOHYDRATE PER SERVING.
SERVE WITH STEAMED BROCCOLI.

226 GRIDDLED MARINATED CHICKEN

2 skinless chicken
  breast halves,
  about 5oz each
6oz fine green beans,
  to serve
salt and freshly ground
  black pepper

MARINADE:
2 tbsp olive oil
1 tsp cumin seeds
1 clove garlic, crushed
1 tbsp lemon juice

1   Mix together the marinade ingredients and season. Add the chicken and spoon over the marinade. Marinate in the refrigerator for at least 1 hour or overnight.
2   Preheat the griddle to high. Reduce the heat and griddle the chicken for 5-6 minutes each side until cooked through. Meanwhile, steam the green beans.
3   Heat the marinade in a saucepan to boiling point. Arrange the green beans on two plates, top with the chicken breasts, and pour over the marinade.

SERVES 2
4.5G CARBOHYDRATE PER SERVING.
SERVE WITH CHEESY ROSEMARY ROASTED VEGETABLES (SEE PAGE 199).

227 PIRI PIRI CHICKEN

2 skinless chicken
  breast halves,
  about 5oz each
salt and freshly ground
  black pepper

MARINADE:
½ red bell pepper,
  seeded and chopped
1 hot red chili,
  finely chopped

1 tsp paprika
2 tbsp red wine
  vinegar
3 tbsp olive oil

1   Put all the ingredients for the marinade in a blender and purée. Season to taste. Put the marinade in a shallow dish and add the chicken. Spoon over the marinade to coat the chicken and leave for at least 1 hour or overnight.
2   Heat a skillet until hot, then reduce the heat to medium. Remove the chicken from the marinade and cook for 4 minutes, turn over the breasts, then cook for another 3-4 minutes.
3   Reduce the heat to medium-low and add the marinade to the pan. Cook the chicken for a further 3 minutes until cooked through and there is no trace of pink in the center.

SERVES 2
2G CARBOHYDRATE PER SERVING.
SERVE WITH SPICY COUSCOUS (SEE PAGE 194).

228   TANDOORI CHICKEN

**2 skinless chicken
  breast halves,
  about 5oz each,
  sliced lengthwise
squeeze of lemon juice
salt and freshly
  ground black pepper**

**MARINADE:
1 tbsp tandoori spices
3 tbsp natural bio yogurt
1 tomato, seeded
1 tbsp lemon juice
1 tbsp extra-virgin olive oil**

1 Put all the ingredients for the marinade in a food processor or blender, then mix until puréed. Put the marinade in a shallow dish, add the chicken and turn until coated. Marinate in the refrigerator for at least 1 hour or overnight.

2 Preheat the oven to 200°C/400°F/Gas 6. Arrange the chicken in a roasting pan and spoon over the marinade. Roast for 12-15 minutes until the chicken is cooked through and there is no trace of pink in the center.

3 Warm the naan bread and split in half. Divide the chicken between the naan and squeeze over a little lemon juice before serving.

SERVES 2

2.5G CARBOHYDRATE PER SERVING.

SERVE WITH 2 SMALL WHOLE WHEAT NAAN BREAD AND

A MIXED LEAF SALAD WITH TOASTED SEEDS (SEE PAGE 56).

229   INDIAN TURKEY WITH SPINACH

**1 tbsp olive oil
1 onion, chopped
2 cloves garlic,
  chopped
1 cup ground turkey
3 tbsp curry paste
  of your choice**

**1 cup canned chopped
  tomatoes
⅔ cup chicken stock
  (see page 30)
½ cup canned
  garbanzos, drained
  and rinsed**

**1¾ cups
  fresh spinach
salt and freshly
  ground black pepper**

1 Heat the oil in a saucepan and cook the onion, half-covered, for 8 minutes. Add the garlic and the ground turkey, and cook over a medium heat for 5 minutes. Stir in the curry paste and cook for another minute.

2 Stir in the tomatoes, stock, and garbanzos, and cook, half-covered, for 15-20 minutes until the sauce has reduced and thickened. Add the spinach and heat through for 3 minutes until wilted. Season to taste before serving.

SERVES 2

11G CARBOHYDRATE PER SERVING.

SERVE WITH BROWN RICE.

230   TURKEY MOUSSAKA

1 small eggplant, sliced
2 tbsp olive oil
1 small onion, diced
½ cup ground turkey
1 clove garlic, chopped
1 tsp dried oregano
½ tsp ground cinnamon

¾ cup dry white wine
½ cup chicken
  stock (see page 30)
1 tbsp tomato paste
salt and freshly
  ground black pepper

⅔ cup natural
  bio yogurt
1 free-range egg, beaten
¼ cup grated Cheddar

1   Preheat the oven to 200°C/400°F/Gas 6. Boil the eggplant in salted water for 5 minutes until tender; drain well.
2   Heat the oil in a saucepan. Add the onion and fry for 8 minutes over a low heat until softened. Add the turkey, garlic, oregano, and cinnamon and cook for 5 minutes, stirring occasionally.
3   Pour in the wine and stock. Cook over a medium-high heat until the liquid has reduced. Reduce the heat, stir in the tomato paste and cook for a further 10 minutes. Season to taste.
4   Layer the meat mixture and eggplant in a baking dish, finishing with a layer of eggplant.
5   To make the topping, beat together the yogurt and egg. Spoon the egg mixture over the eggplant and level with the back of a spoon. Sprinkle with the cheese, and bake for 20-25 minutes until golden.

SERVES 2
11G CARBOHYDRATE PER SERVING.
SERVE WITH A GREEN SALAD.

231   TURKEY FRICASSÉE

2 pieces skinless turkey
  breasts, about 5oz
  each, cut into
  bite-sized pieces
1 tbsp soy flour
1 tbsp olive oil
1 large onion,
  finely chopped

2 cloves garlic, chopped
1 small red bell pepper,
  seeded and diced
2 tsp dried oregano
2 tbsp canned no-sugar
  corn kernels, drained
  and rinsed
⅓ cup dry white wine
⅔ cup chicken

or vegetable stock
  (see page 30)
4 tbsp reduced-fat
  crème fraîche
⅓ cup canned
  flageolet beans,
  drained and rinsed
salt and freshly
  ground black pepper

1   Toss the turkey pieces in seasoned flour. Heat the oil in a large, lidded sauté pan and fry the onion for 8 minutes. Remove the onion and add the turkey pieces to the pan, then fry over a medium heat for 5 minutes, turning occasionally, until browned all over. Add a little stock to the pan if the meat begins to stick.
2   Return the onion to the pan with the garlic, red bell pepper, and oregano, then cook for a further 3 minutes until the bell pepper has softened.
3   Add the corn and white wine, then increase the heat and boil until the liquid has reduced, the alcohol has evaporated, and any smell of wine has disappeared.
4   Reduce the heat, add the stock, and cook, covered, for 10 minutes. Stir in the crème fraîche and beans, and warm through. Season to taste.

SERVES 2
13.5G CARBOHYDRATE PER SERVING.
SERVE WITH BROWN RICE AND STEAMED SUGAR SNAP PEAS.

232 TURKEY & MANGO STIR-FRY

1 tbsp groundnut
  or sunflower oil
9oz turkey
  breasts, cut
  into strips
1 clove garlic,
  chopped

1 bird's eye chili, seeded
  and finely chopped
juice of 1 lime
1 tbsp Thai fish sauce
2 scallions, sliced on
  the diagonal

2 small heads
  pak choi, sliced
1 small mango,
  sliced
chopped fresh
  cilantro, to garnish

1   Heat the oil in a wok. When hot, add the turkey and stir-fry for
    6–8 minutes until cooked through. Transfer to a plate and keep warm.
2   Add the garlic, chili, lime juice, fish sauce, scallions, and pak choi to
    the wok and stir-fry for a further 2–3 minutes. Return the turkey to the
    wok with the mango, and stir to combine. Serve sprinkled with chopped
    fresh cilantro.

SERVES 2
17G CARBOHYDRATE PER SERVING.
SERVE WITH BROWN RICE.

FISH

Fish and shellfish can play a significant part in a weight-loss or weight-maintenance plan and this section includes a wide selection of recipes to suit all tastes. Many of the dishes can be adapted to suit other types of fish or shellfish—feel free to experiment according to your likes and dislikes. You'll find classics, such as Broiled Sole with Herb Sauce, or Moules Marinière; recipes with a fusion twist, including Salmon with Wasabi Drizzle; and Asian specialties, such as Coconut Fish Curry and Chinese Spicy Shrimp.

233 CRISP SEA BASS WITH JAPANESE PICKLED VEGETABLES

4 sea bass fillets
2 tbsp lime juice
1 tsp balsamic vinegar
1 small clove garlic,
   crushed
1 bird's eye chili, seeded
   and finely chopped
salt
fresh basil leaves,
   to garnish

PICKLED VEGETABLES:
1 carrot, finely shredded
2-inch piece
   cucumber, seeds
   scooped out
   and finely shredded
1 scallion, finely shredded
2 tbsp rice vinegar

HOT CHILI DIP:
2 tbsp reduced-fat
   mayo
1½ tsp Thai red
   curry paste
1 tbsp olive oil

1   Place the sea bass, skin-side down, in a shallow pan. Mix together the
    lime juice, vinegar, garlic, and chili. Pour the mixture over the sea bass
    and season with salt. Leave for 30 minutes.
2   To make the pickled vegetables, put the carrot, cucumber, and scallion
    in a small bowl. Pour over the vinegar and mix together.
3   To make the hot chili dip, mix together the mayo, Thai red curry
    paste, and olive oil in a small bowl.
4   Preheat the broiler to high and line the broiler pan with foil. Place the
    sea bass, skin-side up, in the grill pan and brush with the marinade. Broil
    for about 3-4 minutes until the skin becomes crisp.
5   Drain the pickled vegetables. Serve the sea bass with the vegetables
    and dip, sprinkled with fresh basil.

SERVES 2
9G CARBOHYDRATE PER SERVING.
SERVE WITH SOBA NOODLES.

234 BROILED SPICED SEA BASS

4 sea bass fillets
juice of 1 orange

1 tsp grated fresh
   ginger root
1 clove garlic, crushed

1 tbsp olive oil
salt and freshly
   ground black pepper

1   Make 3 diagonal slashes along the skin of each fillet. Mix together the orange
    juice, ginger, garlic, and oil, then season. Spoon the marinade over the skin side
    of each fillet and into the cuts. Marinate in the refrigerator for 30 minutes.
2   Heat the broiler to high and line a broiler pan with foil. Place the fillets
    skin-side down in the pan and broil for 2 minutes until just cooked, then
    turn carefully and spoon over more of the orange marinade. Broil for another
    2-3 minutes until just cooked.

SERVES 2
6G CARBOHYDRATE PER SERVING.
SERVE WITH SOBA NOODLES AND VEGETABLE STIR-FRY.

235 BAKED LEMON COD WITH SALSA VERDE

2 thick cod fillets,
about ½lb each
olive oil, for brushing
4 thin slices lemon
salt and freshly ground
black pepper

SALSA VERDE:
3 tbsp olive oil
1 clove garlic, crushed
3 tbsp chopped
fresh parsley

2 tbsp chopped
fresh mint
juice of ½ lemon

1   Preheat the oven to 200°C/400°F/Gas 6. Rinse and dry each cod fillet and
    brush with olive oil. Place each fillet on a piece of foil that is large enough
    to cover the fish, and make a package. Top each fillet with two slices of lemon
    and season. Fold over the foil to encase the fish, and bake for 20 minutes until
    just cooked and opaque.
2   Meanwhile, to make the salsa verde, put the olive oil, garlic, parsley, mint,
    and lemon juice in a blender and mix until finely chopped. Season to taste.
3   Carefully unfold each package and place on serving plates. Place a spoonful
    of herb sauce by the side of each piece of fish before serving.

SERVES 2

1G CARBOHYDRATE PER SERVING.

SERVE WITH BROWN RICE MIXED WITH WILD RICE AND ROASTED FENNEL (SEE PAGE 195).

236 SOLE WITH QUICK ORANGE SAUCE

2 sole or plaice fillets,	ORANGE SAUCE:	½ shallot, diced
about 6oz each	3 tbsp fresh orange juice	1 tbsp olive oil
sunflower oil, for brushing	2 tbsp chopped	salt and freshly
½ tsp lemon juice	fresh parsley	ground black pepper

1   Preheat the broiler to high and line the broiler pan with foil. To make the orange sauce, mix together all the ingredients and season well.
2   Brush the fish with a little oil and season. Broil for 4-5 minutes. To serve, place on two serving plates, drizzle with lemon juice and spoon over the orange sauce.

SERVES 2
3G CARBOHYDRATE.
SERVE WITH SPICY COUSCOUS (SEE PAGE 194).

237 BROILED SOLE WITH HERB SAUCE

2 sole (or plaice) fillets,	HERB SAUCE:	2 tbsp reduced-fat
about 6oz each	½ cup spinach,	mayo
sunflower oil, for brushing	tough stalks removed	1 tbsp lemon juice
salt and freshly ground	2 tbsp arugula leaves	
black pepper	2 tbsp fresh basil	
½ tsp lemon juice	and flat-leaf parsley	

1   Preheat the broiler to high and line the broiler pan with foil. Steam the spinach and arugula for 1½ minutes until wilted. Rinse the leaves under cold running water and drain well. Squeeze out any water left in the leaves with your hands, then roughly chop.
2   Put the spinach and arugula in a food processor or blender with the remaining ingredients for the sauce, and mix until a sauce consistency.
3   Brush the sole with oil, and season. Broil the sole for 4-5 minutes, squeeze over the lemon juice, and serve with a spoonful of sauce.

SERVES 2
2G CARBOHYDRATE PER SERVING.
SERVE WITH SMALL POTATOES IN THEIR SKINS AND STEAMED GREEN VEGETABLES.

238 MARINATED TUNA STEAKS

2 tbsp olive oil
½ tsp ground coriander
½ tsp ground cumin
2 tbsp lemon juice

2 tbsp chopped
    fresh cilantro
salt and freshly
    ground black pepper

2 tuna steaks,
    about ¼lb each

1   Mix together the oil, ground coriander and cumin, lemon juice,
    and fresh cilantro in a shallow dish. Season. Add the tuna,
    then spoon over the marinade. Marinate in the refrigerator for about 1 hour.
2   Heat a griddle pan until very hot and cook the tuna for about 2 minutes
    each side until cooked on the outside but still pink inside. Heat the marinade
    through and spoon over the cooked fish before serving.

SERVES 2
2G CARBOHYDRATE PER SERVING.
SERVE WITH GARBANZO MASH (SEE PAGE 195).

239 MAPLE-GLAZED TUNA

4 tsp soy sauce
2 tbsp olive oil
1 clove garlic,
    crushed

1 tsp grated fresh
    ginger root
1 clove garlic, crushed
1 tsp maple syrup

2 tuna steaks, about
    ¼lb each
salt and freshly
    ground black pepper

1   Mix together the soy sauce, oil, ginger, garlic, and maple syrup. Season and
    add the tuna steaks. Spoon over the marinade to coat the fish and let marinate
    in the refrigerator for about 1 hour.
2   Preheat the broiler to high and line the broiler pan with foil. Broil the tuna for
    about 2 minutes each side, occasionally spooning the marinade over the fish.

SERVES 2
4G CARBOHYDRATE PER SERVING.
SERVE WITH SESAME NOODLE SALAD (SEE PAGE 51) AND SESAME SPINACH
(SEE PAGE 197).

240 SPEEDY TUNA SAUCE

1 tbsp olive oil
1 large clove
    garlic, chopped
¾ cup dry white wine

14-oz can
    chopped tomatoes
½ cup canned
    tuna fish in olive oil
    or spring water, drained

1 tsp dried oregano
salt and freshly ground
    black pepper

1   Heat the oil in a heavy-based skillet. Fry the garlic for 1 minute.
    Increase the heat, pour in the wine, and boil until reduced and the
    alcohol has evaporated.
2   Reduce the heat and add the tomatoes and oregano, and cook for a further
    10 minutes, stirring occasionally, until thickened. Break up the tuna into large
    chunks, and add to the pan with the seasoning. Cook for another 3 minutes.

SERVES 2
5G CARBOHYDRATE PER SERVING.
SERVE WITH WHOLE WHEAT SPAGHETTI AND A GREEN LEAF SALAD.

241   **SPICY MOROCCAN TUNA**

1 tsp cumin seeds	½ cup water	salt
1 tsp caraway seeds	juice of ½ lemon	chopped fresh cilantro,
1½ tbsp olive oil	4 tbsp tomato paste	to garnish
2 cloves garlic, sliced	2 tuna steaks, about	
1 bird's eye chili, seeded	¼lb each	
and finely chopped		

1   Grind the cumin and caraway seeds in a pestle and mortar. Heat the oil in
    a sauté pan and fry the garlic, spices, and chili for 1 minute. Add the water,
    lemon juice, and tomato paste and simmer for 5 minutes.
2   Add the tuna and spoon over the sauce, then cook for 5-8 minutes, depending
    on the thickness of the fish. Season with salt and sprinkle with cilantro.

SERVES 2
9G CARBOHYDRATE PER SERVING.
SERVE WITH SPICY COUSCOUS (SEE PAGE 194).

242 MEDITERRANEAN TUNA

1 tbsp olive oil	2 tomatoes, seeded and	2 tuna steaks, about
1 red onion, sliced into	chopped	¼lb each
rings	1 clove garlic, crushed	salt and freshly ground
1 red bell pepper, seeded	2 tsp fresh oregano	black pepper
and sliced	1 tbsp balsamic vinegar	basil leaves, to garnish

1   Preheat the oven to 200°C/400°F/Gas 6. Heat the oil in a skillet
    and fry the onion for 7 minutes.
2   Add the bell pepper, tomatoes, garlic, oregano, and balsamic vinegar
    and cook for 2 minutes, stirring continuously.
3   Place the tuna in a shallow baking dish and spoon over the onion and bell
    pepper mixture. Season, and cover the dish with foil. Bake in the oven for
    about 15-20 minutes until the fish is cooked. Sprinkle with basil before serving.

SERVES 2

10G CARBOHYDRATE PER SERVING.

SERVE WITH GARBANZO MASH (SEE PAGE 195).

243 TROUT IN BLACK BEAN SAUCE

4 trout fillets	1 tbsp sunflower oil	2 tbsp black bean sauce
1 tsp lemon juice	1 clove garlic, crushed	1 tsp grated fresh ginger

1   Preheat the broiler to high and line the broiler pan with foil. Arrange the
    trout fillets in the broiler pan, squeeze over the lemon juice and cook for
    about 5-6 minutes, or until cooked, turning halfway.
2   Meanwhile, heat the oil, and fry the garlic over a medium-low heat for 1 minute.
    Stir in the black bean sauce, ginger, and 3 tablespoons of water, and heat
    through until slightly reduced and thickened.
3   Place the trout on serving plates, and spoon the sauce over the top.

SERVES 2

6G CARBOHYDRATE PER SERVING.

SERVE WITH WHOLE WHEAT NOODLES AND STEAMED PAK CHOI.

244 TROUT IN WHITE WINE SAUCE

4 trout fillets	1 tbsp chopped fresh	salt and freshly
1 cup dry white	marjoram	ground black pepper
wine	2 bay leaves	1 tsp butter

1   Preheat the oven to 200°C/400°F/Gas 6. Arrange the trout fillets in a
    baking dish and pour over half the wine. Sprinkle the marjoram over the
    fillets, then lay the bay leaves on top, and season.
2   Cover the dish with foil and bake for about 10 minutes until just cooked.
    Remove the fish and keep warm while you make the sauce.
3   Pour any cooking liquid in the dish into a small saucepan and add the
    remaining wine. Bring to a rolling boil, and cook until slightly reduced.
    Reduce the heat and stir in the butter until melted.
4   Season to taste, and pour the sauce over the trout fillets before serving.

SERVES 2

1G CARBOHYDRATE PER SERVING.

SERVE WITH CANNELLINI BEAN PURÉE (SEE PAGE 197) AND A MIXED LEAF SALAD.

STEAMED TROUT PACKAGES

2 scallions,
  thinly sliced
2 cloves garlic, chopped
1 tbsp grated fresh ginger
1-inch piece lemon grass,
  peeled and finely
  chopped

1 tbsp groundnut
  or sunflower oil
3 tbsp chopped
  fresh cilantro
juice and zest of 1 lime
4 trout fillets, boned
  and skinned

salt and freshly
  ground black pepper
4 large lettuce leaves
1 tbsp sesame
  seeds, toasted
lemon wedges, to serve

1   Fry the scallions, garlic, ginger, and lemon grass in the oil for 2 minutes.
    Remove from the heat and mix with 2 tablespoons of the cilantro and the
    lime juice and zest.
2   Lay the fish fillets on a plate and season. Arrange the scallion mixture
    down the center of each fillet and carefully roll up, the thinnest end first.
    Secure each package with one or two tooth picks.
3   Place the lettuce leaves in the bottom of a steamer and top with
    the fish packages. Steam for about 6 minutes.
4   Arrange the lettuce leaves on 2 plates and top each one with 2 fillets.
    Sprinkle with the remaining sesame seeds and cilantro.

SERVES 2
3G CARBOHYDRATE PER SERVING.
SERVE WITH BROWN RICE.

145

MAIN MEALS

246 RED SNAPPER WITH ROMESCO SAUCE

4 red snapper fillets,
  about 6oz each
olive oil, for brushing
salt and freshly
  ground black pepper

ROMESCO SAUCE:
¼ cup chopped almonds
3 tomatoes, peeled,
  seeded and diced
2 tbsp olive oil
1 small clove garlic, sliced

2 tsp red wine vinegar
handful of fresh
  flat-leaf parsley
½ tsp paprika

1 Preheat the broiler to high and line the broiler pan with foil.
2 To make the sauce, lightly toast the almonds in a dry skillet until golden.
   Put in a food processor or blender with the rest of the sauce ingredients
   and mix until very finely chopped and a sauce consistency; season.
3 Lightly brush the red snapper with oil and broil for about 3 minutes
   each side, then season before serving with the sauce.

SERVES 2
3G CARBOHYDRATE PER SERVING.
SERVE WITH GARBANZO MASH (SEE PAGE 195).

247 JAPANESE-STYLE SALMON

1 tbsp soy flour
1 tsp wasabi powder or
  English mustard powder
½lb salmon fillet,
  skinned and cut into
  large bite-sized pieces
2 tsp sunflower oil

1 clove garlic, chopped
2 tbsp soy sauce
2 tsp sherry vinegar
4 tbsp dry sherry
2 tbsp apple juice
2½ cups fresh spinach,
  tough stalks removed

salt and freshly
  ground black pepper
1 scallion, sliced on
  the diagonal
1 tsp sesame
  seeds, toasted

1 Mix together the flour and wasabi or mustard powder on a plate and dip
   the salmon pieces into the mixture until lightly dusted.
2 Heat the oil in a skillet over a medium-high heat and fry the salmon
   for 2 minutes, turning halfway through.
3 Reduce the heat and add the garlic, soy sauce, vinegar, sherry, apple juice,
   spinach, and 4 tablespoons of water to the pan. Cook for 1-2 minutes until
   the spinach is tender. Season to taste.
4 Transfer to serving plates and sprinkle with scallion and sesame seeds.

SERVES 2
9G CARBOHYDRATE PER SERVING.
SERVE WITH STEAMED BROCCOLI AND SOBA NOODLES.

248 SALMON WITH WASABI DRIZZLE

2 salmon fillets,
  about ¼lb each
lemon juice, for brushing
salt and freshly ground
  black pepper

WASABI DRIZZLE:
2 tsp Japanese wasabi
  paste
1 tbsp rice vinegar
2 tbsp reduced-fat
  crème fraîche

1 Preheat the broiler to high and line the broiler pan with foil.
2 To make the wasabi drizzle, mix together all the ingredients
    in a small bowl and set aside.
3 Place the salmon in the broiler pan and brush with a little lemon
    juice, season, and broil for about 3 minutes each side until
    cooked on the outside but still rare inside. Serve the
    salmon with the dressing drizzled over.

SERVES 2
2G CARBOHYDRATE PER SERVING.
SERVE WITH SOBA NOODLES AND STIR-FRIED VEGETABLES.

249 MARINATED SALMON IN LIME & GINGER

2 salmon fillets,
  about ¼lb each
1 hot red chili,
  sliced into rounds

juice of 1 lime
1 tbsp fresh orange juice
½-inch piece fresh
  root ginger, peeled
  and grated

6oz fine green beans
salt and freshly
  ground black pepper
1 scallion, sliced on
  the diagonal

1 Thinly slice each salmon fillet on the diagonal. Mix together the chili,
    lime juice, orange juice, and ginger in a shallow dish. Add the salmon
    slices and spoon over the marinade. Marinate in the refrigerator for at
    least 1 hour.
2 Steam the green beans.
3 Meanwhile, heat a griddle pan until hot. Add the salmon slices and cook
    for 1½ minutes until just cooked.
4 Divide the green beans between two serving plates. Heat the marinade
    through in a saucepan. Place the salmon on top of the beans and spoon
    over the marinade; season. Sprinkle with the scallion before serving.

SERVES 2
5G CARBOHYDRATE PER SERVING.
SERVE WITH WHOLE WHEAT NOODLES.

250 GLAZED SALMON WITH ASPARAGUS

2 salmon fillets,
about 5oz each
olive oil, for brushing
10 spears asparagus,
ends trimmed
1 tbsp sesame seeds,
toasted

MARINADE:
1 clove garlic, crushed
4 tbsp fresh apple juice
1 tbsp soy sauce
1 tbsp sunflower oil
1 tsp toasted sesame oil
salt and freshly ground
black pepper

1   Mix together the ingredients for the marinade. Place the salmon in
    a shallow dish and pour the marinade over, turning the fish to ensure
    it is completely covered. Let marinate in the refrigerator for at least
    1 hour, turning the fish occasionally.
2   Preheat the broiler to high. Line the broiler pan with foil and place the
    salmon on top. Brush the fish with the marinade and broil for about
    6 minutes, turning once, until just cooked but still pink in the center.
3   Meanwhile, heat a griddle pan and brush with olive oil. Arrange the
    asparagus in the pan and cook for 3-4 minutes until tender.
4   Place the remaining marinade in a small saucepan, and heat until
    thickened and reduced.
5   Arrange the asparagus on two plates, then top with the salmon.
    Spoon the marinade over the fish, and sprinkle with the sesame seeds.

SERVES 2
7G CARBOHYDRATE PER SERVING.
SERVE WITH A MIXTURE OF BROWN AND WILD RICE.

251 POACHED SALMON IN SHALLOT SAUCE

2 tsp olive oil
1 leek, finely sliced
1 shallot, diced
1 bay leaf
1 cup dry white wine
⅔ cup fish stock

2 salmon fillets,
  about ¼lb each
1 tbsp butter
salt and freshly
  ground black pepper

1 Heat the oil in a large sauté pan and fry the leek, shallot, and
   bay leaf over a medium heat for 4 minutes, stirring frequently.
2 Increase the heat and add the wine, then cook at a rolling boil
   until the wine has reduced by half.
3 Reduce the heat, add the stock and salmon, then cover with the
   lid and poach the fish for 6-8 minutes, turning halfway through,
   until cooked. Remove the salmon and keep warm.
4 Add the butter to the sauce and heat though, stirring continuously,
   until the butter has melted and the stock has reduced to form a sauce.
   Remove the bay leaf and season to taste. Put the salmon on serving
   plates and spoon over the sauce.

SERVES 2
4G CARBOHYDRATE PER SERVING.
SERVE WITH CAULIFLOWER MASH (SEE PAGE 129).

252 SMOKED SALMON WITH BROCCOLI SAUCE

1½ cups broccoli florets
1 tbsp olive oil
1 leek, finely chopped
½ cup reduced-fat
  garlic-and-herb
  cream cheese

3 tbsp semi-
  skimmed milk
3oz smoked
  salmon pieces
salt and freshly
  ground black pepper

1 Steam the broccoli for about 6-8 minutes until just tender.
2 Heat the oil in a sauté pan and fry the leek for 5-7 minutes over a medium
   heat until softened. Stir in the cream cheese and milk, and heat through gently.
3 Add the smoked salmon and broccoli, and cook for 1 minute, stirring frequently.
   Season to taste, and serve.

SERVES 2
5G CARBOHYDRATE PER SERVING.
SERVE WITH WHOLE WHEAT TAGLIATELLE.

253 SALMON STEAKS WITH HERB SALSA

2 salmon steaks,
about 5oz each
lemon juice, for brushing
salt and freshly ground
black pepper

HERB SALSA:
2 tbsp extra-virgin
olive oil
1 small clove
garlic, crushed
1 shallot, chopped

3 tbsp fresh
cilantro leaves
1 green chili,
chopped
1 tbsp lemon juice

1 Preheat the broiler to high and line the broiler pan with foil.
2 To make the salsa, put all the ingredients in a blender and mix until
a coarse purée; season.
3 Place the fish steaks in the broiler pan, and brush with a little lemon juice,
season, and cook for 3–5 minutes each side, depending on the thickness
of the fillets. Spoon the herb salsa over the salmon, and serve.

SERVES 2
2G CARBOHYDRATE PER SERVING.
SERVE WITH CANNELLINI BEAN PURÉE (SEE PAGE 197).

254 SALMON FILLETS WITH KIWI SALSA

2 salmon fillets,
about ¼lb each
olive oil, for brushing
salt and freshly
ground black pepper

KIWI SALSA:
1 kiwi fruit,
peeled and diced
1 scallion, finely chopped
½ avocado,
peeled and diced

1 green chili,
seeded and
finely chopped
1 tbsp chopped
fresh cilantro
1 tbsp lime juice

1 To make the salsa, put all the ingredients into a small bowl and stir to combine.
Season and set aside.
2 Preheat a griddle and brush it lightly with oil. Cook the salmon for 2–3 minutes
each side, depending on the thickness of the fillet. Serve with the kiwi salsa.

SERVES 2
6G CARBOHYDRATE PER SERVING.
SERVE WITH BROWN RICE AND A GREEN SALAD.

255 SWORDFISH WITH SUN-DRIED TOMATO PESTO

olive oil, for brushing
2 swordfish steaks,
    about ½lb each
1 tsp lemon juice
salt and freshly
    ground black pepper

PESTO:
2 tbsp sun-dried
    tomato paste
1 tbsp extra-virgin olive oil
1 small clove
    garlic, crushed

1   Preheat the oven to 200°C/400°F/Gas 6. Lightly oil a baking dish, and
    add the fish. Squeeze over the lemon juice and season. Cover with foil
    and bake for 15-20 minutes, depending on the thickness of the steaks.
2   Meanwhile, to make the pesto, mix together the sun-dried tomato paste,
    oil, and garlic in a bowl. Season to taste, and serve with the swordfish.

SERVES 2
4.5G CARBOHYDRATE PER SERVING.
SERVE WITH PURÉE OF ROASTED VEGETABLES (SEE PAGE 198).

256 LIME & CHILI SWORDFISH STEAKS

2 swordfish steaks,
    about ½lb each
salt and freshly
    ground black pepper
1 tbsp chopped fresh mint

MARINADE:
1 tbsp olive oil, plus extra
    for brushing
juice and finely
    grated zest of 1 lime

1 chili, seeded and
    sliced into rounds
½-inch piece fresh
    root ginger, peeled
    and grated

1   Mix together the ingredients for the marinade in a shallow dish and
    add the swordfish. Spoon the marinade over the fish, season,
    and marinate in the refrigerator for 1 hour.
2   Preheat the oven to 200°C/400°F/Gas 6. Put the swordfish in a lightly
    oiled roasting pan, and spoon over half of the marinade. Cover with foil
    and bake for 15-20 minutes depending on the thickness of the steaks.
3   Place the fish on serving plates, spoon over the remaining marinade,
    and garnish with the chopped mint.

SERVES 2
2G CARBOHYDRATE PER SERVING.
SERVE WITH SESAME SPINACH (SEE PAGE 197) AND BROWN RICE.

257 HOKI WITH CHILI-ORANGE GLAZE

2 thick hoki fillets,
  about 6oz each
olive oil, for brushing
2 tbsp orange juice

finely grated zest
  of ½ orange
1 tbsp sweet chili sauce

1 tbsp chopped
  fresh cilantro
salt and freshly
  ground black pepper

1 Preheat the broiler to high and line the broiler pan with foil.
   Brush the fish with oil and season. Broil the fish for 5 minutes,
   then remove from the broiler and turn over.
2 Meanwhile, mix together the orange juice and zest and sweet chili sauce.
   Season well. Spoon half of the orange sauce over the fish and broil for
   another 3-5 minutes.
3 Put the remaining orange sauce in a saucepan, and heat through
   gently until thickened.
4 Serve the fish with the sauce spooned over, and sprinkled with cilantro.

SERVES 2
6G CARBOHYDRATE PER SERVING.
SERVE WITH ROASTED FENNEL (SEE PAGE 195).

258 TILAPIA WITH CILANTRO HOUMOUS

4 tilapia fillets
olive oil, for brushing
1 tbsp lime juice
½ tsp paprika
½ quantity Red Bell

Pepper Houmous (see
  page 74)
2 tbsp chopped fresh
  cilantro, plus
  extra for sprinkling

½ tsp grated lime zest
2 tbsp reduced-fat
  mayo
salt and freshly
  ground black pepper

1 Preheat the broiler to high and line the broiler pan with foil.
   Brush the tilapia fillets with oil and drizzle over the lime juice.
2 Sprinkle the fillets with the paprika and broil for 4-6 minutes,
   turning halfway through, until the fish is cooked.
3 Meanwhile, mix together the houmous, cilantro, lime zest,
   and mayo. Season to taste, and divide between serving plates.
   Top with the tilapia and sprinkle with extra cilantro.

SERVES 2
6G CARBOHYDRATE PER SERVING.
SERVE WITH WARM ORIENTAL SALAD (SEE PAGE 50).

259 SMOKED HADDOCK WITH CREAMY CHIVE SAUCE

2 smoked haddock fillets, about 6oz each, skinned
¼ cup milk
½ cup heavy cream

1 tsp butter
½ tsp Dijon mustard
2 tbsp snipped fresh chives, plus extra to garnish

freshly ground black pepper

1   Put the fish in a sauté pan, and cover with the milk and half the cream. Bring to a simmer and poach the fish, occasionally spooning the cream over the fish, for 8-12 minutes, depending on the thickness of the fillets.
2   Using a fish slice, carefully remove the fish from the pan and set aside. Add the rest of the cream, butter, mustard, and chives to the pan and simmer until reduced to a sauce consistency. Season with pepper.
3   Place the fish on 2 plates, pour over the sauce, and garnish with chives.

SERVES 2
5G CARBOHYDRATE PER SERVING.
SERVE WITH CELERY ROOT MASH (SEE PAGE 200) AND STEAMED BROCCOLI.

260 MACKEREL WITH ORANGE SALSA

4 mackerel fillets, boned
sunflower oil, for brushing
salt and freshly
   ground black pepper

ORANGE SALSA:
1 orange, peeled,
   segmented, and diced
1 shallot, diced
juice and zest of 1 lime

¼ tsp dried
   crushed chili
2 tbsp extra-virgin
   olive oil
4 tbsp chopped
   fresh mint

1   Preheat the broiler to high and line the broiler pan with foil.
2   To make the salsa, put the orange, shallot, lime zest and juice,
    chili, oil, and mint into a bowl. Stir to combine, and season to taste.
3   Broil the mackerel for about 2 minutes each side. Serve with
    spoonfuls of the salsa.

SERVES 2
6G CARBOHYDRATE PER SERVING.
SERVE WITH SEEDED WHOLE WHEAT BREAD AND A GREEN SALAD.

261 BROILED MACKEREL WITH ROSEMARY

1 clove garlic, crushed
grated zest and juice
 of ½ lemon
1 tbsp olive oil

2 long sprigs fresh
 rosemary, plus 1 tsp
 chopped, to garnish
2 whole fresh mackerel,
 gutted and cleaned

lemon wedges, to serve
salt and freshly
 ground black pepper

1 Mix together the garlic, lemon zest and juice, olive oil, and rosemary in a bowl; season well.
2 Using a sharp knife, make 3 slashes on each side of the fish, cutting through to the bone. Place the fish in a dish and pour over the rosemary marinade, rubbing it into the cuts. Cover and marinate in the refrigerator for 1 hour. Remove the rosemary sprigs.
3 Preheat the broiler to high and line the broiler pan with foil. Broil the fish for 5-6 minutes on each side until cooked. Garnish with the chopped rosemary, and serve with lemon wedges.

SERVES 2
2G CARBOHYDRATE PER SERVING.
SERVE WITH CELERY ROOT MASH (SEE PAGE 200) AND STEAMED VEGETABLES.

262 MACKEREL WITH SAUCE VIERGE

4 mackerel fillets
salt and freshly
 ground black pepper
basil leaves, to garnish

SAUCE VIERGE:
2 tbsp extra-virgin
 olive oil
2 shallots, diced
1 clove garlic, chopped

8 small plum tomatoes,
 seeded and diced
2 tsp sherry vinegar
2 tsp lemon juice

1 Preheat the broiler to high and line the broiler pan with foil. To make the sauce vierge, heat the oil in a small pan and fry the shallots for 3 minutes, then add the garlic and fry for another 1 minute.
2 Add the tomatoes, vinegar, and lemon juice to the pan and heat through for 1 minute. Season.
3 Meanwhile, broil the mackerel fillets for 2 minutes each side. Serve with the sauce vierge and garnish with fresh basil.

SERVES 2
5G CARBOHYDRATE PER SERVING.
SERVE WITH PURÉE OF ROASTED VEGETABLES (SEE PAGE 198).

263 MACKEREL WITH HORSERADISH DRESSING

4 mackerel fillets
2 tsp lemon juice
1 tbsp chopped fresh
   parsley, to garnish
   (optional)
salt and freshly
   ground black pepper

DRESSING:
1 tbsp creamed
   horseradish
1 tbsp lemon juice
3 tbsp fat-reduced
   crème fraîche

1   Preheat the broiler to high and line the broiler pan with foil. Arrange the fillets
    in the broiler pan, and squeeze over the lemon juice. Season well. Broil for
    about 2 minutes each side until cooked.
2   Meanwhile, to make the dressing, put the horseradish, lemon juice, and
    crème fraîche in a small bowl. Season well, and mix until combined.
    Serve with the mackerel, sprinkled with parsley, if using.

SERVES 2
2.5G CARBOHYDRATE PER SERVING.
SERVE WITH BEAN & ROASTED RED BELL PEPPER SALAD (SEE PAGE 49).

264 MEDITERRANEAN SARDINES

2 tbsp olive oil
zest of ½ lemon
1 clove garlic, crushed
1 tbsp fresh
   oregano, chopped

1 tbsp fresh
   chives, snipped
4-6 fresh sardines,
   depending on size,
   headed, gutted, and
   cleaned

salt and freshly
   ground black pepper
lemon wedges, to serve

1   Mix together the olive oil, lemon zest, garlic, oregano, and chives
    in a shallow dish large enough to accommodate the sardines.
2   Arrange the sardines in the dish and turn in the marinade. Leave for at
    least 1 hour or preferably overnight in the refrigerator to marinate.
3   Preheat the broiler to medium. Season the sardines and broil for about
    8 minutes, depending on their size, turning halfway through, until
    golden and crispy on the outside. Serve with lemon wedges.

SERVES 2
1G CARBOHYDRATE PER SERVING.
SERVE WITH A SLICE OF TOASTED CIABATTA AND BROILED TOMATOES.

265 HALIBUT WITH TOMATO & RED ONION RELISH

2 halibut steaks,
  about ½lb each
1 tsp lime juice
salt and freshly
  ground black pepper

RED ONION RELISH:
2 vine-ripened tomatoes,
  seeded and diced
¼ red onion, finely diced
1 tbsp lime juice

large pinch dried
  crushed chili flakes
1 tbsp chopped
  fresh cilantro

1 Preheat the broiler to high and line the broiler pan with foil. To make
   the relish, put the tomatoes, onion, lime juice, chili flakes, and cilantro in
   a bowl. Season with salt, and toss well until combined.
2 Put the halibut in the broiler pan. Squeeze over the lime juice and season.
   Broil for 5 minutes each side. Serve each steak with a large spoonful of relish.

SERVES 2
2G CARBOHYDRATE PER SERVING.
SERVE WITH NUTTY COLESLAW (SEE PAGE 55).

266 HALIBUT TRICOLORE

2 halibut steaks,
  about ½lb each
olive oil, for brushing

2 tbsp green or red
  ready-made pesto
1 tomato, sliced
4 slices mozzarella

salt and freshly
  ground black pepper

1 Preheat the broiler to high and line the broiler pan with foil. Brush the halibut
   steak with a little oil.
2 Place the fish in the broiler pan and broil for 3 minutes, turn and cook for a
   further 2 minutes until opaque.
3 Remove from the broiler and place a tablespoon of pesto on top of each steak.
   Arrange the tomato slices and then the mozzarella on top of the pesto.
   Broil for 3 minutes until the mozzarella has melted and is slightly golden.

SERVES 2
2G CARBOHYDRATE PER SERVING.
SERVE WITH AVOCADO, RED ONION, & SPINACH SALAD
(SEE PAGE 58) AND SMALL POTATOES IN THEIR SKINS.

267 POLENTA-CRUSTED SALMON STICKS

½ cup fine polenta
  or cornmeal
1 tsp paprika
2 tbsp freshly grated
  Parmesan

salt and freshly ground
  black pepper
½lb thick salmon fillet,
  skinned
1 free-range egg, beaten
sunflower oil, for frying

DIP:
4 tbsp reduced-fat crème
  fraîche
2 tsp dill sauce
1 tsp fresh lemon juice

1   Mix together the crème fraîche, dill sauce, and lemon juice in a small bowl
and set aside.
2   Mix together the polenta, paprika, Parmesan, and seasoning on a plate.
3   Cut the salmon into six thick fingers. Dip each finger into the beaten
egg, then roll them in the polenta mixture until evenly coated.
4   Pour enough oil to lightly cover the base of a heavy-based skillet
and warm over a medium-high heat. Place the salmon fingers in the pan
and cook for 3 minutes each side until golden and crisp on the outside.
Drain on paper towels, and serve the salmon sticks with the dill dip.

SERVES 2
9G CARBOHYDRATE PER SERVING.
SERVE WITH BEAN & ROASTED RED BELL PEPPER SALAD (SEE PAGE 49).

268 COD WRAPPED IN PROSCIUTTO

4 slices prosciutto
2 thick cod fillets,
  about 6oz each

1 tbsp lemon juice
olive oil, for brushing

freshly ground
  black pepper

1   Preheat the oven to 200°C/400°F/Gas 6. Lay 2 slices of the prosciutto on
a counter and place a cod fillet in the middle, drizzle with half the lemon
juice, then fold over the prosciutto to make a package. Repeat with the
second piece of fish.
2   Put the prosciutto-wrapped fish in a lightly oiled baking dish. Season with
pepper and bake for about 15-20 minutes until the fish is cooked through.

SERVES 2
1G CARBOHYDRATE PER SERVING.
SERVE WITH PURÉE OF ROASTED VEGETABLES (SEE PAGE 198).

269 BROILED FISH WITH WARM VINAIGRETTE

2 thick white fish
  fillets, such as cod,
  hoki, or haddock,
  about 6oz each
olive oil, for brushing

salt and freshly ground
  black pepper

VINAIGRETTE:
2 tbsp extra-virgin
  olive oil
2 tsp balsamic vinegar
1 tsp Dijon mustard
juice of ½ lemon

1 Preheat the broiler to high and line the broiler pan with foil. Brush the cod with oil, and season, then broil for 8-10 minutes, depending on the thickness of the fish.

2 Meanwhile, whisk together the oil, vinegar, mustard, and lemon juice. Pour the dressing into a saucepan and heat through gently. Serve the fish with the vinaigrette poured over.

SERVES 2
3G CARBOHYDRATE PER SERVING.
SERVE WITH CANNELLINI BEAN PURÉE (SEE PAGE 197).

270 COCONUT FISH CURRY

1 tbsp vegetable oil
1 tsp cumin seeds
1 onion, grated
1 green chili, chopped
1 large clove garlic,
  grated
1 tbsp grated fresh root
  ginger

1 tsp ground turmeric
1 tsp ground coriander
1 tsp garam masala
1 cup reduced-fat
  coconut milk
⅔ cup canned chopped
  tomatoes

14oz skinless cod fillets
  or other firm white fish,
  cut into 1-inch pieces
1 tsp lemon juice
salt
1 tbsp chopped fresh
  cilantro, to garnish

MAIN MEALS

1 Heat the oil in a large heavy-based saucepan. Add the cumin seeds and cook until they begin to darken and sizzle. Stir in the onion and cook, stirring frequently, over a medium-low heat, half-covered, for 7 minutes until softened.

2 Add the chili, garlic, ginger, and spices, then cook for 1 minute.

3 Pour in the coconut milk and chopped tomatoes and cook, half-covered, over a medium heat for 5 minutes.

4 Add the cod and cook for a further 10 minutes, stirring occasionally and taking care not to break up the fish, until the sauce has reduced and thickened.

5 Stir in the lemon juice, and season. Spoon into bowls, and sprinkle with the cilantro.

SERVES 2
11G CARBOHYDRATE PER SERVING.
SERVE WITH BROWN RICE AND STEAMED GREEN BEANS.

271　ORIENTAL FISH EN PAPILLOTE

2 thick cod fillets,
　about ½lb each
1 clove garlic,
　thinly sliced
2 thin slices fresh ginger
　root, peeled and cut
　into matchsticks

2 small leeks,
　cut into thin strips
1 small carrot,
　cut into thin strips
¼ red bell pepper,
　cut into thin strips
2 tbsp lime juice

2 tsp light soy sauce
1 tbsp fresh apple juice
½ tsp sesame oil
salt and freshly
　ground black pepper
fresh cilantro,
　to garnish

1　Preheat the oven to 200°C/400°F/Gas 6. Place each cod fillet onto
　a piece of foil or baking parchment large enough to encase the fish.
　Arrange the garlic, ginger, leeks, carrot, and bell pepper on top of
　each piece of cod.
2　Mix together the lime juice, soy sauce, apple juice, and sesame oil, then spoon
　the mixture over the fish. Season to taste, then fold the foil or paper to make
　a loose package. Put the packages on a baking tray and bake for 15 minutes
　until the fish is just cooked. Serve garnished with cilantro.

SERVES 2

5G CARBOHYDRATE PER SERVING.

SERVE WITH BROWN RICE AND SESAME SPINACH (SEE PAGE 197).

272 PLAICE WITH ROASTED SMALL PLUM TOMATOES

1 tbsp olive oil, plus
    extra for frying
10 small plum tomatoes

1 tbsp fresh oregano
2 plaice fillets, each
    about 6oz
soy flour, for dusting

salt and freshly
    ground black pepper
1½ tsp butter
2 tsp lemon juice

1 Preheat the oven to 200°C/400°F/Gas 6. Heat the oil in a roasting pan, and add the tomatoes. Coat them in the oil, and season. Roast for 6-10 minutes until tender. Peel off the tomato skins, and sprinkle the tomatoes with oregano.
2 Dust the fish in seasoned flour. Heat the butter and a little oil in a skillet until very hot. Cook the fish for 4-5 minutes, turning halfway through.
3 Place the fish on serving plates with the tomatoes and squeeze over the lemon juice. Season to taste.

SERVES 2
7G CARBOHYDRATE PER SERVING.
SERVE WITH STEAMED GREEN VEGETABLES.

273 BAKED FISH WITH CRISP CRUMB TOPPING

1 slice whole wheat bread,
    crusts removed
2 tbsp chopped
    fresh chives
2 tsp harissa (chili)
    paste

juice and finely grated
    zest of ½ orange
salt and freshly
    ground black pepper
1 tbsp extra-virgin olive oil
1 fennel bulb,
    thickly sliced

3 small leeks,
    halved lengthwise
2 thick white fish fillets,
    such as cod, haddock,
    or hoki, about
    6oz each

1 Preheat the oven to 200°C/400°F/Gas 6. Put the bread in a blender and process until it forms bread crumbs. Mix the bread crumbs with the chives, harissa, 3 teaspoons of the orange juice, and the zest. Season well.
2 Put the oil, fennel, leeks, and the remaining orange juice in a baking dish. Roast the vegetables for 8 minutes.
3 Meanwhile, spread the bread-crumb mixture over the fish. Place the fish on top of the vegetables and return the dish to the oven to cook for about 15 minutes, depending on the thickness of the fillets.

SERVES 2
18G CARBOHYDRATE PER SERVING.
SERVE WITH TOMATO & BASIL SALAD (SEE PAGE 55).

274 MONKFISH WITH RED BELL PEPPER CRUST

1 tsp butter
1 tbsp olive oil
salt and freshly ground
  black pepper
2 skinless, boneless
  monkfish fillets, about
  ½lb each

RED BELL PEPPER
  CRUST:
2oz red bell pepper,
  chopped
2 tbsp olive oil
1 tbsp fresh parsley
1 pinch paprika

2 tbsp whole wheat
  bread crumbs
½ clove garlic
1 tsp lemon juice

1 Preheat the oven to 200°C/400°F/Gas 6. To make the red bell pepper crust,
   put all the ingredients in a blender, then season and mix until coarsely chopped.
2 Heat the butter and oil in a skillet and cook the monkfish for 1-2 minutes each
   side until golden and sealed.
3 Place the fish in a roasting pan and spoon the red bell pepper mixture
   over the top of each fillet, then roast for 12-15 minutes.

SERVES 2
8G CARBOHYDRATE PER SERVING.
SERVE WITH QUINOA TABBOULEH (SEE PAGE 50).

275 MONKFISH & VEGETABLE ROAST

1 red bell pepper,
  seeded and sliced
½ fennel bulb, sliced
6 shallots, peeled
  and halved
olive oil, for brushing

2 skinless, boneless
  monkfish fillets,
  about ½lb each
salt and freshly
  ground black pepper

BASIL OIL:
2½ tbsp extra-virgin
  olive oil
¾ cup fresh basil
1 small clove
  garlic, crushed

1 Preheat the oven to 200°C/400°F/Gas 6. Put the red bell pepper, fennel,
   and shallots in a large roasting pan and brush with oil. Roast for 15 minutes.
2 Meanwhile, heat a little oil in a skillet over a medium-high heat. Add
   the fish and cook for 1-2 minutes each side until golden and sealed. Place the
   fish on top of the roasting vegetables and cook for a further 12-15 minutes.
3 To make the basil oil, gently heat the olive oil until just warm. Transfer the
   oil to a blender with the basil and garlic and purée; season.
4 Arrange the vegetables on a plate, top with the fish, and drizzle over
   the basil oil. Season to taste.

SERVES 2
8G CARBOHYDRATE PER SERVING.
SERVE WITH STEAMED GREEN VEGETABLES AND WHOLE WHEAT PASTA.

**MONKFISH KEBABS
WITH SPICY COUSCOUS**

1lb monkfish
  tail, skinned, and
  cut into 8 pieces
2 zucchini, thickly
  sliced into 8
1 red onion, cut into
  8 wedges

4 bay leaves
olive oil, for brushing
juice of ½ lemon
salt and freshly
  ground black pepper
1 quantity Spicy
  Couscous, see page 194

1 Preheat the broiler to high and line the broiler pan with foil. Thread
the monkfish, zucchini, onion, and bay leaves onto 4 skewers. Brush
with oil, squeeze over the lemon juice, and season well.

2 Prepare the couscous.

3 Broil the kebabs for 3-4 minutes each side, brushing with more oil,
if necessary, then serve with the couscous.

SERVES 2
36G CARBOHYDRATE PER SERVING.
SERVE WITH A GREEN SALAD.

MAIN MEALS

277 SEAFOOD KEBABS

2 tbsp sweet chili sauce
1 clove garlic, crushed
1-inch piece fresh root
  ginger, peeled
  and grated
½ tsp crushed
  dried chili

zest and juice of 1 lime
8 raw tiger prawns,
  peeled and deveined
5oz salmon, skinned and
  cut into large bite-sized
  pieces

6oz firm white fish,
  skinned and cut into
  large bite-sized pieces
salt and freshly
  ground black pepper
lime wedges, to serve

1 Mix together the sweet chili sauce, garlic, ginger, dried chili, lime juice
   and zest, and 1 tablespoon of hot water in a shallow dish. Add the prawns,
   salmon, and white fish to the dish and turn to coat in the marinade; season.
   Marinate for 30 minutes in the refrigerator.
2 Preheat the broiler to high and line a broiler pan with foil. Divide the fish and
   prawns among 4 metal skewers, starting and finishing each one with a prawn.
3 Arrange the skewers in the broiler pan and spoon over half the marinade.
   Grill for 2½ minutes, turn, and spoon over the rest of the marinade and
   broil for a further 2½ minutes. Place 2 skewers on each plate, pour over
   any marinade left in the broiler pan, and accompany with wedges of lime.

SERVES 2

6G CARBOHYDRATE PER SERVING.

SERVE WITH BROWN RICE AND CHARGRILLED THYME ZUCCHINI (SEE PAGE 194).

278 MALAY SEAFOOD STEW

½ onion, chopped
2 cloves garlic, chopped
1-inch piece fresh root
  ginger, peeled and
  chopped
1 tsp coriander seeds
1 stick lemon grass,
  peeled and finely
  chopped

1 tbsp groundnut oil
1 green chili, chopped
1 tsp turmeric
1 cup reduced-fat
  coconut milk
juice of ½ lime
1 tsp lemon juice
1 tsp Thai fish sauce

3 tbsp chopped
  fresh cilantro
10oz skinless
  white fish, cut into
  large bite-sized pieces
1 cup mixed cooked
  shellfish, such as
  shrimp, mussels, squid
salt

1 Mix together the onion, garlic, ginger, coriander seeds, lemon grass, oil, chili,
   turmeric, and 1 tablespoon of water in a food processor to make a coarse paste.
2 Put the paste in a large saucepan and cook for 4 minutes, stirring continuously.
   Add the coconut milk, lime and lemon juices, fish sauce, and cilantro and bring
   to a boil, then reduce the heat and simmer, half-covered, for 3 minutes.
3 Add the fish and cook for about 10 minutes, stirring occasionally and taking
   care not to break it up. Stir in the shellfish 2 minutes before the end of the
   cooking time, and heat through.

SERVES 2

9G CARBOHYDRATE PER SERVING.

SERVE WITH BROWN RICE AND STEAMED BROCCOLI.

279 SEAFOOD STEW WITH ROUILLE

1 tbsp olive oil
1 onion, finely sliced
1 tsp fennel seeds
²⁄₃ cup dry white wine
scant 1 cup canned
   chopped tomatoes
10oz cod fillets,
   skinned and cut into
   large bite-sized pieces

1 cup mixed cooked
   seafood, such as
   shrimp, squid,
   and mussels
salt and freshly
   ground black pepper
1 tbsp chopped
   fresh cilantro

ROUILLE:
1 clove garlic, crushed
3 tbsp reduced-fat
   mayo
½ tsp harissa
   (chili) paste

1 To make the rouille, mix together the garlic, mayo, and harissa in a bowl.
   Season to taste, and set aside.
2 Heat the oil in a large lidded saucepan and fry the onion for 8 minutes,
   half covered, stirring occasionally. Add the fennel seeds and cook for 1 minute.
3 Pour in the wine and tomatoes and bring to a boil, then reduce the heat and
   simmer, half-covered, for 8 minutes. Add the fish and cook for about 4 minutes,
   then add the seafood and heat through, occasionally stirring gently. Season.
4 Serve in large shallow bowls, topped with a spoonful of rouille and sprinkled
   with cilantro.

SERVES 2
7G CARBOHYDRATE PER SERVING.
SERVE WITH SEEDED WHOLE WHEAT BREAD AND
A MIXED LEAF SALAD WITH TOASTED SEEDS (SEE PAGE 56).

280 THAI-STYLE MUSSELS

1 tbsp olive oil
2 shallots, chopped
2 cloves garlic, chopped
1 stick lemon grass, peeled and finely chopped

2 kaffir lime leaves
½ cup dry white wine
⅓ cup fish stock
juice of ½ lime
2 tbsp Thai tom yam paste

1lb 10oz mussels, scrubbed and thoroughly rinsed
1 tbsp chopped fresh cilantro

1 Heat the oil in a large, deep saucepan and cook the shallots for 5 minutes until softened. Add the garlic, lemon grass, and kaffir lime leaves and cook for another minute.
2 Pour in the wine, fish stock, and lime juice and bring to a boil. Stir in the tom yam paste, reduce the heat and simmer for 5 minutes until reduced.
3 Add the mussels, cover, and simmer over a medium heat for 5 minutes, shaking the pan occasionally, until the mussels have opened. Discard any mussels that have not opened. Serve immediately, sprinkled with cilantro.

SERVES 2
25G CARBOHYDRATE PER SERVING.
SERVE WITH BROWN RICE.

281 SARDINIAN-STYLE MUSSELS

1 tbsp olive oil
1 onion, finely chopped
2 cloves garlic, crushed
¾ cup dry white wine

4 tbsp canned chopped tomatoes
1 tbsp chopped flat-leaf parsley
¼ tsp dried crushed chili flakes

1lb 10oz mussels, scrubbed and thoroughly rinsed
1 tsp lemon juice
black pepper, to taste

1 Heat the oil in a large, deep saucepan. Add the onion and cook for 8 minutes over a medium heat until softened. Add the garlic and cook for a further minute, stirring frequently.
2 Increase the heat, add the wine, and boil for 2 minutes until reduced and the alcohol evaporates. Reduce the heat to medium and add the tomatoes, parsley, and chili flakes. Simmer for 5 minutes until reduced by a third.
3 Throw in the mussels, cover the pan, and cook for 5 minutes, shaking the pan occasionally until the mussels have opened. Discard any mussels that remain closed.
4 Add a squeeze of lemon juice, and season with black pepper, if liked. Spoon into large bowls and pour the juices over. Serve immediately.

SERVES 2
17G CARBOHYDRATE PER SERVING.
SERVE WITH WHOLE WHEAT SEEDED BAGUETTE AND A MIXED LEAF SALAD.

282 MOULES MARINIÈRE

1 tbsp olive oil
1 tsp butter
3 shallots, finely chopped
2 cloves garlic, finely
   chopped

1lb 10oz mussels,
   scrubbed and
   thoroughly rinsed
¾ cup dry white wine

2 tbsp chopped
   fresh parsley
salt and freshly
   ground black pepper

1 Heat the oil and butter in a large, deep saucepan with a lid. Add the shallots
   and garlic and fry for 4 minutes, stirring frequently, until softened.
2 Add the mussels, stir, then pour in the wine. Cover and cook over
   a medium heat, shaking the pan occasionally, for 5 minutes until
   the mussels have opened. Discard any that remain closed.
3 Season to taste, and sprinkle over the parsley before serving.

SERVES 2

15G CARBOHYDRATE PER SERVING.

SERVE WITH WHOLE WHEAT SEEDED BAGUETTE AND A MIXED LEAF SALAD.

283 CLAMS WITH GARLIC & CHILI

1lb small fresh clams
1 tbsp olive oil
2 cloves garlic,
   finely chopped

1 hot red chili,
   seeded and
   finely chopped
1 cup dry white wine

salt and freshly
   ground black pepper
1 tbsp chopped
   fresh parsley
lemon wedges, to serve

1 Rinse the clams well, discarding any with broken or open shells.
   Put the clams in a large saucepan and just cover with water.
   Bring to a boil and cook for 2 minutes. Drain the clams, reserving
   the cooking liquor, and discard any shells that remain closed.
2 Heat the oil in a large sauté pan and fry the garlic and chili for 1 minute.
   Increase the heat, add the white wine and cook until reduced. Add a
   quarter of the reserved cooking liquor, and cook for a few minutes.
   Season to taste.
3 Divide the clams between two shallow bowls. Pour the sauce over
   the clams and sprinkle with parsley. Serve with wedges of lemon to
   squeeze over.

SERVES 2

8.5G CARBOHYDRATE PER SERVING.

SERVE WITH WHOLE WHEAT SPAGHETTI AND A GREEN LEAF SALAD.

284 CALAMARI WITH TOMATOES & OLIVES

2 tbsp olive oil
1 large clove
   garlic, chopped
1 tsp dried oregano
¼ tsp dried crushed
   chili

½ cup dry white wine
1 cup canned chopped
   tomatoes
2 tbsp small
   black olives
10oz squid rings

1 tbsp lemon juice
chopped fresh parsley,
   to garnish
salt and freshly
   ground black pepper

1   Heat the oil in a sauté pan. Fry the garlic for 1 minute, then add the
    oregano, chili, wine, and tomatoes. Bring to a boil, then reduce the heat
    and simmer, half-covered, for 10-12 minutes until reduced and thickened.
2   Add the olives and squid and cook, half-covered, over a low heat
    for 30 minutes.
3   Season to taste, and stir in the lemon juice. Serve sprinkled with parsley.

SERVES 2
10G CARBOHYDRATE PER SERVING.
SERVE WITH WHOLE WHEAT PASTA.

285 SEARED SCALLOPS WITH SHRIMP & TOMATO SAUCE

2 tbsp olive oil, plus
extra for brushing

3 vine-ripened tomatoes,
seeded and chopped

1 clove garlic, crushed

1-inch piece fresh root
ginger, peeled and
grated

2/3 cup cooked shrimp

1 tbsp chopped
fresh cilantro

salt and freshly
ground black pepper

6 scallops

1½ cups arugula leaves

1   Heat the oil in a sauté pan and add the tomatoes, garlic, and ginger.
    Cook over a medium-low heat for 2 minutes. Add the shrimp and
    cook for 1 minute to heat through. Add the cilantro, and season.
2   Meanwhile, heat a griddle pan until hot. Brush the scallops with oil and season.
    Arrange the scallops in the griddle and cook for 1-2 minutes each side.
3   Spoon the tomato and shrimp sauce onto 2 plates and top with the
    scallops and arugula.

SERVES 2

8.5G CARBOHYDRATE PER SERVING.

SERVE WITH HERB & ALFALFA SALAD (SEE PAGE 57).

286 PROVENÇAL SHRIMP

1 tbsp olive oil

1 clove garlic,
chopped

6 tbsp passata

1 tsp sun-dried
tomato paste

¼ tsp dried
crushed chili

2 tbsp small pitted
black olives, rinsed

1⅓ cups cooked
large shrimp

salt and freshly
ground black pepper

2 tbsp chopped fresh
basil, to garnish

1   Heat the oil in a skillet and fry the garlic for 1 minute. Add the
    passata, tomato paste, chili, and olives and cook over a medium-low
    heat for 2 minutes.
2   Add the shrimp and heat through. Season to taste, and sprinkle with basil.

SERVES 2

3G CARBOHYDRATE PER SERVING.

SERVE WITH STEAMED ARTICHOKES WITH GARLIC MAYO (SEE PAGE 202).

287 CARIBBEAN SHRIMP BALLS WITH MANGO SAUCE

9oz firm skinless white
 fish
²⁄₃ cup medium cooked
 shrimp
½ tsp English mustard
 powder
1 shallot, roughly chopped

1 clove garlic, crushed
½ tsp cayenne pepper
juice of 1 lime
1 tsp dried thyme
sunflower oil, for frying
salt and freshly ground
 black pepper

MANGO SAUCE:
½ medium mango, pitted
 and flesh scooped out
 of the skin
1 tsp lemon juice
½ tsp dried chili flakes

1 Put the fish, shrimp, mustard powder, shallot, garlic, cayenne pepper, lime juice, and thyme in a food processor. Season well and mix until a thick paste. Chill for 30 minutes to let the mixture firm up.

2 Form the shrimp mixture into 12 balls, each the size of a large walnut, then flatten the tops slightly. Pour enough oil to lightly cover the base of a large, heavy-based skillet. Heat the oil and fry the balls in two batches for 2 minutes each side until lightly golden. Drain on paper towels, and keep warm while you cook the second batch.

3 Meanwhile, put the mango, lemon juice, and chili flakes into a blender and mix until puréed. Season with salt and pour into a small bowl.

4 Serve the shrimp balls with the sauce on the side.

SERVES 3
8G CARBOHYDRATE PER SERVING.
SERVE WITH SIMPLE BELL PEPPER SALAD (SEE PAGE 56).

288 SPANISH SHRIMP

2 tbsp olive oil
1½ tbsp ground
 almonds
½ tsp dried crushed
 chili flakes
1 clove garlic, chopped

1¹⁄₃ cups large raw
 shrimp, peeled
grated zest and
 juice of ½ lemon
salt and freshly
 ground black pepper

1 tbsp chopped fresh
 cilantro, to garnish

1 Heat the oil in a skillet and add the almonds, chili, and garlic. Cook for 1 minute over a medium-low heat, stirring frequently.

2 Add the shrimp, lemon zest, and juice and cook for 3 minutes until cooked through. Season and serve sprinkled with fresh cilantro.

SERVES 2
3G CARBOHYDRATE PER SERVING.
SERVE WITH CHEESY ROSEMARY ROASTED VEGETABLES (SEE PAGE 199).

MAIN MEALS

289 MALAYSIAN-STYLE COCONUT PRAWNS

2 tsp groundnut
or sunflower oil
½ red bell pepper,
seeded and diced
1 small head pak choi,
stalks thinly sliced
and leaves chopped
1 large clove
garlic, chopped

½ tsp ground turmeric
2 tsp garam masala
1 tsp chili powder
⅓ cup hot vegetable
stock (see page 30)
2 tbsp no-sugar
smooth peanut butter
⅔ cup reduced-fat
coconut milk

2 tsp soy sauce
¾ cup raw tiger prawns,
peeled
1 scallion, finely chopped
on the diagonal
1 tsp sesame seeds,
toasted

1 Heat the oil in a wok or large heavy-based skillet. Add the red bell pepper, pak choi stalks, and garlic and stir-fry for 3 minutes. Add the turmeric, garam masala, chili powder, and pak choi leaves and stir-fry for another 1 minute.
2 Mix together the hot stock and peanut butter until the latter has dissolved and add to the stir-fry with the coconut milk and soy sauce. Cook for 3 minutes until reduced and thickened.
3 Add the prawns to the coconut curry and cook for a further 3–5 minutes until cooked through.
4 Spoon into shallow bowls and sprinkle with the scallion and sesame seeds.

SERVES 4
8.5G CARBOHYDRATE PER SERVING.
SERVE WITH SOBA NOODLES.

290 CHINESE SPICY SHRIMP

2 tsp Sichuan
  peppercorns, crushed
½ tsp chili powder
3 tsp groundnut oil
1 cup large raw shrimp,
  peeled

2 tsp sesame oil
½ red bell pepper, seeded
  and sliced lengthwise
2 heads pak choi, sliced
2 cups bean sprouts
4 tsp soy sauce

1 tsp grated fresh
  root ginger
juice of ½ lime
2 tbsp chopped
  fresh cilantro
salt

1 Mix together the Sichuan peppercorns, chili powder, and oil in a bowl.
   Add the shrimp, season with salt, and stir well until the shrimp
   are coated in the spice mixture. Chill for 30 minutes.
2 Heat a wok or skillet and add the shrimp, then stir-fry for
   about 2 minutes. Remove from the wok and keep warm.
3 Heat the sesame oil in the wok and add the red bell pepper and pak choi.
   Stir-fry for 2 minutes, then add the bean sprouts, soy sauce, ginger,
   and lime juice, and stir-fry for another minute.
4 Divide the stir-fry between two plates, top with the shrimp
   and sprinkle with cilantro.

SERVES 2
7.5G CARBOHYDRATE PER SERVING.
SERVE WITH BROWN RICE.

291 PRAWN STIR-FRY

1 tbsp sunflower oil
1 tsp sesame oil
1 large clove garlic,
  chopped
1 bell pepper, seeded
  and sliced

½-inch piece fresh
  root ginger, peeled
  and grated
4 tbsp dry sherry
4 tbsp fresh apple
  juice

½lb raw tiger prawns,
  peeled
1 tsp soy sauce
1 cup bean sprouts
salt and freshly
  ground black pepper

1 Heat a wok or large skillet and pour in the sunflower and sesame oils.
   Add the garlic and bell pepper and stir-fry for 2 minutes.
2 Add the ginger, sherry, apple juice, prawns, and soy sauce and stir-fry for
   another 2 minutes.
3 Add the bean sprouts and stir-fry for a further minute and season to taste
   before serving.

SERVES 2
7G CARBOHYDRATE PER SERVING.
SERVE WITH SOBA NOODLES OR BROWN RICE.

MAIN MEALS

VEGETARIAN

Vegetable-based dishes are by nature higher in carbohydrates than those dishes that are principally fish-, poultry-, or meat-based. Nevertheless, don't ignore vegetables as they are an invaluable part of a nutritious diet and have tremendous health-giving properties. Some vegetables are lower in carbohydrates than others, as well as lower in the Glycemic index (see page 9). These form a major part of the following recipes, as do valuable protein-based foods in the form of cheese, eggs, nuts, tofu, and seeds.

292 EGGPLANT, SMOKED MOZZARELLA, & BASIL ROLLS

1 small eggplant
2 tbsp olive oil, plus extra for drizzling

¾ cup smoked mozzarella, cut into 6 slices
1 vine-ripened tomato, cut into 6 slices

6 large basil leaves
salt and freshly ground black pepper
1 tsp balsamic vinegar, for drizzling

1 Cut the eggplant lengthwise into 6 thin slices and discard the two outermost slices. Sprinkle the slices with salt and leave for 20 minutes. Rinse under cold running water and pat dry with kitchen towels.
2 Preheat the broiler to medium-high and line the rack with foil. Place the eggplant slices on the broiler rack and brush with oil. Broil for 8-10 minutes until tender, turning once, and brushing with extra oil, if necessary.
3 Remove from the broiler, then place a slice of mozzarella, a slice of tomato, and a basil leaf in the center of each eggplant slice, season to taste. Fold the eggplant over the filling and broil, seam-side down, for 3 minutes until the mozzarella begins to melt. Serve drizzled with olive oil and balsamic vinegar.

SERVES 2
4G CARBOHYDRATE PER SERVING.
SERVE WITH MIXED LEAF SALAD WITH TOASTED SEEDS (SEE PAGE 56).

293 MEDITERRANEAN STUFFED EGGPLANT

1 small eggplant, halved lengthwise
2 tbsp olive oil, plus extra for brushing
1 onion, finely chopped
1 portobello mushroom, finely chopped

½ red bell pepper, seeded and diced
2 tsp dried oregano
2 cloves garlic, chopped
½ cup dry white wine
2 tbsp chopped tomatoes

salt and freshly ground black pepper
¾ cup sliced mozzarella

1 Preheat the oven to 200°C/400°F/Gas 6. Steam the eggplant halves in a saucepan of salted water for 10 minutes, then remove from the pan and drain well. Scoop out the center of the eggplant halves, leaving a shell, then finely chop the flesh.
2 Heat the oil in a large sauté pan and fry the eggplant flesh, onion, mushroom, red bell pepper, oregano, and garlic, covered, for 10 minutes until the vegetables are softened and tender.
3 Remove the lid and add ¼ cup of water, the wine, and the chopped tomatoes. Increase the heat and cook until the liquid has reduced. Season.
4 Lightly brush the eggplant shell with oil and spoon in the vegetable filling. Place the stuffed eggplants in a baking dish. Add 2 tablespoons of water to the dish and cover with foil. Bake for 20 minutes.
5 Remove the foil and arrange the mozzarella on top of the eggplant halves. Bake for another 10-15 minutes until the cheese has melted and is golden.

SERVES 2
9G CARBOHYDRATE PER SERVING.
SERVE WITH A GREEN SALAD.

294 EGGPLANT & GARBANZO TAGINE

1 small eggplant, cut
   into ½-inch dice
2 tbsp olive oil
1 onion, roughly chopped
1 large clove garlic,
   chopped
1 zucchini, sliced into
   thick rounds

1 cup brown cap
   mushrooms, sliced
1 tsp ground coriander
2 tsp cumin seeds
1 tsp chili powder
1 tsp ground turmeric
14-oz can chopped
   tomatoes

1 tbsp tomato paste
¼ cup canned
   garbanzos, rinsed
salt and freshly ground
   black pepper
1 tbsp chopped fresh
   cilantro, to garnish

1 Preheat the broiler to medium. Toss the eggplant in 1 tablespoon of the oil and arrange in a foil-lined broiler pan. Broil for 20 minutes, turning occasionally, until softened – brush with more oil if the eggplant becomes too dry.

2 Heat the remaining oil in a large, heavy-based saucepan. Fry the onion for 8 minutes, then add the garlic, zucchini, and mushrooms and cook over a medium heat for 5 minutes. Add the spices, and cook for a further 1 minute, stirring continuously.

3 Pour in the chopped tomatoes, stir, and add the tomato paste. Bring to a boil then reduce the heat and simmer for 5 minutes until the sauce begins to thicken and reduce.

4 Add the eggplant and garbanzos and cook, half-covered, for a further 10 minutes. Stir the sauce occasionally to prevent it sticking—add some vegetable stock or water if the sauce is looking dry. Season well, and serve the tagine sprinkled with the fresh cilantro.

SERVES 2
14G CARBOHYDRATE PER SERVING.
SERVE WITH SPICY COUSCOUS (SEE PAGE 194).

295 EGGPLANT PARMIGIANA

1 small eggplant, sliced
2 tbsp olive oil
2 cloves garlic, chopped
⅓ cup dry white wine

14-oz can chopped
   tomatoes
large bunch fresh basil
2 tsp sun-dried
   tomato paste

1¼ cups sliced mozzarella
salt and freshly
   ground black pepper

1 Preheat the oven to 200°C/400°F/Gas 6. Steam the eggplant for 8-10 minutes until tender.

2 Heat half of the oil in a sauté pan and fry the garlic over a medium-low heat for 1 minute. Increase the heat and add the wine, then cook until the liquid has reduced and the alcohol evaporated.

3 Reduce the heat and add the tomatoes, basil, and tomato paste. Cook, half-covered, for 10 minutes until thickened, then season well. Pour the sauce into a medium-sized baking dish.

4 Arrange the eggplant slices on top of the tomato sauce, then brush them with the remaining oil. Top with the mozzarella and bake for 30 minutes until golden.

SERVES 2
13G CARBOHYDRATE PER SERVING.
SERVE WITH A GREEN SALAD.

296 OPEN LASAGNE WITH PORCINI MUSHROOMS & OLIVES

1½oz dried porcini
  mushrooms
2 tbsp olive oil
2 cloves garlic, chopped
1 tsp dried oregano
1¼ cups field
  mushrooms, sliced

½ cup dry white wine
3 tbsp canned
  chopped tomatoes
¼ cup small
  black olives
salt and freshly
  ground black pepper

2 fresh lasagne sheets
¼ cup Parmesan
  shavings
basil leaves, to garnish

1   Place the porcini mushrooms in a bowl and cover with boiling water. Let soak for 15 minutes, then drain, rinse, and pat dry.
2   Heat the oil in a large skillet and sauté the porcini mushrooms over a high heat for 5 minutes until they become slightly crisp around the edges. Add the garlic, oregano, and field mushrooms and cook for another 5 minutes.
3   Pour in the wine and tomatoes. Bring to a boil, then reduce the heat and simmer for 5 minutes until reduced and thickened. Add the olives and cook for 2 more minutes. Season to taste.
4   Meanwhile, cook the lasagne in plenty of boiling water until al dente. Drain lightly—the pasta should still be moist.
5   To serve, spoon the mushroom sauce onto each plate. Sprinkle with some of the Parmesan, then top with a sheet of lasagne. Sprinkle with more Parmesan, and the basil.

SERVES 2
26G CARBOHYDRATE PER SERVING.
SERVE WITH A GREEN SALAD.

297 BUCKWHEAT PASTA AND FONTINA BAKE

⅓ cup buckwheat
  pasta shapes
2 cups Savoy
  cabbage, shredded
1½ tbsp olive oil, plus
  extra for greasing
1 onion, chopped

1 leek, chopped
1 clove garlic, chopped
1 cup mushrooms, sliced
1 tsp caraway seeds
½ tsp cumin seeds
⅔ cup vegetable stock
  (see page 30)

½ cup sliced Fontina
  cheese
¼ cup walnuts,
  roughly chopped
salt and freshly
  ground black pepper

1   Preheat the oven to 200°C/400°F/Gas 6.
2   Cook the pasta in plenty of boiling salted water following the package instructions, then add the cabbage in the last minute of cooking. Drain, then rinse under cold running water.
3   Meanwhile, heat the oil in a saucepan and fry the onion and leek for 7 minutes until softened. Add the garlic and mushrooms, and cook for a further 3 minutes, stirring occasionally. Stir in the spices, and cook for 1 minute, stirring continuously.
4   Add the pasta and cabbage to the pan and stir until combined, then transfer to the baking dish. Pour over the stock and sprinkle with the cheese and nuts. Bake for 15 minutes.

SERVES 2
25G CARBOHYDRATE PER SERVING.
SERVE WITH ROASTED CUMIN PUMPKIN (SEE PAGE 195).

298 BELL PEPPER & HALOUMI KEBABS

2 baby zucchini, each cut
    into 4 chunks
8 cherry tomatoes
1 small orange bell pepper,
    seeded and cut into
    8 chunks
5oz haloumi cheese,
    cut into 16 cubes
1 red onion, cut into
    8 wedges

FOR THE MARINADE:
3 tbsp olive oil
2 tbsp balsamic vinegar
1 clove garlic, chopped
3 tbsp fresh orange juice
handful of chopped mixed
    herbs, such as oregano,
    marjoram, and chives

1   If using wooden skewers soak them in water for at least 15 minutes.
    Mix together the ingredients for the marinade in a shallow dish.
2   Arrange the vegetables on the skewers: Thread 2 pieces of zucchini,
    2 cherry tomatoes, 2 pieces of bell pepper, 4 cubes of haloumi, and 2 wedges
    of onion onto each skewer. Place the kebabs in the marinade, and turn to coat,
    then marinate for 1 hour.
3   Preheat the broiler to high and line the broiler pan with foil. Place the kebabs
    under the broiler, spoon over the marinade, and cook for about 8-10 minutes,
    turning occasionally, until tender and browned. Spoon over more marinade
    if the kebabs look dry.

SERVES 2 (MAKES 4 KEBABS)
13G CARBOHYDRATE PER SERVING.
SERVE WITH SPICY COUSCOUS (SEE PAGE 194).

299 VEGETABLE GOULASH

1 tbsp olive oil
1 onion, chopped
1 clove garlic, finely
    chopped
1 small red bell pepper,
    cored, seeded, and diced

⅔ cup butternut
    squash, peeled
    and diced
1 tsp caraway seeds
2 tsp paprika
1 tsp soy flour

1 cup canned chopped
    tomatoes
⅔ cup vegetable stock
    (see page 30)
salt and freshly
    ground black pepper
2 tbsp sour cream

1   Preheat the oven to 180°C/350°F/Gas Mark 4.
2   Heat the oil in a large casserole dish. Add the onion and fry, half-covered,
    for 8 minutes until softened. Add the garlic, red bell pepper, squash, and
    caraway seeds and cook, half-covered, for 10 minutes, stirring occasionally.
3   Stir in the paprika and flour and cook for 1 minute, then add the tomatoes
    and stock. Bring to a boil, then reduce the heat and simmer, half-covered
    for 15 minutes, stirring occasionally, until the sauce has reduced and
    thickened and the vegetables softened. Season to taste.
4   Stir the sour cream into the goulash and heat through.

SERVES 2
18G CARBOHYDRATE PER SERVING.
SERVE WITH STEAMED BROCCOLI.

300 VEGETABLE & BEAN HOTPOT

1 tbsp sunflower oil
1 onion, chopped
1 stick celery,
   finely chopped
²/₃ cup peeled and diced
   butternut squash
1 bay leaf
1 tsp dried thyme

²/₃ cup TVP
1 cup canned chopped
   tomatoes
1¼ cups vegetable stock
   (see page 30)
1-2 tsp vegetarian
   Worcestershire sauce

1¼ cups canned
   flageolet beans, rinsed
salt and freshly ground
   black pepper

1   Heat the oil in a large heavy-based saucepan. Add the onion and cook,
    half-covered, for 8 minutes until tender. Mix in the celery and squash,
    then add the bay leaf and thyme. Replace the lid and cook, stirring
    frequently, for 5 minutes.
2   Add the TVP, tomatoes, stock, and Worcestershire sauce and bring
    to a boil. Reduce the heat and cook, half-covered, over a medium-low
    heat, stirring occasionally, for 25 minutes until the squash is tender.
    Add a little water if the sauce becomes dry.
3   Stir in the beans, season, and heat through.

SERVES 2
22G CARBOHYDRATE PER SERVING.
SERVE WITH BAKED CARAWAY CABBAGE (SEE PAGE 200).

301 EGGS IN RICH SPICY TOMATO SAUCE

1 tbsp olive oil
1 large clove
   garlic, crushed
1 small red bell pepper,
   seeded and finely
   chopped

1 tsp ground cumin
1 tsp ground coriander
1 hot red chili, seeded
   and finely chopped
²/₃ cup dry white wine

salt and freshly
   ground black pepper
1³/₄ cups passata
2 large free-range eggs
chopped fresh cilantro,
   to serve (optional)

1   Heat the oil in a sauté pan. Add the garlic and bell pepper and cook over
    medium heat for 1-2 minutes until softened. Add the cumin, coriander,
    and chili and cook for a further minute. Pour in the wine, bring to a
    boil and cook for 2 minutes until reduced.
2   Reduce the heat, add the passata and cook, half-covered, for 10 minutes
    until reduced and thickened. Season to taste.
3   Make two hollows in the sauce and break an egg into each one. Cover the pan
    with a lid and cook for about 15 minutes until the egg whites have set.
    Serve, sprinkled with cilantro, if using.

SERVES 2
11G CARBOHYDRATE PER SERVING.
SERVE WITH BROWN RICE AND STEAMED VEGETABLES.

302 STUFFED ARTICHOKES

2 artichokes, stems
  removed
1 tsp lemon juice

STUFFING:
½ slice whole wheat
  bread, crusts removed
1 clove garlic, chopped
¼ cup finely grated
  Parmesan

1½ tbsp olive oil
yolk of 1 free-range egg
6 large basil leaves
salt and freshly
  ground black pepper

1 Half-fill a saucepan with water. Add salt and the lemon juice and bring to
a boil. Using a pair of scissors, trim the top of the tough outer leaves
of the artichokes. Place the artichokes stem-end down in the pan of
boiling water and cook, covered, for 20 minutes.
2 Meanwhile, put the stuffing ingredients in a food processor and mix
until combined.
3 Carefully remove the artichokes from the pan using a slotted spoon, and
drain upside down. When cool enough to handle, open out the artichokes
slightly and, using a teaspoon, remove the hairy choke found in the center.
Spoon the stuffing into the middle of each artichoke. Close the leaves
around the filling.
4 Return the artichokes to the saucepan. Cook for a further 10 minutes
until a leaf pulls away easily and the heart is tender.

SERVES 2
10.5G CARBOHYDRATE PER SERVING.
SERVE WITH A MIXED LEAF SALAD WITH TOASTED SEEDS (SEE PAGE 56).

303 BAKED ZUCCHINI WITH TALEGGIO

5 small zucchini,
  halved lengthwise
3 small leeks,
  halved lengthwise
olive oil, for brushing

salt and freshly
  ground black pepper
½ cup sliced
  taleggio cheese,
  rind removed

1 Preheat the oven to 200°C/400°F/Gas 6. Steam the zucchini
and leeks for 2 minutes until nearly tender.
2 Arrange the zucchini in a lightly oiled baking dish. Add the
leeks, season well, and then top with the slices of cheese.
3 Bake for about 15-20 minutes until the cheese has melted and
is slightly golden.

SERVES 2
9G CARBOHYDRATE PER SERVING.
SERVE WITH AVOCADO, RED ONION, & SPINACH SALAD (SEE PAGE 58).

304 HERB RICOTTA FLAN WITH SUN-BLUSH TOMATO PESTO

olive oil, for greasing
3¼ cups ricotta cheese
²/₃ cup finely grated
  Parmesan

3 free-range eggs,
  separated
4 tbsp torn fresh basil,
  plus extra to garnish
4 tbsp fresh oregano,

plus extra to garnish
½ tsp salt
½ tsp paprika
freshly ground
  black pepper

1 Preheat the oven to 180°C/350°F/Gas 4 and lightly grease an 8-inch
   springform cake pan. Mix together the ricotta, Parmesan, and
   egg yolks in a food processor. Add the herbs, season well,
   and mix until smooth and creamy. Transfer to a bowl.
2 Whip the egg whites in a large bowl until they form stiff peaks.
   Gently fold the egg whites into the ricotta mixture and spoon
   the mixture into the tin. Smooth the top with a palette knife.
3 Bake for about 1 hour until risen and the top is golden.
   Remove from the oven and let cool before removing from the pan.
   Brush lightly with olive oil and sprinkle with paprika. Serve cut into wedges
   with the Sun-blush Tomato Pesto (see page 121), garnished with extra herbs.

SERVES 6
3G CARBOHYDRATE PER SERVING.
SERVE WITH SIMPLE BELL PEPPER SALAD (SEE PAGE 56)
AND SEEDED WHOLE WHEAT BREAD.

305 GOAT'S CHEESE & ZUCCHINI TORTILLA

1 tbsp olive oil
1 onion, sliced
1 zucchini, sliced
6 free-range eggs,
   lightly beaten

¼lb firm goat's cheese,
   rind removed and sliced
salt and freshly
   ground black pepper

1 Heat the oil in medium-sized skillet and fry the onion for 6 minutes
   until softened, stirring occasionally. Add the zucchini and cook for
   a further 3-5 minutes until tender. Spread the onion and zucchini
   evenly over the base of the pan.
2 Preheat the broiler to medium-high. Season the beaten eggs, then pour
   them over the onion and zucchini. Arrange the cheese on top and
   cook over a medium heat for 5-6 minutes until the eggs are just set.
3 Place the pan under the broiler (protect the handle with a double layer of
   foil if it is not heatproof) and cook the top for about 3 minutes until lightly
   golden. Serve warm or cold, cut into wedges.

SERVES 3
3G CARBOHYDRATE PER SERVING.
SERVE WITH BELGIAN ENDIVE & RED ONION SALAD (SEE PAGE 57).

306 CREAMY PUY LENTILS WITH POACHED EGGS

½ cup Puy
   lentils, rinsed
1 tbsp olive oil
½ red bell pepper,
   seeded and diced

2 cloves garlic, chopped
juice and zest of ½ lemon
1 tsp dried oregano
3 tbsp reduced-fat
   crème fraîche

salt and freshly
   ground black pepper
1 tbsp chopped
   fresh parsley
2 large free-range eggs

1 Put the lentils in a saucepan and cover with water. Bring to a boil,
   then reduce the heat, cover, and simmer for 25 minutes until tender.
   Drain well and set aside.
2 Meanwhile, heat the oil in a skillet and fry the bell pepper and garlic for
   3 minutes, stirring frequently.
3 Add the lemon juice and zest, oregano, crème fraîche, and 4 tablespoons
   of water. Season and mix over a low heat until combined. Stir in the lentils
   and heat through, then sprinkle with the parsley.
4 Meanwhile, bring a sauté pan of water to a boil. Carefully break the eggs into
   the pan and poach over a gentle simmer for about 4 minutes until lightly
   cooked. Remove with a slotted spoon, and serve on top of the lentils.

SERVES 2
15G CARBOHYDRATE PER SERVING.
SERVE WITH GARLIC & LEMON CHARD (SEE PAGE 202).

307 CRISP CHINESE TOFU

3 tbsp black bean sauce	1 tsp sesame oil
1 clove garlic, crushed	9oz firm tofu,
1 tsp grated fresh root	patted dry using
ginger	paper towel

1 Preheat the oven to 180°C/350°F/Gas 4.
2 Put the black bean sauce, garlic, ginger, and sesame oil in a saucepan. Place the block of tofu in the pan, spoon over the sauce, and heat through over a medium heat for 2 minutes, spooning the sauce over frequently.
3 Transfer the tofu to a roasting pan and spoon over a little of the sauce. Roast for about 20 minutes until golden and crisp on the outside.
4 Serve sliced with the remaining sauce spooned over.

SERVES 2

7.5G CARBOHYDRATE PER SERVING.

SERVE WITH SESAME SPINACH (SEE PAGE 197) AND BROWN RICE.

308 STIR-FRIED LEMON GRASS TOFU

2 tsp sesame oil	1 large clove garlic,	1¼ cups fresh spinach,
2 stalks lemon grass,	thinly sliced	tough stalks removed
peeled and finely	9-oz block firm tofu,	salt
chopped	cubed	1 scallion, thinly sliced
1 green chili, thinly	1 tbsp sunflower oil	on the diagonal
sliced into rounds	1 small red bell pepper,	1 tbsp chopped
	seeded and diced	fresh cilantro
	juice of 1 lime	

1 Mix together the sesame oil, lemon grass, chili, and garlic in a shallow dish. Add the tofu and turn to coat it in the marinade. Cover with plastic wrap and marinate in the refrigerator for 2 hours.
2 Heat the sunflower oil in a wok and stir-fry the tofu for 6-8 minutes, turning occasionally, until golden. Remove the tofu using a slotted spoon and drain on paper towels.
3 Add the red bell pepper, marinade, and lime juice to the wok and stir-fry for 2 minutes. Return the tofu to the wok with the spinach, and stir-fry for another 1-2 minutes. Season with salt.
4 Serve the tofu sprinkled with scallion and cilantro.

SERVES 2

8G CARBOHYDRATE PER SERVING.

SERVE WITH SOBA NOODLES AND PAK CHOI.

309 THAI GREEN VEGETABLE CURRY

2 tsp sunflower oil
1 cup reduced-fat
 coconut milk
²/₃ cup vegetable stock
 (see page 30)
1 cup small
 broccoli florets
1 small red bell pepper,
 seeded and sliced
1 cup spinach leaves,
 shredded

salt and freshly
 ground black pepper
1 tbsp chopped fresh
 cilantro, to garnish

SPICE PASTE:
3 green chilies,
 seeded and chopped
1 stick lemon grass,
 peeled and finely
 chopped

1 shallot, sliced
juice and zest of 1 lime
1 clove garlic, chopped
1 tsp ground coriander
1 tsp ground cumin
½-inch piece
 fresh root ginger,
 peeled and grated
2 tbsp chopped
 fresh cilantro

1 Place all the ingredients for the spice paste in a food processor and
   mix until a coarse paste.
2 Heat the oil in a large saucepan and fry the spice paste for 1 minute,
   stirring. Add the coconut milk and stock, and bring to a boil.
   Reduce the heat and simmer for 10 minutes until reduced.
3 Add the broccoli and red bell pepper. Cook for 3 minutes, then add the spinach
   and cook for another 2 minutes until the vegetables are just tender.
4 Season to taste and sprinkle with cilantro before serving.

SERVES 2
11G CARBOHYDRATE PER SERVING.
SERVE WITH BROWN RICE.

310 LENTIL & VEGETABLE DAHL

1 tbsp groundnut oil
1 onion, finely chopped
2 cloves garlic, chopped
1 small carrot, diced
½-inch piece fresh
   root ginger, peeled
   and grated

1 tsp cumin seeds
1 tsp yellow
   mustard seeds
1 tsp ground turmeric
1 tsp chili powder
1 tsp garam masala
½ cup split red lentils
1 cup reduced-fat
   coconut milk

2 tomatoes, peeled,
   seeded, and chopped
juice of ½ lime
2 tbsp chopped
   fresh cilantro
salt and freshly
   ground black pepper
1 tbsp flaked
   toasted almonds

1   Heat the oil in a saucepan and fry the onion for 8 minutes until softened.
    Add the garlic, carrot, ginger, cumin, and mustard seeds. Cook for 5 minutes,
    stirring continuously, until the carrot begins to soften. Stir in the ground
    spices, and cook for 1 minute.
2   Add the lentils, coconut milk, tomatoes, and 1 cup of water. Bring to a boil,
    then reduce the heat and simmer, covered, for about
    35 minutes, stirring occasionally to prevent the lentils sticking.
3   Add the lime juice and half the cilantro, season to taste, and cook for another
    5 minutes. Serve sprinkled with the remaining cilantro and the almonds.

SERVES 2
24G CARBOHYDRATE PER SERVING.
SERVE WITH A MINI NAAN BREAD.

311 MIXED VEGETABLE CURRY

⅔ cup peeled and cubed
   butternut squash
1 small carrot, cut
   into bite-sized pieces
1 tbsp vegetable oil
1½ tsp cumin seeds
2 cardamom pods, split
1 tsp mustard seeds
1 onion, grated

1 tsp ground coriander
1 tsp ground turmeric
1 bay leaf
1 tsp hot chili powder
2 tsp grated fresh ginger
2 garlic cloves, crushed
½ cup chestnut
   mushrooms, halved
⅔ cup passata

⅔ cup vegetable stock
   (see page 30)
1 cup frozen peas
1 cup frozen spinach
   leaves
salt

1   Steam the butternut squash and carrot until just tender but still
    retain some bite.
2   Heat the oil in a large saucepan and add the cumin seeds, cardamom
    pods, and mustard seeds. When they begin to darken in color and sizzle,
    add the onion and cook for 7 minutes, half covered, until golden.
3   Add the spices, ginger, garlic, and mushrooms and cook for 2 minutes. Add
    the passata and vegetable stock and cook over a medium heat,
    half-covered, for 10-15 minutes until the vegetables are cooked.
4   Add the peas and spinach, then cook for a further 2-3 minutes.
    Season with salt to taste.

SERVES 2
22G CARBOHYDRATE PER SERVING.
SERVE WITH BROWN BASMATI RICE.

312 SPRING VEGETABLE
STIR-FRY WITH CASHEWS

½ tbsp groundnut
  or vegetable oil
splash of toasted
  sesame oil
1½ cups broccoli
  florets
2 scallions, sliced on
  the diagonal

3oz fine green
  beans, trimmed
2 heads pak choi, sliced
  in half
1 clove garlic, chopped
½-inch piece fresh root
  ginger, peeled and
  finely chopped

3 tbsp fresh apple juice
2 tsp soy sauce
⅔ cup unsalted cashew
  nuts, toasted
basil leaves, to garnish

1   Heat a skillet or wok and add both the groundnut and sesame oil.
    Add the broccoli, scallions, and green beans. Stir-fry, tossing the
    vegetables continuously, for 5 minutes.
2   Add the pak choi, garlic, and ginger and stir-fry for another 1 minute.
    Pour in the apple juice and soy sauce, and cook for 1–2 minutes
    (add a little water if the stir-fry appears too dry).
3   Sprinkle each serving with cashew nuts, and garnish with basil.

SERVES 2
13G CARBOHYDRATE PER SERVING.
SERVE WITH BROWN RICE.

313 MUSHROOM, ZUCCHINI, & SPINACH TOWER

4 large flat mushrooms	⅔ cup canned	3 cups fresh spinach,
1 tbsp olive oil, plus	cannellini beans, rinsed	tough stalks removed
extra for oiling	1 tsp dried oregano	4 slices haloumi cheese
4 slices eggplant	2 tbsp reduced-fat	
2 cloves garlic, chopped	crème fraîche	

1   Preheat the oven to 200°C/400°F/Gas 6. Place the mushrooms on a lightly oiled piece of foil large enough to make a package. Top each mushroom with a slice of eggplant. Brush the mushroom and eggplant with oil and add 1 tbsp of water to the package. Season well and fold to enclose the vegetables. Put the package on a baking sheet and bake for 20–25 minutes until tender.
2   Meanwhile, heat the remaining oil in a saucepan and fry the garlic for 1 minute. Add the beans and oregano and heat through. Stir in the crème fraîche and heat through. Purée the mixture in a blender, and keep warm.
3   Steam the spinach for 2–3 minutes until wilted; drain well.
4   To serve, put one mushroom on each plate, top each one with a slice of eggplant and haloumi. Divide the bean purée between the mushrooms, then top with the spinach and another slice of eggplant and haloumi. Finish with the remaining mushroom.

SERVES 2
9G CARBOHYDRATE PER SERVING.
SERVE WITH ROASTED FENNEL (SEE PAGE 195).

314 BAKED MUSHROOMS WITH CILANTRO PESTO

1¾ cups fresh spinach,	2 cloves garlic, crushed	salt and freshly
tough stalks removed	¼ cup roasted	ground black pepper
and leaves roughly	unsalted cashew	4 large flat mushrooms
chopped	nuts, chopped	½ cup feta cheese, sliced
1½ cups fresh cilantro	¼ cup olive oil	

1   Steam the spinach for 2 minutes until wilted. Drain thoroughly and set aside.
2   Meanwhile to make the pesto, put the cilantro, garlic, nuts, and oil in a food processor or blender. Mix until a coarse paste. Season to taste.
3   Preheat the oven to 200°C/400°F/Gas 6. Arrange the mushrooms gill-side up in a shallow, ovenproof dish. Top each one with a spoonful of spinach, then the cilantro pesto. Arrange the slices of feta on top of each mushroom.
4   Add 2 tablespoons of water to the dish and cover with foil. Bake for 20 minutes, then remove the foil and cook for a further 5–10 minutes until the cheese is golden.

SERVES 2
6G CARBOHYDRATE PER SERVING.
SERVE WITH PURÉE OF ROASTED VEGETABLES (SEE PAGE 198).

315 NUT BURGERS

½ cup mixed unsalted
  nuts, including cashews,
  Brazils, and walnuts
2 tbsp sunflower seeds
1 slice whole wheat bread,
  crusts removed

1 onion, grated
1 tsp dried oregano
1 tsp Dijon mustard
½ free-range egg, beaten
salt and freshly
  ground black pepper

soy flour, for dusting
1 tbsp olive oil

1 Grind the nuts and seeds until very fine, then add the bread and
  mix again until it forms bread crumbs.
2 Mix the nuts, seeds, and bread crumbs with the onion, oregano,
  mustard, and egg. Season well, and chill for at least 30 minutes to firm up.
3 Dust a plate and your hands with flour and form the nut mixture into
  2 burgers, lightly coating each one in the flour to prevent it sticking.
4 Heat the oil in a skillet and cook the burgers for 3 minutes each side.
  Drain on paper towels before serving.

SERVES 2
13G CARBOHYDRATE PER SERVING.
SERVE WITH A SMALL WHOLE WHEAT PITTA BREAD AND A HERB & ALFALFA
SALAD (SEE PAGE 57).

316 MIXED NUT ROAST

1 tbsp olive oil
1 onion, finely chopped
1 carrot, grated
1 small parsnip, grated
1 tsp dried mixed herbs
1 tsp dried thyme

½ cup unsalted peanuts
½ cup hazelnuts
1 slice whole wheat bread,
  crusts removed
1 tbsp sunflower seeds
2 tsp vegetarian
  Worcestershire sauce

1 tsp bouillon
  powder
1 free-range egg, beaten
salt and freshly ground
  black pepper

1 Preheat the oven to 200°C/400°F/Gas 6. Heat the oil in a saucepan, add the
  onion and cook, covered, for 7 minutes until softened. Add the carrot, parsnip,
  and herbs and cook for a further 2 minutes. Remove the pan from the heat.
2 Meanwhile, grind the peanuts in a food processor until finely chopped
  then process the bread into crumbs. Stir into the pan with the seeds,
  Worcestershire sauce, and bouillon powder. Add the beaten egg, season,
  and stir until combined.
3 Spoon the mixture into 2 individual greased dariole molds. Bake for
  30 minutes until golden and crisp on top. Turn out before serving.

SERVES 2
21G CARBOHYDRATE PER SERVING.
SERVE WITH STEAMED BROCCOLI AND SMALL POTATOES IN THEIR SKINS.

317 ROASTED VEGETABLES WITH PESTO DRESSING

2 tbsp olive oil
1 tbsp balsamic vinegar
2 sprigs fresh rosemary
1 red bell pepper, seeded and quartered
1 zucchini, sliced lengthwise
2 red onions, quartered

1 bulb fennel, sliced into thin wedges
8 tomatoes on the vine
1 bulb garlic, unpeeled with top sliced off
10 black olives
Parmesan shavings, to serve

PESTO DRESSING:
1 tbsp good-quality ready-made pesto
1 tbsp extra-virgin olive oil
1 tbsp hot water

1 Mix together the olive oil, vinegar, and rosemary in a large shallow dish.
2 Place the red bell pepper, zucchini, red onions, fennel, tomatoes, and garlic in the dish, and toss them in the marinade. Let marinate for at least 1 hour. Meanwhile, preheat the oven to 200°C/400°F/Gas 6.
3 Put the vegetables (except the tomatoes), garlic, and marinade in a roasting pan. Roast for 25 minutes, turning occasionally, then remove the rosemary. Add the tomatoes and olives, then return to the oven and cook for another 10–15 minutes until the vegetables are tender and slightly blackened at the edges.
4 Meanwhile, mix together the ingredients for the pesto dressing. Arrange the roasted vegetables on two plates and drizzle with a little dressing. Top with the Parmesan shavings to serve.

SERVES 2
21G CARBOHYDRATE PER SERVING.
SERVE WITH GRIDDLED WHOLE WHEAT PITTA BREAD.

318 CREAMY BROCCOLI & CAULIFLOWER CHEESE

1¼ cups broccoli, cut into
   small florets
1¼ cups cauliflower, cut
   into small florets
1 tbsp butter

1½ tbsp soy flour
1½ cups semi-skimmed
   milk, warmed
2 tsp Dijon mustard

⅔ cup grated mature
   Cheddar
salt and freshly
   ground black pepper

1   Steam the broccoli and cauliflower for 5 minutes until just cooked.
2   Meanwhile, make the cheese sauce. Melt the butter in a heavy-based saucepan. Stir in the flour and cook for about 2 minutes, stirring continuously, until it forms a thick light brown paste. Remove from the heat and gradually add the warm milk, whisking well with a balloon whisk after each addition. Continue to whisk in the milk to make a smooth, creamy sauce.
3   Return the white sauce to the heat and add the mustard. Cook for about 10 minutes until the sauce has thickened. Mix in two-thirds of the cheese and stir well until it has melted. Season to taste. Pour the sauce over the vegetables in the dish and mix gently until combined.
4   Preheat the broiler to high. Sprinkle the dish with the remaining cheese, then broil for 5-10 minutes until the cheese is bubbling and golden.

SERVES 2
13.5G CARBOHYDRATE PER SERVING.
SERVE WITH FRESH PEAS.

319 ROASTED TOFU WITH FRESH TOMATO SAUCE

9-oz block firm tofu,
   cut into ½-inch cubes
2 tsp sesame seeds,
   toasted, for sprinkling
1 scallion, sliced on the
   diagonal, to garnish

MARINADE:
2 tbsp dark soy sauce
1 tsp vegetable oil
1 tsp toasted sesame oil
1 tbsp sherry vinegar
2 cloves garlic, crushed
1-inch piece fresh root
   ginger, peeled and sliced
1 red chili, seeded and
   finely sliced

SAUCE:
1 tbsp olive oil
8 vine-ripened tomatoes,
   halved, seeded, and
   chopped

1   Combine all the ingredients for the marinade. Place the tofu in a shallow dish and pour the marinade over. Carefully turn the tofu in the marinade making sure it doesn't break up. Marinate for at least 1 hour, turning occasionally.
2   Preheat the oven to 180°C/350°F/Gas 4. Remove the tofu from the marinade using a slotted spoon and place on a baking sheet. Bake for 20 minutes, turning occasionally, until golden and crisp on all sides.
3   Meanwhile, make the sauce. Heat the oil in a saucepan and add the strained marinade and tomatoes. Bring to a boil, stirring, then reduce the heat and simmer for 10 minutes. Mix in a food processor or blender to make a thick, smooth sauce.
4   Serve the tofu with the tomato sauce. Sprinkle with sesame seeds and garnish with scallion.

SERVES 2
12.5G CARBOHYDRATE PER SERVING.
SERVE WITH SOBA NOODLES AND STIR-FRIED GREEN VEGETABLES.

chapter 6

SIDE DISHES

Whether you are looking for a vegetable accompaniment to partner a main course or an alternative to potatoes, white pasta, or rice, this chapter has something for you. Many of the dishes also make an ideal light meal or snack. For lunch, you could serve the Zucchini Fritters with a large mixed salad, and the Spicy Garbanzos and Spinach would make a satisfying supper dish. Pulses are a combination of protein and carbohydrate and provide a nutritious range of vitamins and minerals. They are also very versatile and make the perfect creamy mash or purée, a good alternative to potatoes. Spicy Couscous or Celery Root Mash work well with many of the main meal recipes without sending the carbohydrate count off the scale. It's all too easy to ignore vegetables when restricting your carbohydrate intake but they play a vital role in a healthy, balanced diet. Some are lower in carbs than others and have a more moderate effect on blood sugar levels, hence their use in many of the recipes that follow. Additionally, many of the following dishes have a protein element—dairy produce, eggs, nuts, or seeds—which will help to tame the effect of the carbohydrate on blood sugar levels.

320 CHARGRILLED THYME ZUCCHINI

sunflower oil, for brushing
2-3 zucchini, sliced finely, lengthwise

1 tsp fresh lemon juice
1 tbsp fresh thyme

salt and freshly ground black pepper

1 Preheat the broiler to medium-high and brush with oil. Arrange the zucchini in a griddle pan—you may have to do this in two batches—and cook for 3-5 minutes, turning once, until tender but still crisp.
2 Squeeze over the lemon juice, sprinkle with thyme, and season to taste.

SERVES 2
3G CARBOHYDRATE PER SERVING

321 MINTY ZUCCHINI

2 small zucchini, grated

1 tbsp lemon juice
1 tbsp chopped fresh mint

salt and freshly ground black pepper

1 Steam the zucchini for 1-2 minutes until just tender.
2 Toss the zucchini in the lemon juice, season, and sprinkle with the mint.

SERVES 2
2.5G CARBOHYDRATE PER SERVING

322 ZUCCHINI FRITTERS

2 small zucchini, coarsely grated
1½ tbsp finely grated Parmesan

1 small free-range egg, beaten
1½ tbsp soy flour

salt and freshly ground black pepper
1-2 tbsp olive oil

1 Squeeze the zucchini in a dish towel to remove any water, then combine with the Parmesan, egg, and flour. Season well.
2 Heat the oil in a skillet. Add 2 tablespoons of the zucchini mixture for each fritter to make four in total. Cook for 2-3 minutes each side until golden. Drain on paper towels before serving.

SERVES 2
3G CARBOHYDRATE PER SERVING

323 SPICY COUSCOUS

½ cup couscous
¾ cup hot vegetable stock (see page 30)

2 tsp olive oil
1 clove garlic
½ tsp ground cinnamon
½ tsp mild chili powder

1 tsp cumin seeds
½ tsp ground coriander
small knob of butter

1 Cover the couscous with the vegetable stock in a bowl. Stir and leave for 10 minutes, then fluff up with a fork.
2 Heat the oil in a skillet and fry the garlic for 1 minute, then add the spices. Cook for a further 1 minute. Remove from the heat, and stir into the couscous with the butter until the couscous is coated in the spice mixture. Season to taste.

SERVES 2
36G CARBOHYDRATE PER SERVING

324 MEDITERRANEAN ZUCCHINI

1 tbsp olive oil
1 small onion,
  finely chopped
1 clove garlic, chopped

2 small zucchini,
  thickly sliced
¾ cup canned chopped
  tomatoes

1 tsp tomato paste
1 tbsp toasted pine nuts
salt and freshly
  ground black pepper

1 Heat the oil in a saucepan, add the onion, and fry for 7 minutes until softened. Add the garlic and cook for 1 minute, then stir in the zucchini and cook for another 5 minutes, stirring occasionally.
2 Add the chopped tomatoes and tomato paste and cook over a medium-low heat, half-covered, for 10 minutes until the sauce has thickened and reduced. Season and serve sprinkled with the pine nuts.

SERVES 2
8.5G CARBOHYDRATE PER SERVING

325 ROASTED CUMIN PUMPKIN

1¼ cups peeled,
  seeded pumpkin,
  cut into ½-inch cubes

1½ tbsp olive oil
1 tsp cumin seeds

salt and freshly
  ground black pepper

1 Preheat the oven to 190°C/375°F/Gas 5. Toss the pumpkin in the oil and cumin seeds, then place on a baking sheet. Roast for 35-40 minutes until tender. Season to taste.

SERVES 2
7G CARBOHYDRATE PER SERVING

326 ROASTED FENNEL

1 fennel bulb,
  trimmed and
  thickly sliced

1 tbsp olive oil
salt and freshly
  ground black pepper

1 Preheat the oven to 190°C/375°F/Gas 5. Put the fennel and oil in a roasting pan. Toss to coat the fennel in the oil and roast for 25-30 minutes until tender and beginning to blacken around the edges. Season and serve.

SERVES 2
4G CARBOHYDRATE PER SERVING

327 GARBANZO MASH

1 tbsp olive oil
2 cloves garlic,
  chopped

½ cup canned
  garbanzos, rinsed
2 tbsp semi-skimmed
  milk

salt and freshly ground
  black pepper
2 tbsp chopped
  fresh cilantro

1 Heat the oil in a saucepan and gently fry the garlic for 2 minutes, then add the garbanzos and milk and heat through for a few minutes.
2 Transfer to a blender or food processor and purée until smooth. Season to taste and stir in the fresh cilantro.

SERVES 2
17G CARBOHYDRATE PER SERVING

328   **SPICY GARBANZOS & SPINACH**

3½ cups spinach leaves, tough stalks removed	1 large clove garlic	3 tbsp lemon juice
	1 tsp cumin seeds	¼ tsp chili flakes
	½ cup canned garbanzos, rinsed	salt and freshly ground black pepper
1 tbsp olive oil		

1   Wash the spinach in cold running water and place in a saucepan with nothing but the water that is already clinging to the leaves. Cook, covered, over a medium-low heat until wilted. Drain well.
2   Meanwhile, heat the oil in a skillet and fry the garlic, cumin, and garbanzos for 2 minutes, stirring continuously.
3   Combine the spinach and garbanzo mixture in a serving bowl. Pour over the lemon juice, season well, and sprinkle with chili flakes. Serve warm.

SERVES 2
10G CARBOHYDRATE PER SERVING

329 **SESAME SPINACH**

2 tsp sesame oil
1 tsp sunflower oil

3½ cups fresh spinach,
tough stalks removed

2 tsp sesame seeds,
toasted

1   Heat both the sesame oil and the sunflower oil together in a wok or skillet over a medium heat.
2   Add the spinach and stir-fry for 2-3 minutes until just wilted. Serve sprinkled with sesame seeds.

SERVES 2
2G CARBOHYDRATE PER SERVING

330 **SPINACH WITH HALOUMI**

3½ cups fresh spinach,
tough stalks removed

1 tbsp lemon juice
1 tsp extra-virgin olive oil

freshly ground
black pepper
3 slices haloumi cheese

1   Steam the spinach for 2-3 minutes until wilted. Toss the spinach in the lemon juice and oil. Season with pepper.
2   Meanwhile, heat a griddle pan and griddle the haloumi for about 2 minutes each side until golden. Finely chop the haloumi and sprinkle it over the spinach.

SERVES 2
2G CARBOHYDRATE PER SERVING

331 **CANNELLINI BEAN PURÉE**

2 tbsp olive oil
1 clove garlic, crushed
7oz canned cannellini
beans, rinsed

juice of 1 lemon
1 tbsp fresh thyme
salt and freshly ground
black pepper

1   Heat the oil in a saucepan and fry the garlic for 1 minute. Add the beans, lemon juice, thyme, and 2 tablespoons of water, then heat through, stirring.
2   Transfer the bean mixture to a food processor and mix until smooth. Season, and serve warm or reheat if preferred.

SERVES 2
15G CARBOHYDRATE PER SERVING

332 PURÉE OF ROASTED VEGETABLES

1½ tbsp olive oil
1¼ cups peeled, seeded, and cubed butternut squash

1 onion, quartered
3 sprigs fresh basil
2 tomatoes, halved

3 cloves garlic, unpeeled
salt and freshly ground black pepper

1   Preheat the oven to 190°C/375°F/Gas 5. Place the oil, squash, and onion in a roasting pan. Toss the vegetables in the oil and tuck in the basil, then roast for 20 minutes, turning occasionally.
2   Remove from the oven and add the tomatoes and garlic. Roast for another 15 minutes until the vegetables are tender. Remove the basil.
3   Peel the tomatoes, then remove the skin of the garlic. Purée with the rest of the vegetables in a food processor or blender until smooth. Season before serving.

SERVES 2
16G CARBOHYDRATE PER SERVING

333 SOUFFLÉ TOMATOES

6 vine-ripened tomatoes, top sliced off and seeds scooped out
¾ cup Gruyère cheese
3 tbsp semi-skimmed milk

1 clove garlic, crushed
2 free-range eggs, separated
salt and freshly ground black pepper

few snipped chives, to garnish, optional

1   Preheat the oven to 190°C/375°F/Gas 5. Lightly salt the tomatoes and place upside down on a plate to drain for 10 minutes.
2   Gently heat the milk in a saucepan until just warm, then add ½ cup of the Gruyère, and the garlic and egg yolks. Heat gently, stirring, until the cheese has melted and the mixture thickened. Remove from the heat.
3   Whip the egg whites in a bowl until they form stiff peaks and gently fold into the cheese mixture using a metal spoon. Season to taste with black pepper.
4   Place the tomatoes in a lightly oiled baking dish and spoon in the soufflé mixture. Sprinkle with the remaining cheese and bake for 20 minutes until risen and golden. Sprinkle with chives and serve immediately.

SERVES 3
6G CARBOHYDRATE PER SERVING

334 CHEESY ROSEMARY ROAST VEGETABLES

1 tbsp olive oil
1 red onion, peeled and
   cut into 8
1 yellow bell pepper,
   seeded and sliced into 8

½ bulb fennel,
   thickly sliced
2 sprigs fresh
   rosemary
4 vine-ripened tomatoes

¾ cup sliced mozzarella
¼ cup grated mature
   Cheddar
salt and freshly
   ground black pepper

1 Preheat the oven to 200°C/400°F/Gas 6. Pour the oil into a roasting pan and add the vegetables, with the exception of the tomatoes. Toss the vegetables to coat them in the oil, season, and tuck in the rosemary.

2 Roast the vegetables for 25 minutes, turning once, then add the tomatoes and cook for a further 10-15 minutes.

3 Preheat the broiler to medium-high. Remove the rosemary. Transfer the vegetables to a small gratin dish and arrange the mozzarella on top, then sprinkle with the Cheddar. Broil for 5-8 minutes until bubbling and golden.

SERVES 2

10.5G CARBOHYDRATE PER SERVING

335 **BAKED CARAWAY CABBAGE**

2 cups Savoy
  cabbage, shredded
1 tbsp white wine vinegar

2 tsp olive oil
2 tsp caraway seeds

salt and freshly
  ground black pepper

1 Preheat the oven to 190°C/375°F/Gas 5. Mix together the cabbage, vinegar, oil, and caraway seeds. Season and spoon onto a piece of foil large enough to make a package.

2 Place the package on a baking sheet. Bake for about 10 minutes until tender.

SERVES 2
2G CARBOHYDRATE PER SERVING

336 **CELERY ROOT MASH**

1 large celery root, peeled
  and cubed
2 tbsp lemon juice
pinch of ground nutmeg

2 tsp Dijon mustard
2 tbsp reduced-fat
  crème fraîche
1 tbsp unsalted butter

salt and freshly
  ground black pepper

1 Put the celery root and half the lemon juice in a saucepan. Pour over enough water to cover, and bring to a boil. Boil for 15–18 minutes until tender; drain well.

2 Put the celery root and the rest of the ingredients in a food processor and mix until smooth and creamy. Season to taste.

SERVES 3
8G CARBOHYDRATE PER SERVING

337 **FAVA BEANS & PROSCIUTTO**

1 cup shelled fava beans
2 slices prosciutto
1 tbsp lemon juice

2 tsp chopped fresh mint
salt and freshly
  ground black pepper

1 Preheat the broiler to medium. Steam the fava beans for 3–4 minutes until tender, then pop out of the tough outer shell.

2 Meanwhile, broil the prosciutto until crisp, then break into bite-sized pieces.

3 Toss the beans in the lemon juice and mint, season, and sprinkle with the prosciutto.

SERVES 2
6.5G CARBOHYDRATE PER SERVING

338   CHINESE BROCCOLI

2 cups broccoli florets
1 tsp toasted sesame oil
1 tsp sunflower oil

1 clove garlic, crushed
2 tsp grated
**   fresh root ginger**

1 tbsp soy sauce
2 tsp toasted
**   sunflower seeds**

1   Steam the broccoli for 3 minutes until barely tender.
2   Heat the oils in a wok or skillet and add the broccoli, garlic, ginger, and soy
    sauce. Stir-fry for about 2 minutes (adding a little water if it appears dry)
    until the broccoli is just tender. Sprinkle with the sunflower seeds.

SERVES 2
3.5G CARBOHYDRATE PER SERVING

339   SPROUT STIR-FRY

1 tsp sunflower oil
1 tsp toasted sesame oil
1 small onion, sliced
1 clove garlic, chopped

1 tbsp grated fresh
**   root ginger**
½ cup Brussels sprouts,
**   peeled and sliced**

salt and freshly
**   ground black pepper**
2 tbsp fresh apple juice
1 tsp sesame seeds,
**   toasted**

1   Heat the oils in a wok or skillet and stir-fry the onion for 8 minutes
    until softened.
2   Add the garlic, ginger, and sprouts and stir-fry for about 5 minutes.
    Add the apple juice and stir-fry for a further 3 minutes; season.
    Sprinkle with sesame seeds to serve.

SERVES 2
5G CARBOHYDRATE PER SERVING

340   PAK CHOI IN BLACK
BEAN SAUCE

1 tbsp sunflower oil
1 clove garlic, crushed

2 tbsp black bean sauce
2 pak choi heads, halved
**   lengthwise**

1 tbsp flaked almonds,
**   toasted**

1   Heat the oil in a wok or skillet. Add the garlic, black bean sauce,
    1 tablespoon of water, and the pak choi. Stir-fry for 3 minutes until tender.
    Sprinkle with almonds to serve.

SERVES 2
3G CARBOHYDRATE PER SERVING

341 GARLIC & LEMON CHARD

1 tbsp olive oil
1 large clove garlic,
  finely chopped

6oz Swiss chard, trimmed
  and stalks sliced
juice and finely grated
  zest of ½ small lemon

salt and freshly
  ground black pepper

1 Heat the olive oil in a sauté pan and fry the garlic for 1 minute.
Add the chard stalks and cook for 2 minutes, stirring frequently.
2 Tear the leaves into large pieces and add to the pan with the lemon
juice and zest, and cook for another 3 minutes until tender. Season well.

SERVES 2
2.5G CARBOHYDRATE PER SERVING

342 BRAISED LEEKS

4 small leeks,
  halved lengthwise

½ cup hot vegetable
  stock (see page 30)

1 tsp butter
freshly ground
  black pepper

1 Put the leeks in a sauté pan and add the stock. Simmer for 3-4 minutes until
tender. Remove the leeks with a slotted spoon, and add the butter. Increase the
heat and cook until reduced; pour the liquid over the leeks. Season with pepper.

SERVES 2
3.5G CARBOHYDRATE PER SERVING

343 HAM-WRAPPED LEEKS

1 tsp olive oil
4 slices good-quality ham

4 slim leeks,
  trimmed

freshly ground
  black pepper

1 Preheat the oven to 180°C/350°F/Gas 4. Lightly oil a large sheet of foil.
Wrap a slice of ham around each leek and place seal-side down together
on the foil. Season with pepper and wrap the leeks in the foil.
2 Place the package on a baking sheet, and bake for 15 minutes, then open the
foil and cook for another 5-10 minutes until the ham begins to turn crisp.

SERVES 2
3G CARBOHYDRATE PER SERVING

344 STEAMED ARTICHOKES WITH GARLIC MAYO

2 artichokes
1 tsp lemon juice

GARLIC MAYO:
3 tbsp reduced-fat
  mayo

1 clove garlic, crushed
1 tsp harissa (chili) paste
salt

1 Remove the stalks and hard outer leaves from the artichokes, then slice off
the top ½-inch. Place stalk-end down in a saucepan of boiling salted water. Add
the lemon juice and cook, half-covered, for about 20-30 minutes until
an outer leaf can be pulled out easily.
2 Mix together the mayo, garlic, and harissa, and serve as a dip.

SERVES 2
4G CARBOHYDRATE PER SERVING

345 BRAISED LITTLE GEMS WITH CRISP BACON

**2 slices bacon,
   trimmed of fat**

**½ cup vegetable stock
   (see page 30)**
1½ tsp butter

**2 Little Gem lettuces,
   halved lengthwise
freshly ground
   black pepper**

1   Preheat the broiler to high and line a broiler pan with foil. Broil the bacon
    slices until crisp. Let cool slightly and snip into small pieces.
2   Put the stock and butter into a sauté pan and heat until the butter has
    melted. Place the lettuce halves into the pan, cover, and simmer for
    2 minutes until softened. Remove from the pan with a slotted spoon.
3   Divide the lettuce between 2 plates, scatter over the bacon
    pieces, and season with pepper.

SERVES 2
1G CARBOHYDRATE PER SERVING

SIDE DISHES

chapter 7

DESSERTS

Desserts play no part in many low-carb diets. However, we all deserve the occasional treat and the recipes will help you have just that without compromising your aims. The deliciously indulgent Chocolate Orange Mousse, Chocolate Orange Cream, and Chocolate Hazelnut Whip are all low in carbohydrates, but I don't recommend eating them every day! Reserve them for special occasions, or perhaps a weekend treat. Fruit is also a no-no in some low-carb diets, especially in the induction stages, but fruit, as with vegetables, should form a regular part of our daily diet, providing essential fiber, vitamins, and minerals, and particularly antioxidants that protect us against heart disease and certain cancers. Special attention has been given to relatively low-carb fruit and fruit with a low glycemic index, such as berries, melon, grapefruit, and papaya. Many of the recipes, including Broiled Grapefruit, Peach Crumble, and Red Berry Fool, also make perfect breakfasts, but try to accompany them with a protein food, to help tame their effect on blood sugar levels. Cakes are normally incredibly high in carbohydrates but I've included two recipes that are relatively low because of the absence of flour.

346 CHOCOLATE ORANGE CREAM

1 heaped cup ricotta
  cheese
2 tbsp brandy
1 tbsp fructose
4 tbsp fresh orange juice

1 tsp orange zest
¾ square good-quality
  plain chocolate
  (70 per cent cocoa
  solids), finely grated

fine strips orange
  zest, to decorate

1   Beat together the ricotta, brandy, fructose, orange juice, and zest in a bowl.
2   Spoon a quarter of the ricotta mixture into 2 glasses, and top with half the
    chocolate. Spoon the remaining ricotta mixture into the glasses, and chill
    for 1 hour.
3   Before serving, sprinkle the remaining chocolate on top, then decorate
    with the orange strips.

SERVES 2
12G CARBOHYDRATE PER SERVING

347 CHOCOLATE HAZELNUT WHIP

½ cup heavy cream
4 tsp chocolate
  hazelnut spread

1 tbsp brandy, optional
whites of 2 free-range
  eggs

2 tsp chopped
  roasted hazelnuts

1   Beat the cream, then fold in the chocolate spread and brandy, if using.
2   Whip the egg whites until they form stiff peaks. Fold one large spoonful into
    the chocolate cream using a metal spoon, then fold in the remaining egg white.
    Spoon into 2 glasses, and chill for 1 hour. Sprinkle with the hazelnuts.

SERVES 2
7G CARBOHYDRATE PER SERVING

348 CHOCOLATE ORANGE MOUSSE

3½ squares good-quality
  plain chocolate
  (70 per cent cocoa
  solids)

juice and zest of 1 orange
2 free-range eggs,
  separated

fine strips orange
  zest, to decorate

1   Melt the chocolate in a heatproof bowl placed over a pan of gently simmering
    water; make sure the bottom of the bowl does not touch the water. Let cool,
    then beat in the orange zest, juice, and the egg yolks.
2   Whip the egg whites until they form stiff peaks. Gently fold one large
    spoonful of the egg whites into the chocolate mixture then fold in the rest.
3   Spoon into 2 tall glasses, and chill until set. Decorate with the strips of orange
    zest before serving.

SERVES 2
8G CARBOHYDRATE PER SERVING

349 ORANGE GRANITA

**freshly squeezed juice
of 3 oranges
1 tbsp lemon juice**

**fine strips orange zest,
to decorate**

1   Pour the freshly squeezed orange juice into a shallow freezer-proof container
    with the lemon juice. Stir until combined.
2   Freeze the juice for 40 minutes, then beat the semi-frozen juice with a
    wooden spoon. Repeat this process at 40-minute intervals over a 4-hour
    period to break the ice crystals down into small chunks.
3   Spoon the granita into 2 glasses, and decorate with the orange rind to serve.

SERVES 3
10G CARBOHYDRATE PER SERVING

350 MANGO FOOL

**1 small mango,
pitted, peeled,
and roughly chopped**

**½ cup heavy cream
white of 1 free-range egg
1-2 tsp fructose**

1   Place the mango in a food processor or blender, and purée until smooth.
2   Beat the cream, and whip the egg white until stiff peaks form.
    Fold the mango and fructose into the whipped cream. Fold the
    egg white into the mango cream using a metal spoon.
3   Spoon the mixture into 2 glasses, and chill for about 1 hour.

SERVES 2
16G CARBOHYDRATE PER SERVING

351 MANGO WITH LIME

**½ small mango, pitted,
peeled, and cubed
juice of ½ lime**

**few fine strips
lemon zest,
to decorate**

1   Place the mango in a serving bowl.
2   Pour the lime juice over, and chill for about 30 minutes.
    Decorate with lime zest before serving.

SERVES 2
7.5G CARBOHYDRATE PER SERVING

352 BAKED RICOTTA CAKES WITH BERRY SAUCE

sunflower oil, for greasing
⅔ cup ricotta cheese
2 tbsp fructose

½ tsp pure vanilla extract
whites of 2 free-range
  eggs

1⅓ cups mixed fresh
  or frozen berries,
  defrosted if frozen
4 tbsp apple juice

1   Preheat the oven to 180°C/350°F/Gas 4. Lightly grease 2 dariole molds.
    Beat the ricotta, fructose, and vanilla extract in a bowl using a wooden spoon.
2   Whip the egg whites until they form soft peaks. Gently fold the egg whites
    into the ricotta mixture. Spoon the mixture into the molds. Bake for about
    20 minutes until risen and golden.
3   To make the berry sauce, put three-quarters of the fruit in a saucepan,
    with the apple juice, then heat gently until softened. Press the fruit
    through a sieve to remove the pips.
4   Carefully remove the ricotta cakes from the molds and place on a plate.
    Serve with the sauce, and decorate with the reserved berries.

SERVES 2
22G CARBOHYDRATE PER SERVING

353 RED BERRY FOOL

⅔ cup ricotta cheese
1⅓ cups raspberries, hulled

1-2 tsp fructose
½ cup natural bio yogurt
1 tsp pure vanilla extract

1 Put the ricotta in a blender and mix until smooth, then add all but 2 of the raspberries, the fructose, yogurt, and vanilla. Mix until smooth and creamy. Spoon into bowls, and chill for 1 hour. Decorate with the reserved raspberries.

SERVES 2
12G CARBOHYDRATE PER SERVING

354 CUSTARD VANILLA CREAM

1 tbsp flaked almonds
1 tbsp sunflower seeds
yolk of 1 free-range egg

½ cup thick natural bio yogurt
½ tsp pure vanilla extract

⅓ cup raspberries, hulled

1 Lightly toast the almonds and sunflower seeds in a dry skillet until golden.
2 Put the egg yolk and yogurt in a heavy-based saucepan. Heat gently, stirring frequently, until the mixture begins to bubble. Add the vanilla, and stir until the mixture thickens to the consistency of custard.
3 Divide the raspberries between 2 glasses. Spoon in the custard, and serve sprinkled with the almonds and seeds.

SERVES 1
7G CARBOHYDRATE PER SERVING

355 PEACH CRUMBLE

1 tbsp porridge oats
1 tbsp sunflower seeds, finely chopped
½ tsp ground cinnamon

1 tsp fructose
2 just-ripe peaches, halved and stone removed

1 Preheat the oven to 180°C/350°F/Gas 4. Mix together the oats, sunflower seeds, cinnamon, and fructose. Sprinkle the mixture over the top of each peach half.
2 Arrange the peaches in a baking dish. Add a little water to the dish to prevent the fruit drying out. Bake for 15-20 minutes until the topping is slightly crisp and the fruit is tender.

SERVES 2
18G CARBOHYDRATE PER SERVING

356 RASPBERRY SPARKLE

12 raspberries

2 glasses Prosecco wine

1 Put the raspberries in a bowl and crush lightly with the back of a spoon. Divide between 2 tall glasses. Pour the Prosecco over the top and serve chilled.

SERVES 2
4G CARBOHYDRATE PER SERVING

357 APRICOT SYLLABUB

3 large fresh
apricots, halved,
pitted, and sliced

⅓ cup dry white wine
⅔ cup heavy cream

whites of 2 free-range
eggs
1oz fructose

1 Put the apricots and wine in a pan and bring to a boil. Reduce the heat and simmer, half-covered, for 8 minutes until softened and the wine has reduced. Let cool. Purée the apricots and wine until smooth.
2 Beat the cream and fold in the apricot purée. Whip the egg whites until they form stiff peaks. Whisk the fructose into the egg whites.
3 Carefully fold the egg whites into the cream and apricot purée. Spoon into 3 glasses and chill for 2 hours until set.

SERVES 3
12.5G CARBOHYDRATE PER SERVING

358 MELON WITH GINGER

⅓ cup peeled and cubed
honeydew melon
1 tsp grated fresh
root ginger

sprig fresh mint,
to decorate

1 Put the melon cubes and ginger in a bowl. Using a spatula, turn to coat the melon with the grated ginger.
2 Chill for 20-30 minutes before serving in tall glasses, decorated with the mint.

SERVES 1
3G CARBOHYDRATE

359 MINTED PAPAYA & MELON

¼ cup peeled, sliced,
and seeded papaya

¼ cup peeled, sliced, and
seeded watermelon

2 tbsp freshly squeezed
orange juice
10 small mint leaves

1 Place the papaya, watermelon, and orange juice in a serving bowl, and add the mint.
2 Turn until the ingredients are combined and chill for about 1 hour before serving in frosted glass dishes.

SERVES 2
3.5G CARBOHYDRATE PER SERVING

360 GRIDDLED PEACHES WITH VANILLA CREAM

2 just ripe peaches, pitted and thickly sliced

small knob of butter
1 tbsp fresh orange juice

VANILLA CREAM:
4 tbsp whipped cream
½ tsp vanilla extract

1 Mix together the whipped cream and vanilla.
2 Heat a griddle over a medium heat. Melt the butter, and add the peaches and orange juice. Cook for 2-3 minutes, turning once.
3 Arrange the peach slices in shallow bowls and pour over any juices left in the pan. Serve with a spoonful of vanilla cream.

SERVES 2
10.5G CARBOHYDRATE PER SERVING

361 BROILED GRAPEFRUIT

1 pink grapefruit, halved crosswise

2 tbsp freshly squeezed orange juice

1 Preheat the broiler to medium and line the broiler pan with foil.
2 Cut into each grapefruit half with a small, sharp knife to loosen the segments. Spoon over the orange juice.
3 Broil for 3-4 minutes until beginning to caramelize on top.

SERVES 2
8G CARBOHYDRATE PER SERVING

362 PINEAPPLE CRUSH

1½ cups peeled, cubed, and cored pineapple

2 tsp grated fresh root ginger

1 Finely chop the pineapple in a food processor or blender.
2 Combine it with the ginger, and spoon into a small freezer-proof container. Freeze for at least 2 hours.
3 Mix to break up the ice crystals immediately before serving. Serve in tall frosted sundae glasses.

SERVES 2
8G CARBOHYDRATE PER SERVING

363 BAKED APPLE WITH CAMEMBERT

1 dessert apple, halved vertically and cored
2 tbsp dry white wine

2oz Camembert, sliced and with rind cut off

1 Preheat the oven to 190°C/375°F/Gas 5. Arrange the 2 apple halves on a large piece of foil and spoon the wine over. Fold up the foil to make a package and place in a roasting pan.
2 Bake the apple for 15-20 minutes until tender.
3 Preheat the broiler to medium and line the broiler pan with foil.
4 Remove the apples from their packages and place the Camembert slices on top. Broil for about 3 minutes until the cheese has melted.

SERVES 2
8.5G CARBOHYDRATE PER SERVING

364 ORANGE & ALMOND CAKE

sunflower oil for greasing
6 free-range eggs, separated

3½oz fructose
grated zest of 3 oranges
1¼ cups ground almonds

TOPPING:
juice of 2 oranges
1 tbsp fructose

1 Preheat the oven to 180°C/350°F/Gas 4. Grease and base line an 8-inch square pan. Beat the egg yolks with the fructose, orange zest, and ground almonds in a large bowl.
2 Whip the egg whites until they form stiff peaks. Fold a spoonful into the almond mixture to loosen it, then fold in the remaining egg white. Carefully pour the mixture into the prepared cake pan.
3 Bake for 45-50 minutes until a skewer inserted into middle of the cake comes out clean. Let cool in the pan.
4 To make the topping, put the orange juice and fructose in a small saucepan and bring to a boil, stir once, then cook undisturbed for 6-8 minutes until reduced, thickened, and syrupy. Using a fork, pierce the cake all over, then pour the syrup over the top and let soak in before serving.

MAKES 9 SLICES
14G PER SLICE

365 **MOCHA BROWNIES**

5 squares good-quality plain chocolate (about 70 per cent cocoa solids)	½ cup butter 1 tsp strong black coffee 1 tsp vanilla extract	scant 1 cup ground almonds 3oz fructose 4 free-range eggs

1   Preheat the oven to 180°C/350°F/Gas 4. Grease and base line an 8-inch square pan.
2   Melt the chocolate and butter in a heatproof bowl placed over a pan of gently simmering water, making sure the bottom of the bowl does not touch the water. Stir occasionally until the chocolate and butter have melted and are smooth.
3   Carefully remove the bowl from the heat and stir in the coffee and vanilla extract. Leave to cool slightly, then add the almonds and fructose, and mix well until combined. Separate the eggs. Beat the egg yolks lightly then stir them into the prepared chocolate mixture.
4   Whip the egg whites until they form stiff peaks. Carefully fold a large spoonful into the chocolate mixture, then fold in the rest until completely mixed in.
5   Spoon the mixture into the prepared pan and bake for 20-25 minutes until risen and firm on top but still slightly gooey in the center. Let cool in the pan then turn out, remove the baking parchment, and cut into 12 pieces.

MAKES 12 SQUARES
15G CARBOHYDRATE PER SQUARE

INDEX

Acknowledgments

Many thanks to everyone at Duncan Baird Publishers who helped create this book, especially to Julia Charles for commissioning me and for her continued support and cheery phonecalls. Thanks, too, to Louise Bostock for her patience and editing skills as well as William Lingwood for the excellent photography, and home economist, David Morgan, who transformed the written word into reality.